START AND RUN A PROFITABLE TOUR GUIDING BUSINESS

START AND RUN A PROFITABLE TOUR GUIDING BUSINESS

Part-time, full-time, at home, or abroad:
Your step-by-step business plan

Barbara Braidwood
Susan M. Boyce
Richard Cropp

Self-Counsel Press
(a division of)
International Self-Counsel Press Ltd.
USA   Canada

*Self-Counsel Press acknowledges the financial support of the Government of Canada
through the Book Publishing Industry Development Program (BPIDP) for our publishing activities.*

Printed in Canada

First edition: 1996
Second edtion: 2000

Canadian Cataloguing in Publication Data

Braidwood, Barbara, 1952-
Start and run a profitable tour guiding business

(Self-counsel business series)
ISBN 1-55180-284-8

    1. Tour guides (Persons)   2. Tourism — Management
I. Boyce, Susan M., 1956- II. Cropp, Richard, 1952- III. Title. IV. Series.

G154.7.B72 2000   338.4'791'068   C00-910814-9

Self-Counsel Press
(a division of)
International Self-Counsel Press Ltd.

1704 N. State Street   1481 Charlotte Road
Bellingham, WA 98225   North Vancouver, BC V7J 1H1
USA   Canada

CONTENTS

APPENDIXES

CHECKLISTS

SAMPLES

TABLES

WORKSHEETS

ACKNOWLEDGMENTS

Many people generously spent time with us helping to make this book possible. We would especially like to thank Marianne Gagel, Barbara Mansell, Shara Street and Amrit Chidakash, Jeff Veniot, and Len Webster for sharing their experiences and firsthand knowledge of the tour guiding industry.

Special acknowledgment also goes to Maureen Wright and Nancy Brenner of the Pacific Rim Institute of Tourism and Catherine Prather of the National Tour Association who so willingly gave their time and expertise to this project.

To Dick Cropp, the ultimate tour guide of life. I couldn't have made it this far without your leadership.

Rick

To Rick's father, Dick Cropp. You guided him well and I thank you.

Barbara

For Dick Bellamy, who puts up with my erratic schedule, reminds me to eat when I'm working late, and is always willing to bring me a cup of tea and oatmeal cookies.

Susan

INTRODUCTION

Imagine a life filled with golden sandy beaches, sparkling ski resorts, priceless art treasures, and exquisite wonders of nature. Glamour! Romance! The adventure of exotic destinations and fascinating people. This week Paris, next week Rome or perhaps Hawaii. On days when you are not globe-trotting, you sport a great tan and are a sought-after guest at parties, where you dazzle everyone with tales of your travels.

Better yet, imagine someone paying you to live this lifestyle!

Sound exciting? You bet it is!

Travel schools, tour operators, and librarians all report that tour guiding is one of the most asked-about careers in the tourism industry. The life of a tour guide or tour director can be fun and rewarding, not to mention thrilling.

This book will give you a realistic idea about what it takes to be a tour director or guide. First we provide some industry background, describe what is involved in tour guiding, and tell you how to get a job as a tour guide or director. Then we give you tips on how to develop your own tours to your favorite destination and outline the planning you must do no matter where you are going. And finally we include a blueprint for the entrepreneur who wants to run a larger organization.

We do recommend you read the whole book. Readers who want a job with a tour company will get a good idea of what problems their employer faces behind the scenes. Knowing how things work and what the issues are can make all the difference to the kind of assignments you get. Entrepreneurs determined to set up a larger tour operation will benefit from learning the daily nitty-gritty of a tour organization.

By the way, if you decide the tour guiding business is perfect for you, you will find yourself being called a —

- ⊕ tour director,

- ⊕ tour guide,

- ⊕ tour escort,

- ⊕ tour host,

- ⊕ tour leader, or

- ⊕ tour manager.

Although the industry has specific definitions for each phrase, these terms are often used interchangeably. In this book we use the term "tour guide" for a person who leads a local day tour and "tour director" for someone who leads a tour that includes at least one night of accommodation.

One caveat: Everything changes in the travel business. We have tried to be accurate but we know that by the time this book goes to press, some item of information that has been the same for the last 20 years will have changed. Rather than relying on this book for every detail, use it to highlight those things you must research for yourself. The facts may change, but the principles will be the same.

1
BEFORE YOU QUIT YOUR DAY JOB

1. WHY GROUP TRAVEL?

Group travel is as old as humanity, a heritage passed down from the days of nomadic prehistory. The glorious quests of the Crusaders, the wandering routes of gypsy caravans, the Wild West migrations across North America, even the voyage of Noah's Ark can all be thought of as group travel.

These groups formed because of common interests, needs, and goals. While it is unlikely (but not impossible) you will ever find yourself in charge of a group whose sole purpose is to recover the Holy Grail, many of the reasons people banded together in the past still apply today. If you want to be successful as a tour professional, it is essential to understand these reasons.

Tours are an increasingly popular option for people who would rather pay someone else to look after the planning and deal with any problems along the way.

1.1 Convenient, hassle-free travel

The single biggest reason most people choose group travel is because someone else takes care of all the planning. They want a sense of luxury, the feeling that Jeeves or Max is constantly available to attend to minor details and inconveniences.

The word *travel* is actually related to the French word *travailler*, meaning "to work." For people with limited annual vacation time to relax from the stress of today's work environment, work is the last thing they want to do during their holidays.

Hassle-free travel can be enticing and worth paying for. People expect to be buffered from all worries, including the following specific concerns:

(a) What happens if my plane gets delayed?

(b) I've never been here. I'm afraid of getting lost.

(c) I can't even pronounce anything on the menu. I certainly don't have any idea what it is. What am I going to eat?

(d) How will I talk to people and make myself understood when I can't speak the language?

(e) How much should I carry in cash and traveler's checks? What about my credit cards? Will my bank debit card work?

(f) How much should I tip the waiters and hotel staff? Should I still leave a tip even if the service was lousy?

(g) What kind of clothes will I need? Should I bring formal evening wear or just casual, comfy clothing?

(h) Will the hotel be up to North American standards?

(i) There is so much to see and I don't want to miss any of it. How will I ever visit everything?

1.2 Companionship

We live in a world of ever-faster travel and communications. Ironically, it is also a world of ever-increasing isolation. Many people travel solo because they have no one to accompany them, and travel becomes a lonely experience. Tours allow travelers to share the joys of experiencing a new destination with other people. If your passion is painting, it is more fun to chat about the wonders of the Louvre with another enthusiast over a cup of cappuccino or a leisurely dinner than to be closeted in a room with no one but room service for company.

1.3 Safety

Safety in numbers may be a cliché, but it is a cliché based on truth. Travel in a foreign city or the wilderness can be dangerous, sometimes even life-threatening, for a solo traveler.

1.4 Affordability

Many first-time tour participants are surprised by the affordability of group travel. Because tour operators receive the benefits of group discounts and repeat booking bonuses, they can often provide first-class packages at economy prices. Costs other than personal spending are known up front, so there are no nasty surprises on arrival in a foreign country. That means additional savings for everyone who can resist the urge to spend three times as much on souvenirs.

1.5 Knowledgeable leader

Group travelers are confident their tour director's knowledge and experience will help them enjoy all the traditional sights as well as some they might not otherwise see — the "back rooms" of museums and theaters, for example. Vacation memories are almost as important as the holiday itself, and a competent, knowledgeable tour director will ensure there are many pleasant ones.

2. DIFFERENT TYPES OF TOURS

2.1 Cruising

A cruise is one of the easiest group tours to arrange and manage, ideal for the first-time tour director. It is the ultimate all-inclusive package: once your group is aboard there is no checking in and out of hotels, no luggage problems, no arranging meals, and entertainment is available on board virtually 24 hours a day. In fact, it is often easy to forget this is a working trip. A tour director's job on a cruise is more of a congenial host than a manager.

2.2 Rail tours

The days of the Orient Express are returning with a vengeance! Travel by rail has a unique, soothing sense of intimacy. Space on board is more restricted than on a cruise ship, but there is still room to move around, avoiding the cramped inactivity often associated with air travel. The sense of intimacy encourages people to strike up friendships with fellow

Tour participants, especially those travelling solo, want to feel safe in a foreign environment.

passengers. As well, scenery is more dramatic because you are so close to it physically. For example, there is an amazing difference between viewing remote areas of the Canadian Rockies by train and by road. When you are on a bus there is a sense of separation, but on a train it often seems you are alone in the wilderness, so close to the trees that you could reach out and touch them as they whisk past.

2.3 Bus tours

Also known as motorcoach tours, travel by bus is a perennial favorite group tour method. For the guide, it is also more demanding than cruise or rail travel. You will be checking your group in and out of hotels daily throughout the trip, so organization and superb planning skills are essential, and you will be responsible for the logistics of the entire tour (e.g., route, entertainment, accommodation).

2.4 Adventure/eco tours

"Getting back to the land" is enjoying a new wave of enthusiasm. According to the National Tour Association, based in Kentucky (see Appendix 1 for information on the NTA and other travel organizations), wilderness travel now ranks among the five most popular types of tours in North America, along with evening entertainment, historical, heritage/cultural, and beautiful gardens. Many city dwellers want to experience nature but lack the survival skills to travel safely in remote areas.

With the rapidly expanding interest in eco-tourism, many urbanites want to experience the Great Outdoors but lack the necessary skills to do so safely on their own.

While the sound of an eagle's cry overhead may be awe-inspiring, the reality of packing 60 pounds of gear dims the exhilaration all too quickly if the traveler is not accompanied by an expert to look after things such as firewood, shelter, food, and water.

2.5 City tours

City tours are usually four- to eight-hour bus tours conducted by a local step-on guide, though some are walking tours. They give tourists an overview of the history and interesting features of a city.

2.6 Theme tours

Most tours have some element of theme, but a true theme tour is organized around one idea — anything from the latest science fiction fad to Chocolate Lovers Anonymous. One example is a recent gravesites tour arranged for a group of Korean War vets.

3. DIFFERENT TYPES OF GUIDES

There are two basic divisions in the tour guiding business — local guides and tour directors. Both guides and directors can work on their own or for a tour operator.

3.1 Local guide

Local guides are on the front line for sightseeing adventures. They are the ones who give commentary and make visitors feel welcome in a specific destination. They can be divided into four subcategories.

(a) Site guide

Site guides work at a specific location such as an historical site (the Little Bighorn battlefield) or an entertainment attraction (Paramount Studios). They are often volunteers but are sometimes employed directly by the owner/manager of the attraction. A site guide is responsible solely for providing commentary to people going through the attraction. This is a great way to gain some volunteer experience.

(b) Step-on guide

City tours and single-day events require a step-on guide — literally someone who steps onto the bus and provides commentary. These are often freelancers working on contract but may also be guides employed directly by a tour company and paid an hourly rate. Many people break into professional tour guiding here. Some love it and stay without ever having a desire to become a long-distance tour director. A step-on guide works close to normal hours, is home every evening, and still has all the excitement of meeting people from around the world. If you want to see how you like this type of work, try taking a group of out-of-town relatives or friends around your hometown. Better yet, take a group of people who live there. If you have uncovered enough fascinating information to hold their attention and can impress them with the charm and wit of your delivery, you have taken the first big step to becoming a successful step-on guide.

(c) Driver guide

A driver guide does all the same things a step-on guide does, but drives the bus as well.

(d) Meet-and-greet guide

Just as the name implies, a meet-and-greet guide assists when groups are arriving and leaving a destination. Visitors arriving at an airport will often be welcomed by a meet-and-greet guide who will ensure everyone is present and all luggage has arrived, then assist with customs clearance and transportation to hotels, cruise ships, or other accommodations where the tour director will take over.

3.2 Tour director

Tour directors must be organized, physically fit, have an endless supply of patience, and be able to laugh at almost anything.

Multiday tours require a tour director. Also called tour manager, tour escort, tour leader, or tour host, this is the job most people are envisioning when they say "tour guide." A tour director is a guide with all the additional headaches of planning accommodation, meals, and long-distance travel. This is a demanding job which requires outstanding organizational skills, endless patience, physical stamina, and a great sense of humor about life's foibles. Chapters 5 through 10 describe the demands on a tour director in detail.

3.3 Tour operator

Tour operators — also known as tour companies, tour packagers, tour brokers, or tour wholesalers — design and market tours that they sell either direct to the public or through travel agencies. (Chapters 14 through 23 provide information on setting up as a tour operator.) Whether you work as a direct employee or as a freelancer on contract, you will most likely be working for and paid by one or more tour operators. Since most people who become tour guides or directors are bored by sameness and routine schedules in their workplace, it is common in the industry to freelance for several different operators at the same time. What is not wonderful with one company will be fantastic with another.

2
CAN YOU REALLY DO THIS DREAM JOB?

The travel industry is built on dreams — dreams of exotic destinations, thrilling adventures, and eternally happy people. Being a tour guide or director will allow you to become part of this incredible world most people only dream of.

But, and it is a very big but, there are also long, long hours behind the scenes, high levels of stress, frequent burnout, intense physical demands, and often not a lot of money.

In short, there are many nonglamourous aspects to this glitzy profession. Before you decide to quit your day job and make the leap into the tour guiding business, let's look at some of the realities behind the myths.

Tour guiding is a
demanding profession
but rewards you with the
flexibility and freedom to
see the world and get
paid for it.

1. THE REWARDS

1.1 Freedom

Whether you want to travel 12 months or two weeks a year, whether your ideal is tropical climates or icy mountaintops, luxury hotels or backpacks and hiking boots, tour guiding is one route to traveling where and when you like. You set your own timetable and pursue your own itinerary. It takes creativity, planning, and sometimes endless patience, but you are essentially the master of your own destiny and travel plans.

1.2 Challenge and excitement

No matter how many times you visit a favorite destination or how many new wonders you discover, there will always be something new to learn and enjoy. Foreign languages, different cultures and traditions, new friends — there is challenge and excitement packed into every day.

At home, travel and tour guiding associations provide a place to network and update skills and knowledge. They can also be a place to share stories and get excited again after the "Trip from Hell." Appendix 1 contains a list of organizations which may have local chapters in your city. Check listings in the Yellow Pages, or contact the chamber of commerce if you live in a major city, to see what your area offers.

1.3 Creative opportunity

Designing and/or running the perfect tour is an artistic endeavor as much as a business venture. The extra touches only you can add make your tour stand out from your clients' other travel memories. Out of ten architecturally unusual hotels, the one that will be talked about years later is the one you pointed out that has a dash of intrigue and mystery in its history. Imagine the quick intake of breath as you describe how Howard Hughes and his retinue once rented a floor and stayed for six months in the very hotel you are driving past (the Westin Bayshore in Vancouver, British Columbia). Actually, it was six months less a day — Hughes would have had to pay residency taxes if he stayed six months, so he left.

1.4 Sharing the joy of a destination

Tour guides and directors share a common joy and exuberance for travel. They glow with excitement when they talk about favorite places in their hometown or abroad. Even after years of leading the same tour, many say they cannot wait for the guiding season to get into full swing. Well-loved destinations stay fresh because each new group brings a unique perspective.

1.5 Meeting people

If you love meeting people, the guiding industry may be an almost perfect vocation. Not only will you meet people at the various destinations you visit, but group travel, especially long-distance travel, also encourages long-term friendships. Tour guests who feel welcome and well cared for will often return for another excursion, sometimes bringing along another friend or family member. Sometimes people keep in touch for years after.

1.6 Tax write-offs

You do not need a fancy office to be a tour guide or director. A space for organizing your paperwork and a love of travel are the only two essentials. Later in this book we will suggest how you can make your office more efficient and convenient. But whether you work out of a closet in the basement or rent the entire top floor of an office building, there are many expenses you can write off. Talk to your accountant for specific details.

If you love exploring new destinations and telling others about them, you already have the basic requirements to become a tour guide.

2. DAY TO DAY — THE REALITY

2.1 Long hours

A smoothly running tour requires long hours and dedication from the tour director. Guests do not want to know about any unexpected glitches. They have paid you to take care of it and they expect it to appear effortless. As one tour director put it, "No matter what headaches we have, they expect and deserve to be cruising easy."

To preserve this image, you will be up early and usually late to bed. You must be ahead of the first early bird and behind the last straggler for everything — flights, day trips, bus departures, or the final curtain of the opera. One cruise tour director we spoke with said it was not unusual to be up at 5:30 in the morning and not in bed until 1:30 a.m. for long stretches of time. It is certainly not uncommon to put in well over 80 hours a week for long periods during the touring season.

Even if it is just you, your tour participants, and Mother Nature for a ten-day wilderness or adventure tour, there will always be tents that will not go up, fires that will not light, and uncooperative weather. Add these unexpected but unavoidable glitches to the normal necessities such as campsite care, cooking in the bush, medical problems from blisters to bee stings, and generally encouraging footsore, weary urbanites, and you will find your days stretching into long, tiring ones. When everyone else is asleep or enjoying an afternoon of unstructured time, you will often be catching up on paperwork, planning for the next day, or solving problems.

2.2 You are never off duty

You are expected to be accessible to every member of the tour at all hours of the day and night. If someone has a problem with accommodation, needs information about the next day's itinerary, feels ill, or is simply lonely, guess who they will come looking for? If you think it is anyone but you, guess again.

2.3 Be prepared for complaints

It does not happen often, but eventually you will have a person on your tour who is disgruntled with life and looking for someone to blame. The tour director makes a handy target. You will be the focus of any complaints — whether or not they are legitimate. You must have solutions for bad weather, the "awful" color of the hotel room, and the inability to get a decent hamburger in the middle of a desert just as readily as you deal with problems such as lost luggage and illness.

Most people understand some things are beyond the control of even the most experienced director. Airlines experience mechanical failures, clouds or fog hide magnificent views, and entertainers do get sick like everyone else. Keeping people informed in a calm, unruffled manner will go a long way to smoothing the path to a solution.

Be prepared to handle complaints of all sorts, even ones that are completely beyond your control.

2.4 You are not going to get rich

Becoming a tour professional is far from a get-rich-quick career. Even though you are getting paid to travel, you likely will not be getting paid much, especially when you factor in the long hours. For many people, the nonmonetary rewards far outweigh financial compensation. If, on the other hand, you are going into tour guiding for a fast buck, there are dozens of other professions you should consider first.

2.5 Home is where the laundry is

Unless you are working as a step-on or site guide, you will be living out of a suitcase. While cruising and rail tours allow you some stability, you must be prepared to spend few nights in your own bed during the touring season. Usually you will stagger home after a tour, run all the dirty clothes through the wash, then repack them into your suitcase or packsack, ready to head out again.

3
GETTING THE JOB

1. ASSESSING YOURSELF

Tour guides and directors are an irrepressibly enthusiastic bunch. They are walking encyclopedias filled with tantalizing tidbits of information and amazing stories of places and people, and they love to share those stories. Whether they are elbowing through the cacophony of sounds and smells in a teeming Hong Kong market or watching for benevolent ghosts in a medieval British castle, tour guides and directors love the people, mystique, and history of the places they go. They love their work. This is a life path, not a job.

1.1 Characteristics of success

It is sometimes said that the best test for anyone who wants to become a tour professional is to ask yourself, "Would I do this for free?" In fact, before you read any further you should ask yourself, "If I didn't get paid to take people traveling, would I be traveling anyway?" If you can honestly answer "Yes!" then at worst you will be doing something you would do in any case. At best, with careful planning, lots of hard work,

A passion for travel is an essential quality. If you can honestly say you would still be travelling even if you weren't being paid for it, then this may just be the perfect profession for you.

13

and just a smidgen of luck, you will have someone else pay your way and put a few dollars in the bank as well.

Nothing can guarantee success, but there are certain personality traits that will make success as a tour professional more likely. Work through the questions on Worksheet 1. Be honest — brutally honest — when you do. Forget what you have been conditioned to think you "should" be like. If you cheat, only you will know and only you will lose.

1.2 Sticking to your goals

Goal setting has become increasingly popular over the last few years, probably because to succeed in any enterprise you need to work toward clearly defined goals. You will have tough times as a tour professional, guaranteed, just as you would have in any other business. Goals will help you weather the days when you wonder why on earth you ever thought about getting into this crazy business. The following are only highlights of goal setting. If you want more detailed information, there are hundreds of books available at libraries and bookstores.

(a) Put your goals down on paper

Writing out your long- and short-term goals gives them importance and makes them easier to stick to. Be realistic and concrete. It is easy to say you will become a successful tour guide "one day." The trouble is, in 20 years "one day" is usually still in the future. Give yourself a specific time frame. How many tours do you want to have under your belt after the first season? The second season? The first five years?

(b) Review and revise

Written goals are a road map, not an immutable ball and chain. Lucky breaks occur to people every day; circumstances change — for good and bad — just as often. Be open to opportunities around you and capture them before they are lost. Then sit down and review your goals. Perhaps you will decide to change some part of them. Make the change and then celebrate.

(c) Learn from your mistakes

Nothing is a better teacher than making a mistake. If the luggage was late getting to the rooms each night on your first trip, figure out what went wrong and modify it. If everyone asked about an attraction you

WORKSHEET 1
CAN I MAKE MY DREAM A REALITY?
SELF-ASSESSMENT TEST

For each of the follow statements do you:

1. Agree strongly

2. Agree somewhat

3. Feel neutral

4. Disagree somewhat

5. Disagree strongly

	1	2	3	4	5
I love to travel anywhere and everywhere.	☐	☐	☐	☐	☐
I enjoy meeting and working with people of all backgrounds and ages.	☐	☐	☐	☐	☐
I see unexpected problems as challenges, not as obstacles.	☐	☐	☐	☐	☐
I am resourceful and creative when faced with an unexpected difficulty.	☐	☐	☐	☐	☐
I have a steady, even temperament and seldom become flustered.	☐	☐	☐	☐	☐
I am able to make decisions quickly when necessary and am willing to stand by my decisions.	☐	☐	☐	☐	☐
I am intrigued by and respectful of different customs, even those that seem strange to me.	☐	☐	☐	☐	☐
I am a detail-oriented, well-organized planner.	☐	☐	☐	☐	☐
I remember names, faces, and facts easily.	☐	☐	☐	☐	☐
I can laugh at myself.	☐	☐	☐	☐	☐
I love talking to strangers. I can talk to anyone.	☐	☐	☐	☐	☐
I have a good sense of direction.	☐	☐	☐	☐	☐
I am a self-starter and work well without direct supervision.	☐	☐	☐	☐	☐

	1	2	3	4	5
I can plan and stick to a timetable, but I am also flexible and creative when I see unexpected opportunities.	☐	☐	☐	☐	☐
I am free to travel without family obligations and/or my partner is free to travel with me.	☐	☐	☐	☐	☐
I seldom take a complaint personally, especially when it is about something I cannot control.	☐	☐	☐	☐	☐
I am in good health.	☐	☐	☐	☐	☐
I have a great sense of humor as well as endless enthusiasm and energy.	☐	☐	☐	☐	☐
I am a good listener.	☐	☐	☐	☐	☐
I have a strong sense of ethics.	☐	☐	☐	☐	☐
I enjoy being "on stage" in front of others.	☐	☐	☐	☐	☐

If you agreed or agreed strongly with most of these statements, you have the temperament and outgoing personality necessary for the tour business. With solid preparation and lots of hard work, you will likely be a success and enjoy yourself in your career as well. If, however, you disagreed or were neutral about most of the statements, the tour guiding and tour directing business is probably not for you. It is possible in some careers to be less than enthusiastic about the work and still be moderately successful, but this is not one of them. You are always being watched and judged by your clients. They will see through your bluff in no time, and the stress will probably burn you out in only slightly more time.

bypassed on a city tour, use it as a stepping stone to improve the itinerary for next time. Then be confident your next trip will be better because of your mistake.

1.3 Do your homework

(a) Network

Talk! Talk to anyone and everyone. If your neighbors went on a tour last spring, find out what they liked and didn't like about it. Talk to your local travel agent — most are very willing to help. When you are on a tour yourself, ask the guides how they got into the business and what they love about it. Don't be afraid to ask lots of tough questions. Better to find out what the problems are sooner rather than later.

(b) Associations and organizations

In any industry there are associations, organizations, and publications you should be aware of. Get your name on mailing lists for local functions and when you go... ask questions! Appendix 1 contains a list of organizations and associations while Appendix 3 lists relevant publications. Use these as a starting point to begin developing your own data base, and add to it at every opportunity.

(c) Read and research

There is no getting around it: you are going to become an information snoop and scrounge. One day you will find yourself trying to spirit a magazine out of your doctor's office because it has a great write-up about a new museum you have been crazy to add to your next tour. Your face should become so well-known at every library, tourist bureau, bookstore (new and used), and magazine stand within a hundred miles that the staff know your first name and exactly how you like your coffee while you are reading. Valuable new information is everywhere and endless. Keep open to every possible avenue of improving your knowledge base.

2. FORMAL EDUCATION

As the travel industry grows, so does the number of schools offering travel training. Just take a look in the Yellow Pages under Travel Schools and you will see how popular they have become. This may appear to make it easier for would-be tour professionals to gain some formal education. The reality is that many of these schools, while offering an excellent curriculum for a generalist or someone focusing on one of the

Celebrate your successes and learn from your mistakes.

Making the time to attend trade functions, get on media lists, and ask for referrals should be an ongoing part of your marketing strategy.

Check the curriculum closely before enrolling in an educational program. Many do not devote enough time to developing the skills required by a tour guide to make it worth your time and financial investment.

more structured areas of tourism, provide little in-depth training specifically aimed at tour guides and directors.

Before you invest in what are often high fees, assess how well the training will advance your personal goals. Exactly how much time will be devoted to tour guiding? How much will be spent on other subjects? If 95 percent of the time is spent learning how to be a travel agent, you will probably want to look elsewhere, unless becoming a tour guide is only a side interest for you. Do not be afraid to ask how many of the school's graduates secure work in the industry. A history of grads finding themselves hard at work as restaurant staff or forklift drivers after completing the course should set off warning bells.

The first and currently the only school in North America devoted *entirely* to training professional tour directors and guides is the San Francisco-based International Tour Management Institute (ITMI). Modeled after training schools in Europe, ITMI was established in 1976 and now has training facilities in San Francisco, Los Angeles, and Boston. Of the more than 250 tour directors and guides ITMI trains each year, approximately 80 percent find work in the industry. As one successful and now employed graduate put it, "The contacts you make there are something you can't buy at any price."

For further information contact:

International Tour Management Institute
Administrative Headquarters
#810 - 625 Market Street
San Francisco, CA 94105
Tel: (415) 957-9489
www.itmitourtraining.com

3. THE IMPORTANCE OF LANGUAGE

One of the most important assets you can have as a tour guide or director is fluency in a second, third, or even sixth language. When you start talking to tour operators, directors, and guides, you will discover that, almost inevitably, the first thing they mention is "second language."

Even if you can't visualize yourself sharing a bowl of pasta and chitchat in a small, nonEnglish-speaking Italian village or trekking through the Himalayas with only Tibetan-speaking monks for company, the number of tourists traveling into North America is enormous and growing. Although we often believe everyone speaks English, many of these guests do not. As a result, sometimes the language requirements of an area are not what you would expect at first glance. Certain destinations may be popular with a particular country even though the area itself has few local residents of that nationality. For example, Canada's West Coast and Rocky Mountains are extremely popular with German tourists; a fact which has sent the demand for German-speaking tour guides skyrocketing.

3.1 Learning a language

Language studies come in many formats. For starters, you could try a night school course. Most community colleges, universities, and continuing education programs offer some form of basic instruction to get you going.

Many good computer stores offer a variety of language courses on CD-ROM. We have not heard any first-hand reports about the usability of these learning tools, but if you have a computer already, this is an option worth investigating.

If you are really serious about becoming multilingual and are willing to invest the time and money, look into the schools that specialize in language instruction. Berlitz Language Schools have facilities in most major centers throughout North America and have long been regarded as one of the best language institutes available. Other popular immersion courses are offered by Dartmouth College's summer Accelerated Learning Programs (Contact: Dartmouth College, 6071 Wentworth Hall, Hanover, NH 13755-3525. Tel: (603) 646-2922 <www.dartmouth.edu\~rassias>) and the Language Immersion Institute at the State University of New York (Contact: College at New Paltz, JF916, New Paltz, NY 12561. Tel: (914) 257-3500).

For a comprehensive list of language instruction options, check out *Smart Vacations: The Traveler's Guide to Learning Adventures Abroad*, compiled by the nonprofit Council on International Educational Exchange and published by St. Martin's Press.

If you can't speak the language of a country you are visiting, a willingness to attempt some basic phrases will usually win approval (and often a broad smile at the accent) from the local people (see Table 1). A pocket dictionary/phrase book should be part of your standard equipment — especially if you are anything less than totally fluent in that language.

TABLE 1
SOME IMPORTANT PHRASES

You and your tour members should know these basic phrases in the language of the country you are visiting.

(a) Please.

(b) Thank you.

(c) Hello. My name is _____.

(d) Goodbye. Thank you for your hospitality.

(e) I don't speak _____ very well. Please talk slowly.

(f) I'm sorry. I don't understand.

(g) Would you show me in my phrase book please?

(h) Do you speak _____ (your own first language)?

(i) Can you show me where the washroom is, please?

(j) May I have the check, please?

It is tempting to include questions such as "Can you tell me how to get to attraction ABC?" in this list, but be aware that if you ask a question requiring a detailed answer, you may receive a precise and complete answer — all willingly passed on to you in a language you do not understand!

Tip: One way to get around asking for directions in a foreign language if you are trying to find a site not on the itinerary (during "free time," for example) is to carry a city map, mark the location of your hotel and any other places you need to find, then ask a local to show you on the map how to get from where you are to where you want to be. Many hotels, especially in major centers, will supply you and your tour members with free city maps.

3.2 Body language

Don't forget that language is not made up only of words. Every culture has idioms, gestures, and other nonverbal language. Here is a sample of some unusual customs and body language you may experience:

(a) In Portugal you may discuss business over lunch but never at dinner.

(b) Do not send flowers to thank your Chinese host. Except when brought to the hospital, a bouquet is believed to bring misfortune to the recipient.

(c) In Australia, the thumbs-up sign we use in North America to say "great" is more vulgar than the middle finger — something former US president George Bush learned to his lasting embarrassment while on a diplomatic trip Down Under.

(d) In Malaysia, pointing at an object with your index finger is rude. Use your thumb instead.

(e) In Israel, Singapore, Egypt, and Saudi Arabia, crossing your legs so someone can see the sole of your shoe is an insult.

(f) Fijians consider it a sign of respect for a person to talk with arms crossed over his or her chest.

(g) A smile is universal. Show yours frequently!

Cross-cultural faux pas can be embarrassing for both host and guest, so prepare before you go. Talk to other guides or make friends with someone who was born in the country. You might want to take a look at books in the series *The Simple Guide to Customs & Etiquette in...*, published by Global Books.

Customs and taboos vary dramatically from country to country. A sheet listing local Dos and Don'ts can save members of your group from making embarrassing and potentially dangerous mistakes.

4. YOUR RÉSUMÉ

Résumé writing is a skill all on its own, and there are dozens of books on the subject. The following very basic list will help you catch the eye of a potential employer, but if you are at all uncomfortable about your résumé-writing skills, pay a professional. The investment will be worth it!

(a) Use plain, white paper — fancy colors, sparkles, or other gimmicks label you as an amateur in any field. Choose a type font and size that will be easy to read. Serif fonts tend to be easier on the eye than sans serif, for example, and any size less than ten point will make your reader squint. Twelve point is even better. If you do not have a laser printer, find someone who does and is willing to let you print out your résumé.

Fluency in a second language is a much sought after skill.

(b) Keep it short, to the point, and, above all, accurate. A résumé should be no longer than two pages except in the most unusual circumstances. A single, well-written page is best. Be sure it is grammatically correct and completely free of typos or spelling mistakes.

(c) Your name, address, phone number, and, if appropriate, fax number and e-mail address should appear centered at the top.

(d) State your objectives clearly. If you want to work locally only, say so. If you are willing to travel anywhere, any time, tell them that.

(e) Use active verbs such as developed, achieved, or organized when talking about previous experience.

(f) Special skills should be shown prominently and early in the résumé. Languages are especially big attention grabbers for a tour operator, but be sure to list all certificates and training such as first aid, CPR, and current licenses to drive motor-coaches or other vehicles.

(g) Volunteer work shows commitment to your goals and a willing attitude. If your neighborhood has a volunteer bureau it can save you many hours of door knocking and searching for some practical experience. While it is not as easy to find as other types of volunteer work, you *can* gain guiding experience this way. For example, many cruise line meet-and-greet guides are volunteers. Or you can contact local museums, botanical gardens, historical attractions, and art galleries. Many are chronically short of cash and welcome volunteers.

(h) Include hobbies if they are relevant and demonstrate experience. If you say you have been a member of Toastmasters for six years, a potential employer will know something important about your public speaking ability.

(i) This is a people industry. Whenever possible, drop your résumé off in person so at least one person knows what you look like and how you present yourself. Always be polite, professional, and immaculate in your appearance. Skilled receptionists and secretaries frequently eliminate sloppily dressed or rude applicants before the first round of job interviewing starts.

(j) Have some references available to show a potential employer during the interview. Be shameless about asking past employers or other responsible individuals for a letter of reference which will show you as levelheaded, energetic, reliable, and competent. If you organized a city tour for your church group or your son's baseball team, the minister or coach will likely be more than happy to help you out.

No book can teach you how to have the personality tour operators are looking for when they hire guides. Once you are invited for an interview, be prepared before you go in, be natural during the process, and remember that "fit" within the company is just as important as skills and experience — sometimes even more important. Many guides, when talking about past interviews, have told us about "great" interviews which ended with the tour operator explaining, "You have a wonderful future in this business, but you're not quite what we are looking for." Do not get discouraged and always ask if your interviewer can recommend another company you should apply to.

5. A STARTING POINT

The best starting point for any job search is in your own community. While the newspaper is traditionally downplayed as a source of employment leads, it is still worth looking at. Sometimes you can strike paydirt in the local daily.

Don't forget to surf the net during your job search and learn how to use a search engine effectively.

Visit your local travel agent — he or she will know if there are any tour companies locally who might be hiring guides. If you see a bus sporting a sign that says "ABC Tours," note down the company's phone number and give it a call. All tour companies hire guides from somewhere, so why not put your name in front of as many of them as possible. Other sources are the Yellow Pages (yes, they really are a great reference), your local chamber of commerce, and departments of tourism (municipal, provincial or state, and national). Appendix 2 lists some of the major tour operators you should contact. Don't be put off by a company just because it is located on the other side of the continent. Tour operators need reliable guides everywhere because tours are created everywhere.

6. HOW MUCH WILL I MAKE?

6.1 Pay rates

Payment varies widely throughout the industry, usually by region. According to research by the National Tour Association, rates are highest in the northeast, Great Lakes, mid-Atlantic, and southern regions. The northwest, west, and Pacific coast areas tend to be at the lower end of the pay scale. While it is possible to earn up to $65,000 per year (including tips) if you are employed by one of the major tour companies, a more realistic figure is probably $20,000 to $35,000. As an overall average, you can expect to make $100 to $150 per day as a tour director or $10 to $20 per hour as a local guide. Gratuities can add a substantial amount to your income, but they are unreliable. One group may tip lavishly, the next give nothing at all, and certain groups simply do not ever tip. Students, for example, are usually on a tight budget themselves, and some cultures consider tipping unnecessary or insulting.

Another factor to consider is the seasonal nature of tour guiding. Only 20 percent of tour guides or tour directors work full time, year-round. For others, 150 days in a year would be considered a heavy work schedule. Regardless of location, the main tour season runs from May to October, ideal for people who want to pursue other interests or kick back and relax for six months out of the year. Some typical winter jobs are ski instructor, student, semi-retired go-getter, and artist.

Bill Newton, cofounder of the International Tour Management Institute (ITMI), has found that many of the best tour guides and directors are the ones who integrate tour management with other pursuits. "If you're doing this year-round," he says, "it often becomes just another job. The ones who pursue other interests as well do this because they love the work. That makes them much better guides than people who are doing it only to make the payments."

6.2 Contracts

Written contracts for freelancers are surprisingly uncommon. Most tour directors and guides are hired verbally on the basis of their résumé and a personal interview. It is not unheard of for someone with experience and good references to get the job after only a phone interview.

7. OCCUPATIONAL STANDARDS

7.1 Canada

In early 1996, the Canadian tour industry ratified a set of voluntary national standards. Long-term professionals in the industry established minimum proficiency levels in all areas of tour guiding and tour directing. The standards are divided into three sections:

(a) Core skills

(b) Tour director

(c) Tour guide

Maureen Wright of the Pacific Rim Institute of Tourism (PRIT) in Vancouver, British Columbia, one of many people who worked on setting the standards, believes they will be invaluable for self-regulation within the industry, could become key components for training and educational purposes, and will provide a solid basis for job descriptions. Copies of the standards are available from PRIT for CDN$25 each or CDN$75 for all three sections. Write to:

Pacific Rim Institute of Tourism
Box 12101
930 - 555 W. Hastings Street
Vancouver, BC V6B 4N6
Tel: (604) 682-8000
Fax: (604) 688-2554

PRIT also began a testing/certification program in 1996 which will recognize qualified guides. The test involves a written exam (15 percent Canadian knowledge, 25 percent provincial knowledge, 65 percent local knowledge) and an on-site assessment by an independent evaluator who goes on tour with the applicant. This pilot project could ultimately be used to certify local guides in all major centers across the country.

Montreal and Quebec City are, at present, the only cities in Canada with formal regulations for tour professionals. Both cities require local tour guides to be licensed, and impose fines for violation.

7.2 United States

There are no formal federal or state regulations governing tour directors in the United States. However, local guides in Washington (DC), New Orleans, and New York City must be licensed.

7.3 Europe

Most European countries regulate tour guides and tour directors. In many places, there are heavy fines for anyone — foreign or local — caught conducting a tour without the appropriate certification.

Be sure you check local licensing and registration requirements before you take a tour out. Some countries fine heavily if you're caught without the proper certification.

4
MEET THE PLAYERS

Whether you are putting together your own tours, guiding tours for someone else, or starting a tour company, you will need to know the players in the travel industry. Knowing what goes on behind the scenes will put you in a better position to solve problems when they arise and give you some understanding of what your employer deals with. And of course, if you are running your own tours, this information is essential.

1. THE TRAVEL SUPPLIERS

A travel supplier is any company or person selling a travel product. Airlines offer airline seats, travel insurers offer travel insurance, and tour guides offer escort services. But as you will see, definitions are flexible and it is not uncommon to find one company acting as several different kinds of supplier. A tour operator may also be a retail travel agency as well as a wholesaler of airline tickets or a consolidator, all under one roof! When you are designing your own tours, you may deal with a number of these suppliers individually or choose to work through an existing tour operator who offers an already assembled package.

Knowing what goes on behind the scenes will put you in a better position to solve problems.

1.1 Airlines

Airlines come in all sizes and use a multitude of equipment. Some, such as the national airlines and megacarriers, serve hundreds of locations, are well known, and maintain their own sales staff to sell directly to the public. Good examples are American Airlines or Air Canada. Some large airlines do not sell to the public at all, but charter their planes to other companies that in turn sell seats to tour operators, travel agencies, and the public. They receive little public recognition, but these charter airlines have a major impact on seat availability, especially to popular destinations during peak times (e.g., to Europe during the summer months or to hot spots during the winter).

Most airlines selling through tour operators and agencies adhere to the rules and regulations of the International Air Transport Association (IATA), which governs everything from commission rates to ticketing restrictions. Typically, airlines pay a commission to the tour operator or travel agency that sells tickets on its flights. Commissions for selling tickets start at 5 percent with a cap on the maximum amount you can earn that varies for domestic and international tickets. Be aware that there are many exceptions. As well, airlines are notorious for changing commission rates. You may find a profitable tour is suddenly no longer worth the effort because the airline changed its commission structure overnight. Keep current.

Some airlines (particularly charter companies) use net pricing, a method of selling in which the airline acts as a wholesaler, setting a ticket price for an intermediate buyer (a tour operator or travel agency, *not* the general public). The buyer then sells the ticket for whatever price the market will bear or packages the ticket with one or more other travel products and resells this package to the public after adding a profit. In the end, a tour operator will earn about the same amount from commissions or net pricing.

Airlines also pay higher incentive commissions, called overrides, if an agency's volume is high enough or if it belongs to a consortium (a group of agencies acting as one high-volume buyer to get higher commission rates). Usually overrides are on a sliding scale and open to negotiation. They are also subject to sudden termination or modifications as market conditions change.

If you are an independent contractor running someone else's tour, you probably will not know what kind of commission your company gets. However, when you put your own tours together, the rate of commission will be all-important when you decide what price to charge for the tour package. You must be sure you are making enough per ticket to cover all your expenses and still make a profit. If you are putting together your own tours through a travel agency, the override commission rate is something you should take into consideration when you are selecting an agency to work with (for more on this, see chapter 11). Overrides allow you to make a little extra money to compensate for other elements of your tour that may not generate much cash.

1.2 Consolidators and wholesalers

Consolidators and wholesalers sell airline tickets either at a discount or at a much higher commission than the airlines will give you. These companies provide a means for the airlines to sell large numbers of tickets at one time. Essentially, the wholesaler makes a commitment to sell a certain volume of tickets in return for a lower price, negotiating the best deal directly with the airlines. Although the airline is, in a sense, setting up competition for itself, the economics of the arrangement are worth the lost revenue.

Airlines never used to admit they engaged in such practices and would tell you, without blinking, that only they sold the airline tickets and that pricing was completely standardized. Airline employees would intimate that tickets not supplied by the airline were probably illegal imports from some distant country. Now, however, some airline reservation departments will tell you that you can get a better price from XYZ Consolidator and Wholesale Company. In effect, consolidators and wholesalers have become the reservation department for some of the airlines, who can then reduce staffing expenses.

1.3 Tour operators

Tour operators are companies that put together two or more travel suppliers' products. For example, a tour operator may commit itself to filling a large number of hotel rooms in Hawaii and a certain number of airline seats during a specific time period to get a preferred price. By combining these two purchases into a "package," the tour operator can sell it to the public for less than if the pieces were purchased separately from each of the travel suppliers. Sometimes it is possible to get the same airline seat through either the airline or a tour operator, but the tour operator's seat may be cheaper!

Tour operators come in all sizes and their products range from escorted tours to airline seats. Packaging tours is a fiercely competitive business with thin margins. Rules change quickly and agreements are canceled with little or no notice.

Commission overrides allow you to make extra money to compensate for elements of your tour that may not generate much cash.

Many of the major airlines have their own tour companies — legally separate companies with a different address, staff, and administration. These firms are dedicated to the airline, however, and use the parent company's equipment most of the time.

If you are just starting to run tours, you may decide to use existing packages instead of designing your own. One of the advantages of working through large tour operators, especially airline-owned ones, is the clout they have with the airlines. As a matter of policy, you may want to play it safe and book your clients only with major tour companies. In a crunch (if you are stranded in a foreign country, for instance), you may be able to count on the tour operator's connections for help. Smaller tour companies, on the other hand, sometimes pay you more than the large companies to entice you to deal with them. In the end, you will have to decide whether the added risk is worth the extra profit. Although it often is, this is far from a hard and fast rule — sometimes security is priceless.

Tour operators come in all sizes and their products range from escorted tours to airline seats.

Tour operators generally specialize in either inbound or outbound markets. As the name implies, inbound tours originate in another country and come to the local area. Outbound tours leave the local area and go to another country. Whether focusing on inbound or outbound, tour operators offer their clients several different types of packages ranging from simple combinations of airfare, hotel, and transfers between the airport and hotel to all-inclusive, fully escorted extravaganzas. Here are the basic divisions you should be aware of.

(a) Group Inclusive Tour (GIT)

A Group Inclusive Tour (GIT) includes transportation to and from the destination, plus transportation needed while traveling, hotel-airport transfers, accommodation, sightseeing, and usually at least some of the meals. These highly structured tours offer western-style accommodation and dining, English-speaking staff at all stops, and limited free time. They are ideal for travelers on their first trip to truly foreign destinations such as the Far East or Muslim countries where customs and cultures are radically different from the tourist's home, or for the person who simply wants to have the comfort of familiar surroundings.

(b) Foreign Independent Travel (FIT)

Foreign Independent Travel (FIT) is a customized group tour. A group of wine connoisseurs might arrange a FIT tour of the Loire Valley of

France. Several members of the group would work out the details, tailoring the itinerary to the group's interests, then leave it up to the tour operator to arrange appropriate bookings and local guides.

(c) Independent Tours (IT)

Independent Tours (IT) are for people who want prearranged rates for the basics (airfare, accommodation, and ground transportation) but complete freedom and no guide at the destination. A couple honeymooning in Acapulco on an IT know their hotel and rental car are waiting on arrival at the airport but are free to explore (or stay at the hotel) as they fancy.

(d) FAM

FAM trips are just one of the marvelous perks of being in the tour guiding business. These are subsidized or free trips to a destination or attraction which FAMiliarize tour operators, directors, and tour guides with its features. For example, a new theme park might provide several nights' accommodation and admission to all rides and exhibits so that tour professionals will promote and show off the park to maximum advantage throughout the season.

1.4 Hotels and car rental agencies

Hotels and car rental agencies sell not only to the public through their own offices and toll-free telephone numbers but also to tour operators. Commission rates range from 5 percent to 12 percent.

1.5 Insurance

Insurance suppliers generally provide medical, accidental death, lost baggage, and cancellation insurance to the industry. This is a wonderful source of revenue as commission rates vary from 10 percent to more than 40 percent on a policy. It is also a necessary protection for you and your clients, especially for travel in foreign countries. Many tour operators insist their clients carry complete insurance in order to join a tour, while others require clients to sign a waiver if they choose to travel without insurance.

1.6 Cruises

There are more cruise ships being built now than at any time in the last 50 years. As a floating luxury resort, each line tries to set itself apart from the others by stressing price, quality, luxury, or differences in the exotic destinations and sidetrips they offer. Ticket prices for a cruise are normally above $1,000 per person, so commissions for each sale start at $100.

2. AGENCY SPECIALTIES

If you are going to run your own tour operation, you will need to find a travel agency to work with. You may deal directly with airlines and hotels in some states and provinces, but in others it is illegal to accept money for travel unless you are either a registered agency yourself or are working under an existing agency's license. (For more information on working with a travel agency, see chapter 11; on laws and registration procedure, see chapter 15.)

The days of the general full-service travel agency are not over. However, the complexity of the industry today has spawned thousands of agencies specializing in particular areas and types of travel. It is to your advantage to focus on those agencies that best represent what you are aiming for. If you want to put together a tour of England, don't go to an agency specializing in African safaris. Keep in mind that the contacts of the travel agency you have chosen will make all the difference to the quality of your tour and to the amount of money you make. If you are going after a certain kind of client, a specialized travel agency may be able to do a better job at a better price than a full-service agency. The specialized agency will have clearly defined target markets and will aim its marketing at these potential clients. This will work to your advantage as you try to fill seats for your tour.

3. TRAVEL REGULATORS — IATA, BSP, IATAN, AND ARC

In the United States, the accreditation bodies you need to be concerned with are the International Airlines Travel Agent Network (IATAN) and the Airlines Reporting Corporation (ARC). In Canada and the rest of the world, the International Air Transport Association (IATA) and the Bank Settlement Plan (BSP) are the major players in accreditation. None of these are government agencies.

In Canada, an IATA appointment automatically means you are accepted by BSP. In the United States, an accreditation by IATAN does not mean acceptance by ARC. A separate application must be made to ARC, which has its own stringent requirements.

You may deal directly with airlines and hotels but in some states and provinces you must be working under a registered agency.

Although you do not need to be accredited by IATA/BSP or IATAN/ARC to be a tour operator, an appointment means your company may issue tickets for many of the association's member airlines and participate in the money settlement plans ARC and BSP provide. Companies appointed by IATA, ARC, and IATAN must meet minimum financial, security, and experience criteria.

As the names imply, IATA, ARC, and IATAN are concerned only with air transport. They have no bearing on cruises, hotels, or car rentals. (IATA, BSP, IATAN, and ARC are discussed at more length in chapters 11 and 15.)

5
WHAT DOES IT TAKE TO BECOME THE PERFECT TOUR DIRECTOR?

What does it take to become the perfect tour director? The long version (**Warning!** Inhale deeply before attempting to say this): The ability to ensure the smooth running of all transportation, luggage handling, sightseeing, activities, accommodations, group meals, customs clearances; to negotiate the best rates for all of the preceding; to promote communication and camaraderie between fellow travelers from the minute the tour begins till the moment the last person heads home.

If you can say it all in one breath, you have probably already passed the lung capacity test to be a tour guide.

The short version (for those in a hurry to read on or who skipped operatic voice training): Everything!

Well-run tours don't just happen. They are the result of superb organization by the tour operator and precision choreography by the tour

Patience and attention to the most minute details are essential qualities for tour guides and tour directors.

guides and directors. It is the tour professional's enthusiasm and attitude that set the tone for any tour, and he or she is solely responsible for making everyone feel comfortable and well cared for. The director or guide is the person tour members interact with, and he or she must be prepared to be ambassador, diplomat, entertainer, historian, psychologist, translator, mind reader, and miracle worker.

The next seven chapters will give you an overview of the duties and responsibilities you can expect when you embark on a career in tour guiding and tour directing. Some of what you read here will be a surprise, while other information may seem self-evident or will not apply to everyone (for example, a step-on guide may wish to skip the sections about cruising). But remember, it is usually the self-evident things that get overlooked in any project, things that are so "obvious" people forget about them. And it is usually those obvious but forgotten considerations that cause the biggest problems.

1. GENERAL DUTIES

1.1 Present a professional image at all times

Whether your route takes you around your hometown or around the globe, you are on display every minute when conducting a tour. People may not consciously notice if you are well groomed and courteous, but they certainly will notice if you are not. Your outward appearance and manners must be immaculate at all times.

(a) Learn everyone's name

It is human nature. People love to hear the sound of their own name, so learn all your clients' names, preferably within the first day or two. Use names frequently — when you greet people, thank them, or acknowledge a question. No one will complain that you have overused their name, but they might comment if they think you did not bother to find out what it was.

(b) Encourage everyone to feel they belong

If you learn something special or unusual about one of your clients, try to find some way of acknowledging it. It does not have to be as lavish as buying roses for a couple celebrating their 50th anniversary (although this could certainly be appropriate under some conditions). It could be no more than asking a gardening enthusiast if he or she had a chance to enjoy the chrysanthemums in the hotel garden, but it will show you are a caring professional and will help you develop rapport with the group.

When people tend to hang back, make a special attempt to draw them into the group, but never force the issue. On one wilderness tour, the director noticed a woman lagging behind the main group. Concerned their arduous hiking pace was overtaxing her, he made sure he was always close by whenever she fell back. It took a day and a half before she politely informed him, "I'm really tired of seeing you. I just want to take some photos in peace."

(c) Mind your p's and q's

Use the words "Please" and "Thank You" frequently. They can never be said too often.

(d) Avoid comparisons with other companies

Even if you are dissatisfied with some aspect of the company you are working for, keep it to yourself. Griping or comparing your company to another one never wins friends. It simply shows you in an unprofessional light and will likely lose you your contract.

(e) Don't show favoritism

When one of your clients is interested in a subject you feel passionate about, it is easy to spend more time talking with that person than with someone who does not share your interest. This can leave some members feeling left out or ignored. Everyone has paid the same price and is entitled to the same service, so you cannot let one or two people monopolize your time and affect the quality you present to all the others. Most tour directors make a point of sitting with hotel staff, the bus driver, or other guides once they have greeted their group for meals and found everyone a place to sit. This not only avoids even the most unintentional hint of favoritism but also gives the tour director some well-deserved and much-appreciated time away from the demands of the job.

If an unexpected opportunity comes up or you feel like doing something that is not on the itinerary, either do it alone on your free time or extend an open invitation to everyone in the group. It could be nothing more extravagant than a sunrise walk along the beach, but if you want to invite one person from the tour, you must invite everyone. You may end up with three or four people, most of the group, or just one companion, but you will not be accused of favoritism if everyone was given the chance to go.

Look for and take every opportunity to make the people on your tour feel special.

(f) Do not take sides

Even if you are the debating champ of your Toastmasters club, as a tour guide or director you must not give in to the urge to get involved in a verbal contest. You must remain neutral on controversial subjects and must never make jokes which could be taken offensively. Politics, race, gender, and religion are obvious subjects to avoid.

(g) Always be immaculately groomed

Clothes should be clean, pressed, and conservative — no flashy jewelry, excessive make-up, or overpowering perfume or after-shave. Keep skin, hair, and teeth clean, and remind yourself constantly that good posture is healthy and looks far more pleasing to the eye than a slouch. If you must chew gum or smoke, do so in private on your own time. Both habits can be extremely offensive, and a growing number of people are more than willing to speak out loudly against them.

To many people, worn down or scuffed shoes are a sign of poor grooming. Pay attention to your looks from head to toe.

While it makes sense to protect your eyes with high-quality sunglasses, especially in tropical or snowbound areas, those "cool" mirrored sunglasses will rapidly annoy most people. The same holds true for haircuts hiding your eyes. No matter what the current trend in eyewear or hairstyles, your face and eyes should always be clearly visible.

1.2 Encourage people to experience the uniqueness of a destination

It may be as simple as trying a native curry dish for the first time or as daring as strapping on a parachute and leaping out of a low-flying airplane. If you help people feel motivated and secure about stretching their personal limits, you will put your unique stamp on any tour. It is often these special highlights, things someone may never have dreamed possible, that become the most talked-about, most remembered part of a tour.

1.3 Be environmentally aware

There is an ever-increasing and long overdue awareness of environmental issues, and the tourism industry as a whole is working hard to promote this awareness. Tour guides and directors have a responsibility to encourage the protection of our fragile planet.

   (a) *Do not litter.* Manmade garbage is just as big a problem in the city as the wilderness. If you pack it in, pack it out — even in town. And make sure members of your group follow this rule too.

(b) *Reduce, reuse, recycle.* Help keep pollution under control whenever possible by observing the Three R's — reduce, reuse, recycle. Watch for energy efficient power alternatives such as propane buses, or perhaps you could walk the two blocks to the restaurant rather than busing everywhere. It is also wise to encourage your driver to turn off the bus engine whenever possible. This is not only for environmental reasons but also for your clients. We were once on a tour where the only way to see the view at one site was to stand directly in front of the spot where the fumes poured out of the bus's exhaust system. It made a big impression. Too bad it was not the right one.

(c) *Do not pick the flowers.* Don't allow tour participants to take flowers, artifacts, or other "souvenirs" from natural or historical sites. Make sure they don't feed wildlife, as this can disrupt the animals' natural feeding habits. Remember the principle: "Take only pictures; leave only footprints."

1.4 Hurry up latecomers

Travelers who are less than punctual should be dealt with politely, promptly, and firmly. Since a late start usually cannot be made up at the end of the day, everyone comes out losers when one person constantly holds up the rest of the group. If you set a good example by always being on time or early, most people will do the same.

1.5 Keep written, daily reports

In addition to whatever daily reports your tour operator requires, it is to your own advantage to document anything unusual, different, or new. You never know what tidbit of information may be useful on your next trip — quality of service, new or improved attractions (how long did the gondola take now that it has finally been overhauled?), weather, food, road conditions (that new bridge under construction will slow down traffic for the next six months — maybe it is time to find an alternate route), and, of course, expenses. Once you are home, transfer everything into your files for future use.

1.6 Have map, will travel

Maps are like hieroglyphics, and learning to read them efficiently and accurately is a survival skill for any tour professional. Here are some of the points to consider.

Always be environmentally aware and encourage tour participants to be so as well.

- Don't litter
- Remember the 3 R's: reduce, reuse, recycle
- Don't disturb the local flora and fauna

There are many excellent sources of maps available on the Internet, but be aware of any possible copyright infringement before distributing them to your group.

(a) Learn how scale and direction translate from the printed page to what is in front of you. You must be able to look at a map and know which side of the bus an attraction will be on or how far away the hotel is — even when you are reading the map upside down.

(b) Certain conventions are common to most maps (for example, north is usually at the top). If you are familiar with the conventions, you will adjust more easily to the idiosyncrasies of a particular map.

(c) Cities and even villages sometimes change overnight. Roads are built or built over, and a shopping mall may spring from what was once open countryside. Several years ago, members of a cycling tour made plans to tent overnight in a small town called Farmer. They arrived at what was supposed to be the center of town, but the only buildings in sight were an abandoned gas station and a farmhouse. Since night was approaching, the tour director knocked on the door of the farmhouse to get directions. "Farmer?" said the owner with a laugh. "Heck, Farmer burned down six years ago." Make sure your map is up-to-date.

(d) Maps can be a source of information about attractions to include in the tour. Watch for historical site markers and information included in sidebars or inserts.

2. WELCOME TO TODAY'S DESTINATION — PROVIDING COMMENTARY

How many steps are there to the top of that pyramid? Is the water safe to drink here? How much is this painting worth? What time is dinner tonight? How long did it take to carve Mount Rushmore?

People on tour expect their guide to know everything — everything about getting to the destination, every obscure bit of history, every plan for the future, every species of flora and fauna, even some questions that will leave you shaking your head in bewilderment, like the guide taking a group on a 20-minute ocean ferry ride who was asked how far above sea level they were.

All right, so you don't know the juicy details about the miller's daughter who had an affair with the lord of the manor's son in 1567. What do you tell the tourist who is not going to be happy until you have given an answer?

At one time people said, "If you don't know, smother your guilt and feelings of inadequacy, remember it's a losing battle to keep ahead of all the questions, and fake it." Tales with sex, thievery, and religious persecution are hard to check and sound plausible almost everywhere. The danger of this approach is that a different version of the story may show up on the postcard rack at the next stop. A better, more professional approach is simply to admit you don't know but will make every attempt to find out — and then follow through!

One guide taking a group of German tourists around the lakes of central British Columbia was asked a technical question about tying flies for fly-fishing. The guide was not a fisherman, so he didn't know the answer. That evening he checked with a local fishing enthusiast who not only supplied the answer but also passed on a copy of *The Fisherman's Calendar* for the upcoming year. The German was ecstatic and the guide learned something new about a popular subject.

Of course, it helps if you are a historian or have already made many trips to the area you are traveling through. But even if you aren't or haven't, there is an easy solution. Read, read, read before arriving at any destination. Most guides already have a passionate interest in the areas they travel to, so research is a pleasure, not a chore. With minimal effort you will discover hundreds of excellent guidebooks on popular destinations and almost as many on most of the obscure ones. Several lightweight reference books can be tucked into a guide's shoulder bag or kept close at hand on the office bookshelf. To start off your own resource library, here are some names to watch for:

Learn some of the local legends and myths as well as the history. These not only give insight into an area's cultural treasures, but they add spice to your commentary.

- Baedeker publications
- Berlitz's Executive Travel Guides
- Birnbaum guides
- Canadian and American Automobile Association publications
- Fielding's guides
- Fodor's travel guides
- Frommer's Comprehesive Guides
- Michelin guides
- Passports Illustrated Travel Guides (from Thomas Cook)
- Rick Steves' European travel guides

- Triptiks road map and guide books

- Tourism and tourist bureau publications

For entertaining and obscure facts, the *Guinness Book of Records* is often overlooked, as are a host of other trivia books. If you want to add some lighthearted anecdotes, these books can be fun and educational.

Experts are often willing to share information and personal experiences which add a special dimension to your commentary. See if you can arrange a tour with, or a brief talk from, someone at the local archives, museum, weather bureau, college, indigenous peoples' organization, forestry and parks department, theater and entertainment facilities, or even religious institutions. Go ahead, ask for an hour of the planetarium curator's time or for a backstage tour of the Metropolitan Opera. The worst that can happen is the person will be too busy or say no.

Keeping current is essential to your success. Tourism offices, visitors' bureaus, and chambers of commerce help you keep up to the minute about an area. Radio and TV broadcasts, magazines, and the local daily newspapers are sources of current information, but so are the "freebies" published in most towns and cities. Don't thumb your nose just because they don't cost anything.

What kind of information do people want? Someone will eventually ask you for anything you can think of — and much that you cannot imagine — but there are a few standard questions you need to prepare yourself for.

2.1 The area's natural environment

People don't need to be biologists or zoologists to want information about the area they are traveling through. Questions will likely include:

- What kind of local flora and fauna will I see?

- What about the geology? (Just how was the Grand Canyon formed?)

- What is the weather like? This is not just a conversation opener on tours. People are interested in climate, seasons, and temperature.

- Is the water safe to drink here? Water quality is becoming a concern everywhere, not just in third world nations.

Keep up with changes and current events in all the areas that you take tours to.

2.2 Sociology

- How is the government structured and where are the centers of power? Is it a democratic system or a form of dictatorship?

- How do people earn their living and how much does it cost to live here? What kinds of jobs and industries are there? What does a house cost? How much is food and entertainment? If I lived here, could I put my kid through college? If I got sick here, what are the medical services like?

- What kinds of community services are available? These services can be anything from art festivals and recreational facilities to ATM/bank machines. Experienced tour guides know they must have information on churches, laundry and dry cleaning, libraries, liquor stores, museums, shopping malls, sports stadiums, and restaurants.

- What are the predominant religions?

2.3 The area's history and current statistics

How many people live here? How big is the country? What happened here 100 years ago? 500 years ago? 20 years ago?

2.4 Transportation

What kinds of transportation are available? Participants on one Vancouver, BC, tour were so fascinated by small shuttle boats bobbing across False Creek that the tour guide added the 15-minute ride to her next tour's itinerary. It was one of the highlights because it was so unique.

2.5 Taxes

Everyone loves to hate taxes. Otherwise calm, mild-mannered people have been known to take on the characteristics of an angry war god when faced with a 15 percent tax bill on their souvenirs. Be sure to warn your group about the local taxes when entering a new country. There are three common forms of taxes:

(a) Local sales tax is usually set by province, state, or municipality.

(b) Value-added tax (VAT) is common in European countries.

(c) Goods and services tax (GST) is less common but similar to VAT. GST is added to all services including laundry, rentals, and postage.

The good news is that foreigners can often receive refunds for the tax they pay by applying at customs when leaving the country, state, or province.

3. IT'S ALL A MATTER OF COMMUNICATION

You have done your research. You have pored over all the printed material you could find. You have interviewed locals, experts, and every member of the visitor's bureau. You have confirmed that all your facts are current and accurate. You're ready!

Or are you?

No matter how much information you have prepared, you must be able to deliver it in a way that sparks people's interest and keeps them clamoring for more. Successful tour guides and tour directors are skilled communicators who project an infectious enthusiasm through their commentary.

3.1 Keeping their attention

Your commentary is like live theatre — it must be entertaining just as much as it must be informative.

Here are some tips from experienced guides to help you prepare sparkling commentary that will keep everyone listening eagerly.

(a) A four-hour lecture read directly from notes is boring to both you and the tour members. Be as dramatic as your comfort level and professionalism allow. Build suspense and excitement. Deliver your commentary with different inflections and gestures, and vary the pace, being sure to use and explain any colorful or unusual local jargon such as "the briny," a British term for the sea.

(b) Stay on topic, but be aware of each group's individual interests. One first-time guide was amazed to discover his group was more interested in golf and souvenir shopping than anything he had to say about the Grand Canyon.

(c) Encourage questions, then paraphrase and repeat them back to the entire group before you answer. This allows everyone to understand what you are answering. It also acknowledges the merit of the question, and makes the person who asked it feel they are a valued member of the group. Questions can spark new areas for you to research, which will benefit all future tours. If one person is curious about the way an earthquake-proof building is constructed, you can be sure others are too.

(d) Personal anecdotes add spice. Personal opinions can be annoying or even insulting.

(e) We use many empty qualifiers and sweeping generalizations in day-to-day speech. *Best, worst, a lot of, nice, fantastic,* or *pretty* are all phrases to avoid. They add fluff but no substance and are often inaccurate. A comment such as "A lot of pretty nice flowers are in this fantastic botanical garden" will curl most anyone's hair whether they are interested in flowers or not.

(f) We have five senses, so draw on all of them. Is it hot or cold? How does the freshly cut hay smell, or the roast duck from the market? Is it so silent you can hear the leaves rustle or are jackhammers pounding behind you? Is the fabric spun by local weavers silky smooth or coarse and abrasive?

3.2 Can everyone hear me?

Microphones and on-board communication systems make delivering commentary much easier and less physically exhausting than it once was. However, they have their quirks like any other machinery. Here is how to work with, not against, your communication equipment.

(a) Test the system before your tour members arrive. The driver will probably know when there is a problem, but you should run a quick check all the same. (It never hurts...)

(b) We have all heard it — the piercing shriek when someone turns the volume on an amplifier too high and creates audio feedback. It certainly gets everyone's attention, but it is attention you would be better off without. Adjust the volume and balance ahead of time so you know where the feedback areas are and so people in one part of the bus are not fishing out their earplugs while others are straining to hear what you are saying.

(c) Cordless systems run on batteries. Make sure the battery is charged and always carry a spare.

(d) If you are not fortunate enough to have a cordless microphone, be aware of where the cord is. Anything that dangles in the aisles will eventually get tripped over — most likely by you.

(e) Video equipment may need to be focused or repositioned so everyone can see.

3.3 The strange case of the missing voice

Like any other activity, speaking for long periods of time may strain unprepared muscles. You might be saying to yourself, "No problem, I'm used to talking for hours." You will make this mistake only once. A tablespoon of honey mixed with several drops of lemon and glycerin is a wonderful folk remedy for the week-long bout of laryngitis you will probably suffer if you do talk too much.

Never attempt to shout over a loud noise or outside interruption. Usually people still won't be able to hear you, and you may seriously damage your voice.

You must learn to protect your voice. When there is a lot of outside noise or if people are talking loudly around you, pause in your commentary instead of attempting to talk over it. Shouting for prolonged periods can seriously damage your vocal chords, and no one will pay attention in any case. Whether you have access to a microphone or not, project your voice from your diaphragm, not your throat. Allow your breathing patterns to help the sound of your words flow instead of blocking them. Drama or voice classes are an excellent investment if you feel your voice does not carry well. For guides who want to learn some techniques to keep their voices fit and flexible, we have found *The Right to Speak* and *The Need for Words* by Patsy Rodenburg, head of the voice departments at both London's Royal National Theatre and the Guildhall School of Music and Drama, have many easy but effective voice exercises. Ask for other recommendations at any bookstore or library, or contact a local chapter of Toastmasters.

4. KEEP PEOPLE INFORMED ABOUT ALL ACTIVITIES

Next to providing commentary, this is one of the most important duties a tour professional has. While it becomes more important as the length of the tour increases, making sure everyone knows exactly what is happening and what is expected of them during the next few hours is just as important as announcing tonight's dress code for dinner or reminding people to have passports and travel visas handy for tomorrow's shopping trip across the border into Tijuana. For instance, there will be times when you must be away from the group for short periods. Always indicate when you expect to be back, since some people become nervous if they haven't seen the tour director for a quarter of an hour.

Always let your group know if you will not be available and for how long.

Be specific. If you have ever waited for an unpleasant task to end, you will know that "We'll be at our hotel soon" means very different things to different individuals. One person may assume you will arrive in an hour or so, while another will expect to be in the front lobby within five minutes. "We'll be at our hotel at 5:30" is clear to everyone. Likewise, "The gray high rise with the statue in front, which you can see to your right" may sound like overkill but is far easier to understand than "The tall building over there." Just where is "over there" anyway? If possible, a written daily itinerary helps avoid such misunderstandings as "But it's only 9:15. Didn't you say breakfast started at 9:30?" Post a notice beside the elevator or in some other prominent location, and then give everyone verbal reminders several times throughout the day.

The key to passing on information effectively is to give it to the entire group as a whole. This saves you time because you don't have to repeat yourself, ensures no one misses a crucial set of instructions, and avoids giving the impression of any form of favoritism. Never assume everyone can hear you, even if you are all crammed into a small waiting area or lobby. Always ask, "Can everyone hear me?" Many people, seniors especially, are hard of hearing but hate to admit to it. Here are some of the obvious and not-so-obvious details that your clients will want to know about, even if they haven't yet thought to ask you.

- What time is lunch and what restaurant will it be at?

- When should I get my wake-up call and how do I get one?

- Should I put my bags in the hallway or will the bellhop (or room steward) get them from my room?

- What time does the bus leave tomorrow morning?

- Is there a washroom at the next stop? How far away is it?

- How much time will I get to spend in the air museum we are visiting today? Will we be going through on our own or will the curator be with us so I can ask questions?

- I've run out of money. Where can I cash a traveler's check and know I am not getting ripped off? (Sometimes hotels offer better rates than banks. If you can find out the current exchange rate, you will impress your group even more.)

- Help, I'm suffering from shopping withdrawal. Where's the nearest mall?

- I'm really bored. I have no idea what to do with my free day. Can I rent a bike around here?

- My room is on the top floor. Where are the elevators?

Always reconfirm the details before you arrive. The biggest to the smallest plans sometimes go awry, and if you have even a few hours of warning you'll be that much more likely to smooth things over so your tour group hardly notices anything went wrong.

⊕ I want to have lunch at the beach. Will the hotel make me a picnic basket?

5. CONFIRM AND RECONFIRM ALL RESERVATIONS

The most detailed, well-planned reservations sometimes go awry. A tour professional should reconfirm every reservation, from the largest hotel to the smallest attraction, prior to arrival. (One possible exception is a step-on guide who shows up twice a day for the entire season at the same two museums and botanical garden.)

Early evening, after you have settled into the hotel and before dinner, is often a good time for this activity. Tour participants are unpacking and relaxing and less likely to bother you. Remember, though, that certain attractions will already be closed, so some directors confirm one or two reservations at each stop throughout the day.

You will likely find some combination of these two methods works best for you. Whatever method you decide on, a form similar to Sample 1 will help you keep track. When confirming any reservation, from a major worldwide airline to an all-but-unknown craft museum, always find out who you are speaking with and make a note of the name. It is amazing how much faster people respond to a problem when you are able to say, "I spoke with Martha Black at 5:30 yesterday to confirm this booking." Toll-free numbers are there to be used, so use them without hesitation whenever possible. Your tour operator will most likely give you a list of relevant numbers, but it is wise to build your own list and add to it every trip. In North America, the continent-wide toll-free directory can be reached at 1-800-555-1212.

6. BE PREPARED

Lord and Lady Baden-Powell had a great idea when they made "Be prepared" the motto of the Boy Scouts and Girl Guides. Almost anything can, and usually does, happen in the most unlikely places. While it would be wonderful to look into one of those mystical crystal balls and know exactly what will happen during your next tour, that is still a skill found only in fantasy novels. As mere mortals, we are able only to guess. Checklist 1 does not give you a window into the future, but it does list a few easy-to-carry items that will help you be prepared for some of the things you will encounter.

DAILY CONFIRMATION SHEET

Day # _____ Date: _____

Special needs:

meals: _____

_____

accomodations: _____

_____

Breakfast at: _____

    Confirmed with: _____ On: _____ a.m./p.m.

Lunch at: _____

    Confirmed with: _____ On: _____ a.m./p.m.

Dinner at: _____

    Confirmed with: _____ On: _____ a.m./p.m.

Hotel: _____

    Confirmed with: _____ On: _____ a.m./p.m.

Attractions:

No. 1: Local guide: _____

    Confirmed with: _____ On: _____ a.m./p.m.

No. 2: Local guide: _____

    Confirmed with: _____ On: _____ a.m./p.m.

No. 3: Local guide: _____

    Confirmed with: _____ On: _____ a.m./p.m.

Problems: _____

_____

Additional comments: _____

_____

CHECKLIST 1
TOUR DIRECTOR'S SURVIVAL KIT

These are things you should carry with you on every tour. You may wish to provide a similar checklist to your tour members, since it would be good for them to carry many of these items as well. While you may think this amount of stuff will fill a large suitcase, with some practice you can fit it all easily into a small briefcase or overnight bag.

- [ ] Extra bandages of varying sizes
- [ ] Aspirin or equivalent
- [ ] Antibacterial lotion or spray for minor injuries
- [ ] Motion sickness treatment
- [ ] Diarrhea treatment
- [ ] Skin moisturizer
- [ ] Sunscreen
- [ ] Sunburn treatment (aloe vera is still one of the best, most effective treatments for any type of burn)
- [ ] Throat and cough lozenges
- [ ] Insect repellant
- [ ] Moist towelettes or singly packaged baby wipes
- [ ] Nail file
- [ ] Tweezers
- [ ] Bobby pins
- [ ] Laundry soap in a small container
- [ ] Several small, zip-lock plastic bags for dirty or wet clothes
- [ ] Sewing kit with a few spare buttons of various sizes (many larger hotels supply kits no larger than a matchbook in the rooms)
- [ ] Safety pins
- [ ] Duplicate address book (ALWAYS leave your original at home)
- [ ] Local stamps (you may have to buy these when you arrive)
- [ ] Small supply of birthday, anniversary, and thank-you cards
- [ ] Spare pens and pencils
- [ ] Paper clips

- [ ] Small, solar-powered calculator
- [ ] Business cards (always carry A LOT and hand them out freely)
- [ ] Inexpensive items "typical" of your country that you can give away generously as thank-you gifts (perhaps a brooch or lapel pin showing your national flag, a small booklet of native legends, or even postcards of home)
- [ ] Inexpensive, fun prizes for any on-tour contests or games
- [ ] Journal/diary (most experienced travelers use one faithfully every trip to record first impressions and anything else that captivates their interest)
- [ ] Personal organizer/planner (many people still prefer a manual organizer, but there are also many cheap electronic ones which can double as a phone book, message pad, and a variety of other recordkeeping items)
- [ ] Enough film for the trip with some to spare (it is usually much cheaper to buy at home and take it with you)
- [ ] Spare disposable camera, camera battery, and flash
- [ ] Dictionary/phrase book
- [ ] Lightweight Swiss army knife (or equivalent)
- [ ] Penlight (small flashlight the size of a pen)
- [ ] Book of matches and a small candle in a plastic bag
- [ ] Sink/bathtub stopper (honest, many places don't have these)
- [ ] Earplugs (especially if you have trouble sleeping while traveling)
- [ ] Emergency fold-up raincoat
- [ ] Emergency space blanket (especially on wilderness tours)

6
YOU'RE ON YOUR WAY

At last! You are on your way with your very first group. Weeks of preparation and planning are all about to pay off.

1. AT THE AIRPORT (OR OTHER TERMINALS)

Many tours begin and end in an airport terminal. Here is where you will create a first impression and leave a lasting one. You want them both to be good. Here's how. Checklist 2 will help you keep track of all the details.

1.1 Confirm your group's reservation

Several days before departure, confirm your group's reservation and advise the airline of special needs such as vegetarian meals or wheelchairs. These items must be booked in advance. Now is also a good time to find out what meals will be served (full meals or just a snack), exactly how long the flight will take, and what famous landmarks might be visible along the way. Rest assured you will be asked for this information many times, both when your group arrives and during the flight.

CHECKLIST 2
AIRPORT CHECKLIST

SEVERAL DAYS BEFORE DEPARTURE

☐ Confirm group's reservation

☐ Confirm all special requests/needs (e.g., meals, wheelchair)

☐ Confirm aisle seat for yourself

☐ Draw up seating plan

DEPARTURE DAY

☐ Make sure all tour members have arrived

☐ Check tour members and luggage against master list

☐ Ensure everyone has all travel documents (e.g., passport, visa)

☐ Make sure baggage is tagged correctly

☐ Oversee and help with group check-in

☐ Announce departure time and gate number

☐ Hand out boarding passes and explain that they are not replaceable

☐ Check nothing has been left in the departure lounge

DURING THE FLIGHT

☐ Introduce yourself to flight crew

☐ Make sure everyone is comfortable

☐ Make sure that anyone seated next to an emergency exit is willing to assume the responsibility

☐ Encourage people to move around and drink lots of water

☐ Help with customs forms if necessary

ON ARRIVAL AT THE DESTINATION TERMINAL

☐ Make sure everyone has rejoined the group

☐ Take group through customs if applicable

☐ Confirm luggage count

☐ Find a porter to help with luggage

☐ Assist with luggage claims if necessary

☐ Find local guide or bus driver

☐ Reconfirm tour members and luggage count as the group boards

If possible, get seat assignments and plan where everyone will sit. Most airlines assume the tour director will want to sit with the rest of the group and will automatically place the entire tour in the same section of the aircraft. However, many experienced tour directors suggest it is better for the guide to sit away from the main group. You will probably need to make a special request for a separate seat, but it will be worth the minimal inconvenience. Not only does this give you some time to yourself but it also helps you avoid the appearance of favoritism right from the start. Always request an aisle seat for yourself so you can move around the cabin to check on your group during the flight.

1.2 Departure day

Stress levels rise at airports. The red tape, lineups, and noise at most airport terminals can cause frayed nerves and flaring tempers among even the most seasoned travelers. Never forget that the reason many people take a tour instead of traveling on their own is so someone else — namely you — takes care of tension-causing details. The more organized you are, the easier it will be to keep your clients calm and relaxed before takeoff.

Arrive early at the airport or other point of departure.

Be sure you arrive early. You must be at the airport well ahead of the first early bird from your tour — at least two hours before departure for a domestic flight and three hours before for international travel. As your group arrives, check each person's name off against your master list. During this process it is your responsibility to:

(a) Confirm everyone has all the necessary travel documentation: e.g., passport, travel visa, and proof of citizenship.

(b) Make sure all old destination tags have been removed from luggage and replaced with new ones. Remind all tour participants that they must be able to handle their own luggage if no porters are available. If any carry-on bags are oversized, make arrangements to have them checked through to the final destination.

(c) Point out where the washrooms, duty free shops, eateries, newsstands, public phones, and money exchanges are located in the terminal. If there is some free time to explore after check-in, be sure to give a specific time when everyone must congregate at the departure gate lounge. A smart director sets the time at least 15 minutes earlier than is absolutely necessary to allow for stragglers.

(d) Ensure everyone remains with the group until all tour members are checked in and boarding passes are issued.

1.3 Checking in

You will be working with one of three types of check-in at most airports.

(a) Each person checks in separately as a regular passenger.

(b) Once all members of the tour have arrived, the group checks in at a special group check-in counter. Group members present their own tickets, luggage, and travel documentation, but everyone goes through at the same time.

(c) Once all members are present, the tour director presents everyone's tickets and travel documentation at the counter while the group waits in a lounge or other holding area. At one time, this option was preferred by most airlines. Today, however, with increasing concern about security at airports worldwide, many airline officials want to see each person with his or her travel papers and own luggage before issuing a boarding pass.

Whichever system is used by the airport your tour flies from, make sure each tour member understands the value of the boarding pass. Once it has been issued, it is almost impossible to get a replacement if it is lost or stolen. One-way tickets to destinations even a few hundred miles away, let alone halfway round the world, are notoriously expensive. Watch carefully when the flight coupon for the current part of the trip is being detached. It is all too easy to take out two coupons by mistake — a situation that will create enormous problems at the next departure. Also, make sure the departure gate and time are clearly marked on the boarding pass and that each tour member knows exactly when they must be at the departure gate.

If you are using a group check-in counter, it helps speed things along and creates goodwill between you and the airline staff if you work with the agent and your clients at the counter. If you appear helpful and not overbearing, the airline staffperson will welcome your assistance and you may receive preferential treatment next time you are dealing with that same person.

1.4 Boarding

Some airlines allow a tour to board at the same time as passengers needing special assistance. Check with the departure gate staff as soon as you arrive to find out if they extend this courtesy. It does not always work out, but if the airline agrees to your request it will be an immediate

Pay attention when detatching flight coupons. If you take two parts out by mistake, you'll have a serious problem when it's time to board the next flight.

boost to your group's confidence in your ability — and to their desire to feel pampered.

Before heading down the ramp to the aircraft, make a final check to be sure everyone is present and that no purses, bags, books, umbrellas, or other personal materials have been left behind.

1.5 During the flight

During the flight, introduce yourself to the flight supervisor and crew, and reconfirm any special meal requests. If anyone in your group has been seated by an emergency exit and is not able or willing to assume the necessary responsibility during an emergency, arrange with the flight crew to have that person moved.

It is ironic and vaguely absurd, but sitting still on long flights leaves most people exhausted. It leaves many people cranky as well, so it is wise to encourage your group to circulate up and down the aisles of the plane during your flight. This will help build a sense of belonging as well as reduce the discomfort of sitting in one place for long periods. Table 2 describes some quick and easy exercises everyone can do during long flights (or when you are caught in a lengthy traffic jam on board a bus). Consider printing up a "stress busters" sheet to hand out before your group boards, perhaps decorated with a cartoon or a sketch of your first destination to entice everyone to read it.

Plane travel can be dehydrating, so be sure to drink lots of water yourself and suggest everyone else do the same. It is a common misconception that drinking tea and coffee is as good as drinking water. They may be emotionally soothing, but tea, coffee, and alcohol may aggravate the problem of dehydration even more.

If necessary, help your group fill out customs forms prior to landing.

Light exercise helps alleviate the fatigue and irritability many people experience during a long airflight.

1.6 On arrival at the destination terminal

On arrival at the destination terminal —

(a) Wait in an obvious and visible area until everyone has deplaned. Once the entire group is together, shepherd everyone toward the baggage claim area and, if necessary, to customs and immigration.

(b) Baggage claim areas are always crowded with people anxious to retrieve their suitcases and be on their way. The fewer people milling around the carousel, the better for you and everyone

TABLE 2
STRESS BUSTERS FOR AIRLINE TRAVEL

Here are some simple exercises everyone, including you, can do to help alleviate the stiffness, fatigue, and boredom of a long flight.

A.

Begin with feet flat on the floor, knees slightly apart. Raise heels as far as possible while keeping your toes on the floor. Repeat. Now raise toes while keeping heels on the floor. Repeat.

Repeat series five times.

B.

Lift right foot several inches off the floor and rotate five times clockwise and counterclockwise from the ankle.

Repeat with left foot.

C.

Try to shrug shoulders so high they touch the bottom of your ears. Then push back so they touch the seat.

Repeat five times.

D.

Turn your head and look as far to the right as possible. Hold for a count of five. Turn to the left, look, and hold for five.

Repeat series five times.

E.

Contract your buttocks and abdomen. Hold for a count of five and relax.

Repeat five times.

F.

Squeeze your hands into tight fists. Hold for a count of five. Now spread your fingers as wide apart as possible and hold for five.

Repeat five times.

G.

Open your mouth as wide as you can and let your eyes bug out. Now squeeze mouth and eyes shut as tightly as possible.

Repeat three times. (Most people prefer to move into the washroom or wait until the lights dim for the movie before they attempt this one!)

else. Seat your group as far outside the main flow of traffic as possible while you arrange for porters to gather everyone's bags.

(c) Horror stories about mauled baggage are plentiful. Check for damage caused during transit at the same time you make sure all luggage actually arrived. If any bags are missing or damaged, file a report immediately with the airline representative on hand. Never attempt to file a claim after leaving the airport — you must do it on the spot.

(d) If appropriate, find the local agent and/or bus driver you will be working with, and introduce yourself. Watch for signs bearing the group's name (Orchid Growers of America), the tour operator's name (ABC Tours), or even your own name when you are trying to locate the local contact. Although it is becoming less common, the local agent will sometimes be allowed inside the baggage claim area to help. More often you will be on your own until you have cleared customs and immigration.

(e) It never hurts to take one more head count! We cannot overemphasize the importance of this advice. Before leaving the airport, double-check one more time that all tour members and their bags are loaded on the bus — as you will be doing throughout the rest of the trip. A great way to make an irreparably bad impression is to start a tour with one member still at the airport.

2. HOTELS

A hotel check-in that is anything less than smooth will leave tour participants grumpy. Here's how to keep the fuss to a minimum and everyone happy. Checklist 3 will allow you to coordinate it all, effortlessly.

2.1 On arrival

There is something about arriving at a hotel which breeds impatience. People want to get to their rooms, the restaurant, the lounge, or the swimming pool, and they want to get there within minutes. Although some tour directors have their groups congregate in the front lobby, most ask everyone to remain on the bus while they check the group in, collect room keys, confirm any meal or entertainment vouchers, and review the rooming list. Also check for mail and messages. Even though tourists who can't stand to be without their mail and daily copy of the *Wall Street Journal* or *Financial Post* are stereotypes, you may have a couple

Use checklists to ensure you don't overlook important details.

CHECKLIST 3
HOTEL CHECKLIST

ON ARRIVAL
- [ ] Confirm master room-list is accurate
- [ ] Confirm all special requests/needs
- [ ] Check for mail and messages
- [ ] Brief group about meals and hotel amenities
- [ ] Brief group about local customs if applicable
- [ ] Remind people about cost of mini-bar service
- [ ] Remind people not to leave valuables in their rooms
- [ ] Announce time and location of next activity
- [ ] Announce your room number
- [ ] Hand out room keys
- [ ] Hand out local maps if applicable and mark the hotel location
- [ ] Post itinerary
- [ ] Schedule next day's wake-up calls
- [ ] Oversee luggage distribution
- [ ] Confirm next day's reservations and activities

ON DAY BEFORE CHECK-OUT
- [ ] Remind front desk your group will be checking out
- [ ] Confirm luggage pickup time with hotel staff
- [ ] Announce luggage pickup time and procedure to group
- [ ] Remind tour members to settle personal charges
- [ ] Remind tour members to collect anything in the hotel's safety deposit box
- [ ] Make any special arrangements necessary for early breakfast

CHECK-OUT DAY
- [ ] Confirm bill is accurate
- [ ] Confirm all tour members have paid personal charges
- [ ] Confirm all room keys are returned
- [ ] Leave forwarding address in case of lost or forgotten items
- [ ] Check bus is clean and ready
- [ ] Count luggage
- [ ] Count tour members

on your tour, or a member of your group may be expecting a delivery. And while everyone hopes it never happens to them, emergencies do occur.

The hotel should have room keys waiting in envelopes, tagged by name and ready to hand out. Many will even sort them alphabetically for easy distribution. It is a helpful touch with one potential problem — Mr. and Mrs. Zylan. They have lived a lifetime of being last in line and have either developed the patience of ten saints (in which case you have no problem) or have become snide and bitter (in which case you, your tour operator, and everyone else will hear about it). When you hand out room keys, vary the letter you start with — perhaps P to Z, then A to O one day, E to Z and A to D the next. Or borrow a cap from one of the tour members and draw names at random. Some tour directors find the second method helps them remember names faster.

Don't forget to hand out local maps and any vouchers (for meals, shopping, and attractions) you have for the group. Many hotels will give you free maps with their name, address, and phone number prominently marked and highlighted. If members get lost during a free-time exploration, they will be able to find their way back to the right hotel if they have one of these maps handy for reference. Before everyone gets off the bus, brief the entire group about meal arrangements, the location of ice machines and other details, and any events planned for that evening or the following morning. If the hotel has a mini-bar in each room, remind everyone to check the contents and the price before indulging — this is usually an expensive way to have a predinner cocktail. Give directions to the elevators and announce your room number. It is also a good idea, especially for the first couple of nights, to remind people it may take longer than ten minutes for their bags to arrive.

Remain in the lobby and available to your clients for at least 20 minutes after everyone has a key. It is surprising how often people will request room changes or have other concerns about the accommodations. Here are some of the most common complaints:

⊕ I can't stand the noise from the elevator, street, neighbor's shower, hotel pub, pub across the street, etc.

⊕ The room attendant hasn't cleaned up yet. I've got some guy's wet towels all over the washroom floor.

⊕ I know I said double occupancy, but I meant with someone on the tour. This room's already occupied.

⊕ I asked for two double beds, not one queen.

Make sure you are available for 20 to 30 minutes after you check in to answer questions and solve last minute problems.

- ⊕ My door lock doesn't.

- ⊕ It's over a 100°F in the shade and my air conditioning doesn't work.

- ⊕ This place smells like a tobacco shop. I asked for the nonsmoking floor.

- ⊕ I paid for a room with a view. You call this a view?

- ⊕ What time did you say breakfast was?

- ⊕ How do I get a wake-up call?

- ⊕ My TV is on the fritz.

Problems such as these can usually be resolved by getting a different room assignment, but in some cases this may not be possible. If the hotel is fully booked, you will have to placate the client as best you can and then make sure he or she gets the best room possible at the next stop. One option which could restore you to the good graces of a disgruntled tour member is to trade rooms. Sometimes just offering to trade is enough.

Before you leave the lobby, be sure you:

(a) schedule any wake-up calls necessary,

(b) confirm check-out time,

(c) arrange luggage pickup with guest services, and

(d) tell food services about any special dietary requirements and group dining arrangements.

2.2 Moving on, checking out

The night before you leave the hotel, make sure all your tour members know what time to have their luggage ready and what the pickup procedure is. Some hotels want bags in the hallway by a certain time; others will collect them from inside the rooms. In either case, if one or two rooms are away from the main group, perhaps on a different floor or in another wing, be sure to double-check so no one's bags are overlooked. (For tips on keeping track of luggage, see section **3.**)

For a very early morning departure you may need to make special breakfast arrangements. If the dining room or coffee shop will not be open before you leave, try to arrange room service — even if it is only coffee and doughnuts or muffins. And remind everyone to be considerate of other hotel guests who may still be asleep.

When your group is not scheduled to leave the hotel until long after the normal check-out time, you will need to figure out what to do with all the luggage. If you are lucky, you may convince the hotel to allow an extended check-out for the entire group. In the middle of high season, though, your chances of success are small. Many hotels will compromise by allowing the tour director to keep his or her room so it can be used for storage.

Always allow plenty of time to check out — most tour directors recommend at least an hour. Verify all charges are accurate and confirm tour members have paid for any incidentals such as phone calls, bar bills, and meals that were not part of the package. Check that all room keys have been returned and anything left in the hotel safety deposit box has been collected. Leave a forwarding address in case lost or forgotten items are discovered after your group has left.

Before your group boards, give the bus a quick inspection to make sure it is clean and ready for travel. Count and confirm the pieces of luggage as your driver puts them aboard. Finally, count your tour members and you are on your way to the next destination.

3. LUGGAGE

If you have ever been stranded without so much as a toothbrush or clean underwear, you will be able to empathize with the traveler whose baggage has vanished into the great, dark void. Your client will be panic-stricken and looking for constant reassurance until the missing piece (or pieces) shows up.

3.1 Precautions

At the beginning of any trip, remove old luggage tags and supply each traveler with new ones. Since tags are easily torn off or damaged, always carry extras. Sample 2 shows the front of an easy-to-use luggage tag which you can customize to each tour.

While the owner's address must be on all tags, it should be hidden from direct view. It is far more common than we like to admit for thieves to mingle with large groups as they check in (especially at airports), glancing at the luggage tags as the bags are processed. A 20-minute stint may yield an extensive list of houses which will be empty over the next week, allowing thieves to break in at their leisure. Smart travelers also use initials only, rather than first names in full. "M. Brown" gives no clue to the owner's sex nor, therefore, to the bag's possible contents.

Always confirm that all room keys have been returned and that no one has left valuables in the hotel safe.

Make sure each tour participant has only current luggage tags on their suitcases.

LUGGAGE TAG FOR TOUR MEMBERS

Please attach securely to your luggage.

Tour:

_____

Member name:

_____

ID #:	
Day 1	Day 2
Day 3	Day 4
Day 5	Day 6
Day 7	Day 8
Day 9	Day 10

Note: Every morning, fill in the name of the hotel where you will be staying that evening.

Put a sheet of paper with the owner's name and contact information for the tour group they belong to on the inside of each suitcase. If a luggage tag gets torn off, this provides an easy way to identify the correct owner.

It is unfortunate but true — not all baggage handlers are completely honest, especially in countries where bribery and theft are a way of life. All suitcases and checked luggage must be securely fastened, preferably locked. While this should be stressed in predeparture information, you need to double-check, especially on the return home when luggage tends to be bulging with souvenirs.

Clients should be encouraged to leave anything of value (whether monetary or sentimental) at home. One tourist discovered burglars had broken into her hotel room while she was lounging at the poolside. They stole the TV, her purse, and a large suitcase. Most of the items were discovered in a trash can close by, but her cash and the only copy of her address book were gone. The financial loss was minimal; the sentimental one was priceless.

3.2 Keeping track while on tour

Without careful planning and monitoring, checking in and out of hotels on a daily basis can be a logistical nightmare. Always count luggage and cross-check each piece against your master tour-member list before you leave a hotel or when your group is transferring between vehicles. Unless the luggage compartment has been opened during the day, you don't actually need to count when you arrive in the evening because you will know everything is there from your morning count. However, this is one of those "it never hurts to check" situations.

The basic way to keep track is by total count: 38 bags arrived, 38 bags are loaded back into the bus the following day. All's well. Right? But suppose Ms. Green accidentally left a bag in her closet and Mr. Brown stuffed the large, heavy, wool poncho he purchased last night at the market into a collapsible carry bag he had hidden in his main suitcase? You will still count 38 bags, but Ms. Green will be left with little choice of wardrobe for the next day's exploration of the pyramids.

A better method is to assign a code to every tour member and put that code on the baggage tags on each piece of the member's luggage. Keep the codes simple — a numeric code such as 101, 102, 103 is easy to work with. At the beginning of the tour, count up the total number of bags for each member. When your group checks into a hotel, check off each piece of luggage for each member in the appropriate "In" box as the driver unloads. When you check out, simply follow the same procedure, checking bags off in the "Out" box as they are loaded back on board. By comparing totals in each box, you will know not only if any pieces are missing or added but you will know also exactly whose pieces they are. It is then a simple procedure to check that person's room for the lost suitcase, or to add another bag to the total count to accommodate yesterday's shopping blitz (see Sample 3). (Some guides use only one box for both check-in and check-out. In this case, when you arrive at a hotel you mark one half of an X or any other two-part symbol you find easy and quick to print. When checking out, you complete the second half of the figure.)

Whichever method you choose, you will need one of these forms for each day of the tour. Since tour members' names and code numbers will not change from day to day, you can photocopy your original list and fill in only room numbers and checkmarks for each day's baggage count.

Even though it is not technically part of your job, working with the hotel staff lets you speed up luggage distribution and keep everyone happy, and may even allow you the luxury of a few moments to yourself.

BAGGAGE TRACKING FORM
(To be used with a master tour-member/room list)

Tour name: _Wine Tasting in the Okanagan_

Date: _October 17, 2000_ Day _1_ of _10_

Hotel: _Viewpoint's Inn_ City: _Kelowna_

Tour member name(s)	ID #	Total # pcs	Rm #	In	Out
M/M Ahmed	101	2	112	//	//
M/M Brown	102	3	204	///	//

In this example, the Browns have forgotten or misplaced one of their bags. You can now save time for yourself and the hotel staff because you know exactly which room they should look in for the missing luggage.

Some different two-part symbols for tracking baggage

Tour member name(s)	ID #	Total # pcs	Rm #	In/Out
				X X /
				¢ ¢ C
				Ø Ø O

3.3 A lifesaver tracking tip

You have counted the bags as they were unloaded in the lobby; you have cross-checked them against your master list to prevent musical suitcases; you have been checked in for two hours and Mr. Bell just called to tell you his suitcase still hasn't arrived in his room. You know it is in the hotel — the question is, where?

Before you panic or launch an all-out search involving bellhops, managers, and everyone else you can round up from the hotel, try a simple trick used by many experienced directors. Often all that has happened is an overworked, exhausted bellhop has transposed two digits of the room number. Room 135 becomes room 153 or even 315. If this doesn't work, look for numbers that are similar shapes to other ones. A hastily scrawled 3 can easily be read as 8 or a 1 misinterpreted as 7. These techniques don't always work, but in a surprising number of cases they do.

3.4 Lost luggage

If a suitcase is lost in transit, there is little you can do other than wait. Once you realize a piece is lost, whether you are at a rail, bus, or air terminal, contact the appropriate official and have the tour member fill out a claims form immediately. Tell the company official where you will be staying so the missing piece can be forwarded to the appropriate hotel once it has been located, and then follow up later the same day or early the next morning.

Usually lost luggage is found within a few hours. If it is truly lost, the airline or company responsible should replace the contents under its insurance plan, but it is up to the claimant to provide a list of contents to be replaced. The sooner the person makes a list, the more likely he or she is to remember everything. There are baggage liability limits which are clearly stated on the back of the airline ticket. These limits are usually based on a dollar figure per pound or on a total payout per traveler. Fragile or perishable articles will probably not be covered at all. Make sure everyone understands it is unlikely they will be reimbursed for their $200 designer jeans unless they have taken out luggage insurance in advance.

4. DINING

A well-known proverb proclaims "An army travels on its stomach." Napoleon, to his ruin, allowed himself to be distracted by other considerations. You cannot afford to do the same — the effect will be identical.

Sometimes "missing" luggage has simply been delivered to a room number where one or more of the digits have been transposed — 46 instead of 64, for example.

Know the limits and restrictions of your group's luggage insurance.

4.1 Seating

Meals are traditionally a time for getting to know fellow tour members without the "hurry up" feeling often present during a busy day of sightseeing. Large, round tables encourage relaxed conversation far more than rectangular ones do. It is easy to see everyone, and no one is stuck on a corner while his or her only neighbor flirts with the person opposite or remains more interested in the dinner plate than in chatting.

It is up to you to decide if you will assign seating at each meal. If you let people sit wherever they like, keep an eye out for tour members who are constantly eating by themselves or with others who are too shy to make conversation. If that happens, orchestrate things at the next meal so you can seat the shy members with a more outgoing group.

4.2 Considerations for group dining

There are several things to consider for group dining:

⊕ Are there enough tables to accommodate everyone on the tour at one sitting? It is rare that you will have enough time to allow two seatings for a meal.

⊕ Is there bus parking and a place for the driver to turn around in easily? Many places catering to tours have pull-through parking lots for exactly this purpose.

Sometimes assigned seating is the only way to ensure that the less outgoing members of your tour aren't left out.

⊕ Does the restaurant serve enough variety to accommodate special-needs diets? Not so long ago, requests for kosher foods were probably the only ones tour directors had to deal with. Attitudes have changed dramatically in recent years. People are becoming more aware of the health implications of certain foods, and religious or cultural beliefs are being acknowledged openly and proudly. You are likely to have at least one tour member, if not more, who will require a vegetarian, low sodium, low cholesterol, reduced sugar, or low lactose diet, or some other form of special preparation for religious or health considerations.

⊕ Does the restaurant want groups? Some do not. It may not want the hassle of 40 people all arriving at the same time; it may be concerned by what it perceives as a high percentage of canceled bookings; the owner may have had a bad experience with one tour and said "Never again!" Whatever the reason, be sure any eating establishment is looking for group business before unloading a bus load of hungry people.

4.3 Menus

There are four basic menu types for group dining.

(a) Set menu: Everyone is served the same meal and there are no deviations.

(b) Group menu: People can choose between two or three choices.

(c) Buffet: People serve themselves from a wide variety of choices.

(d) À la carte: People are free to order any item off the menu. If the cost of the meal is included in the tour price, there are often certain restrictions imposed (e.g., tour members cannot order the $45 lobster dinner when most items on the menu run $20 or less), although individuals may be able to pay the extra price for more expensive choices.

There is a fifth option that is often, unfortunately, dismissed as being an emergency measure only. Picnic lunches can be a marvelous alternative to restaurant meals, especially on informal, fun days when you are at the beach or hiking in alpine meadows. Some hotels will make up picnic baskets on request, and there is also a growing number of companies specializing in putting together gourmet picnic baskets.

When planning menus, try to avoid offering what is essentially the same meal two days in a row. Chicken à la king on Tuesday and roast lemon chicken on Wednesday (or even on Thursday) will be sure to bring a chorus of "Chicken again???"

4.4 Take regular breaks

Traveling is a hungry business. Be sure to schedule regular snack stops, even if they are just 20 minutes to grab coffee and a doughnut. One rule of thumb is to have a break after two hours on the bus, which means once between breakfast and lunch, and once between lunch and dinner if you are not stopping at attractions. For these mini-breaks, it is best to stay away from areas where people may be tempted to wander off exploring. Try getting 40 people back on a bus in half an hour when the restaurant is part of a major shopping mall!

4.5 The "best" place to eat may not be

Sometimes it becomes habit to eat at a particular restaurant. After all, it is familiar, it is safe, you know what is on the menu, and you can predict to the second how long it takes for your group to get its meals.

Regular breaks for snacks and a stretch are a must on any bus tour.

If the tour has "always" stopped at the Mountain Top Café for lunch on Day Two, but you find you aren't really happy with the food, talk to the locals — even one of the staff at the good old Mountain Top. You can be sure they will know where the best places really are, so if they whisper "Hillside Grill" under their breath, it is well worth checking out. It's not uncommon for one tour to start a new trend by moving to a different eatery.

5. BORDER CROSSINGS AND OTHER WILD ANIMALS

Before you take a group across any border, know the rules. The relatively easy crossing we enjoy between Canada and the United States lulls people into a false sense of comfort about international boundaries. There are few international borders with completely unrestricted access, and customs regulations vary dramatically both in procedure and intensity. In particular, third world and communist countries often have standard policies Westerners find bewildering or even frightening. One woman, ready to enjoy her first trip to one of the more remote areas of China, was horrified to discover she faced a four-hour wait on hot tarmac. When she finally reached customs, she was subjected to what she considered barely less than an interrogation by an already irritable customs official — not the best way to start a vacation, but apparently a routine event for the area she was in.

5.1 Passports and travel documentation

Prior to arrival at customs, you must ensure that every member of your group has the appropriate paperwork. It is unlikely that an entire group would be turned away if one person forgot a passport, but it is not unheard of. If your group is refused entry, it leaves you, the tour director, in an uncomfortable position.

More usually, only the person without a passport will be turned away, and someone — the tour director again — must make alternate arrangements for the person in question. If it is the beginning of the trip and the client lives in the city you are starting from, you will have to arrange for him or her to catch up to the trip as soon as possible. If the person is from out of town, or if you are already several stops into the trip, it is going to require some fancy footwork to resolve the problem, and you will likely be the one who has to stay behind tap dancing.

5.2 Restricted items

This is not limited to obvious items such as firearms. Canada prohibits ivory, crocodile shoes, and anything made from turtles. These items can and will be confiscated. Importing plant life will almost certainly be prohibited at international borders, but is sometimes banned across state lines as well. California and Hawaii are two states that do not want foreign plants brought in. So don't let anyone in your group innocently declare "no plant life" to an overworked Immigration or Department of Agriculture official while the perfume from an orchid lei wafts lazily across the room. (We actually saw this happen.)

5.3 Register valuables

When leaving their own country, all participants should register the brand and serial number of valuables such as cameras, video equipment, or laptop computers. Registration is a simple process of filling out a Y-38 form in Canada or a 4455 form in the United States. The form provides proof that goods were not acquired abroad and are not subject to import duties.

5.4 Duty free

Bringing home a cheap bottle of expensive perfume or liquor is one of the perks many travelers look forward to at the end of a vacation. The feeling of legally getting something tax-free appeals to most people as much as the pleasure of buying the item. However, the allowable value of duty free items varies with the amount of time away and the nature of the goods, so you must make sure everyone in the group knows exactly what they may bring back. For example, there are limits on the amount of liquor and the number of cigarettes that can be imported into either Canada or the United States without paying hefty duties.

5.5 Keep all receipts

It is up to tour members to prove what they spent for any goods obtained abroad. Taxes and duty are paid on the actual sale price, but if there is a dispute about the value, the customs official will have the final say. Be sure all tour members have their receipts ready before arriving at the customs counter, and remind them they will be holding up the entire group, not just themselves, if they have to scrabble through all their luggage for an errant sales slip.

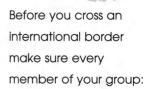

Before you cross an international border make sure every member of your group:

- has all correct documentation
- has receipts for goods purchased
- has registered any valuables such as cameras or laptop computers
- is not carrying any restricted items

5.6 Carry only what is yours

Never allow anyone to carry anything across an international border for someone else. This is an open invitation to big trouble — the kind of trouble that can get you thrown into very unpleasant jails, or worse.

6. SELLING OPTIONAL EXCURSIONS

No matter how all-inclusive a tour is, there will usually be some choices available for optional add-on excursions. Add-ons are frequently, but far from always, arranged and paid for at the time of the original booking. Once on tour, people who passed on the add-ons will get caught up in the spirit or ambience of a destination and in the other tour members' enthusiasm. Suddenly it is crucial for them to view Paris from the highest point of the Eiffel Tower or to watch horse racing at Ascot with the rest of the tour members. For some events or attractions, you may find clients hammering at your door to find out where they can sign up.

On other occasions, the tour director might arrange a spontaneous excursion in response to requests from tour members. (Some tour operators do not allow this; many do.) White-water river rafting may not be on the itinerary, but if half your group has asked about it, why not see what you can work out on the spot?

This will make you a star in the eyes of your clients, but you might find yourself in possession of what can amount to large sums of money in cash, checks, and credit card slips. Make no mistake: you are responsible for every penny of it. The best and safest method of handling this money is to deposit it immediately into the nearest branch of your tour operator's bank (the operator should have provided you with the necessary banking information for direct deposit before the beginning of the tour). If there is no branch of the bank close by, or if the bank is closed, have the money locked up in the hotel's or ship's safety deposit box until regular banking hours.

What happens if the banks are closed and the hotel has no safe? One guide we spoke to said she once arranged a spontaneous sidetrip during a trip to Banff, Alberta, and ended up carrying almost $10,000. The nearest branch of the correct bank was two days and several hundred miles away. Her solution was to conceal the money and credit card receipts in a fanny pack and sleep with it strapped securely around her waist.

Whenever you are handling money, issue receipts immediately, especially for a cash payment. For credit card transactions, have the client sign the slip, then call the issuing company for an approval number. Once you have the number, give a copy of the credit card slip to the client.

7. IT'S PARTY TIME

Everyone loves a good party, and tour groups are certainly no different. Get-acquainted and farewell gatherings are tour traditions which are not only fun but will also contribute to the smooth running of your tour.

7.1 Hello, my name is...

Welcoming parties get people in the vacation spirit, set the tone of the tour, and create a sense of bonding both within the group and with you, the tour director. At the beginning of a tour there are usually one or two people who are shy or have some hesitancy about group travel. As the host, it is your job to encourage everyone to get into the spirit of the adventure. Mingle, but never spend too much time with any one person or one group. You will be amazed how much useful information you can discover about the people you are traveling with just by listening — okay, call it eavesdropping if you must! If you hear two clients discussing their grandchildren or theater or the latest bestselling book, it gives you an immediate conversation opener later in the trip and proves you are genuinely interested.

If you are using nametags, a welcoming party is the place to distribute them (unless you already handed out nametags at the arrival or check-in point). It is also the perfect opportunity to give some background about yourself and explain what people can expect from the tour. Let your own excitement about the destinations and attractions along the way shine through. Enthusiasm is contagious, and you want your trip to begin with eager anticipation from everyone. You should also include the following tips and warnings from this chapter in your briefing:

(a) Highlights of the tour's itinerary

(b) Daily procedures such as wake-up calls, luggage handling, and sightseeing

(c) Local details such as currency exchange and what side of the road traffic drives on

(d) Reminder about punctuality

(e) Explanation of emergency procedures

A get-acquainted party is a traditional, fun way to break the ice at the beginning of a tour.

(f) Tips on general safety, such as:

    (i) Do not wander into unknown areas, especially after dark.

    (ii) If you want to explore on your free time in the evening, always travel with at least one other person.

    (iii) Carry wallets in a front pocket and purses securely under your arm to minimize the chance of theft.

    (iv) Never leave passports or money unattended in a hotel room.

    (v) Have a local map and the name of the group's hotel with you at all times (better yet, carry a packet of matches or other publicity item with the hotel name printed on it).

Although this might sound a bit dry for a party, a few carefully chosen anecdotes will get your points across without diminishing the mood in the slightest.

7.2 Good-bye; I'll write soon

By the end of a successful tour, many new friendships have been formed. Some last only as long as the tour, but one tour director tells of two couples who, seven years after the trip, still get together once or twice a year, even though they are separated by over 3,000 miles.

Farewell gatherings allow people to reminisce about their experiences on the tour, share and show off pictures, and exchange addresses. You might want to acknowledge special achievements such as one tour member's first bungee jump or another's bargaining skills which caused a ripple of awe in every open-air marketplace. This last evening of good fellowship is often punctuated by laughter and the odd tear as people say good-bye. It is also a chance for you to promote upcoming tours. Go ahead — it is fine to push for more business as long as you don't leave people with the impression they are at a sales presentation.

7
OVER LAND AND SEA

Tour types and themes are limited only by your imagination. We give you some basic ideas in this chapter, but let your creativity shine when you are thinking about how and where you want to take a group of people on tour.

1. CRUISING

Cruising is no longer the exclusive pastime of semiroyalty or the independently wealthy. In any group of a dozen people, the odds are good that at least one or two have been on some form of cruise. In fact, one travel agent we spoke to believes cruising is rapidly becoming the vacation of choice throughout North America.

1.1 All aboard

Whether you meet your group at the cruise ship terminal or the airport, you will be doing all the same things outlined in sections **1.2** and **1.3** in chapter 6 — make sure everyone is there, check travel documentation, look after the luggage, and handle the check-in process.

1.2 Getting to know your floating hotel

After people have had time to settle in, hold a get-together in one of the lounges (they are everywhere on most cruise ships). This is a perfect chance to explain hours for on-board shopping and dining, entertainment schedules and locations, policies on things such as tipping, and details of the optional sidetrips that are available. It is also a fun and professional touch to hand out a list of nautical terms to your tour members. Many will readily confess to not knowing the difference between port and a porthole. See Table 3 for a list.

Cruise ships are often so large it takes a day for people to figure out where the amenities are — and there are lots of them! Spa, swimming pools, casino (usually a popular spot), theater, health center, beauty salon, library, card room, and the list goes on. The exotic feeling of luxury and pampering most people feel aboard the "Love Boat" or her kin makes them curious to know more. If you can satisfy their curiosity about their floating hotel, it will reflect well on both you and your tour operator. It is best to arrange a tour before boarding, but even if you or your tour operator have not set up a special tour, officers on board are usually more than happy to show off their ship. Contact the chief purser or cruise director.

1.3 The send-off party

It is traditional for cruise ships to put on a ship-wide "get acquainted" party the first evening, but it is a professional touch to have one exclusively for your group members. Many cruise lines provide a complimentary champagne reception for private groups of 35 or more. If this is not on the itinerary from your tour operator, be sure to find out several weeks ahead of time if it is possible to include one.

1.4 Shore excursions

Tour directors always accompany their groups on any optional shore excursions. Make sure you have a bus booked so your group can stay together; some of the popular excursions can fill a dozen or more vehicles. If a tour participant did not book an excursion through the tour operator but is suddenly seized by the urge to find out what a sea lion looks like close up or to experience the revelry of a Mexican fiesta, you may need to help him or her sign up. Be sure to add the name to your master list so you don't forget this person ashore when you return to the ship.

A ship tour helps your group get to know each other and the place they will be spending their vacation.

TABLE 3
NAUTICAL TERMS

Aft: Near or at the rear of the ship

Afterdeck: The part of a deck toward or at the stern

Amidship: Near or at the middle of the ship

Athwartships: Running across the ship from side to side

Beam: The width of the ship at its widest point

Bells: The system used to tell time on a ship. A certain number of bells are rung at half-hour intervals throughout the day (e.g., one bell at 12:30, two at 1:00, and so on until eight bells at 4:00, when it goes back to one bell at 4:30)

Bow: The front point of the ship

Bridge: The captain's command center

Brig: Stay out of here! This is the ship's jail

Bumboat: A small boat used by local merchants in port to sell items to the ship's crew

Davit: A crane at the side of the ship that hoists lifeboats, anchors, or cargo on board or overboard

Fantail: An overhang shaped like a duck's bill that hangs over the back of the ship

Fathom: The nautical measurement for six feet

Free Port: A port with no customs or duties

Gale: A strong wind of 30 to 55 knots (32 to 63 mph)

Galley: The place where all the incredible food is produced (the kitchen)

Gimbal: This keeps the ship's compass stable in rough seas

Hatch: A door or door covering

Helm: A lever or wheel for controlling the ship's rudder

Horse latitudes: An area on either side of the equator where westerly winds change to trade winds and reverse direction

Leeward: The side of the ship sheltered from the wind

Lubber's knot: A square knot that didn't work (usually tied by a landlubber)

Make sail: Begin the voyage! (originally Raise sail or Set sails)

Nautical mile: 1.15 statute miles (1.85 km)

Orlop deck: The lowest deck of a ship with four or more decks

Port: The left side of the ship as you face forward

Put about: Reverse direction

Quarterdeck: A ceremonial open space on the afterdeck

Sextant: An optical instrument that measures the sun's angle to determine latitude

Sick bay: This is where you go when the swells are too large — the ship's infirmary

Starboard: The right side of the ship as you face forward

Stern: The very back of the ship

Swell: Rolling waves that send many people to the sick bay

Tender: Small shuttle boats used to ferry passengers ashore

Windward: The side of the ship that wind blows against

Theme tours are always a popular tour option.

1.5 Making it unique

Once you are aboard, the cruise staff will handle many of the day-to-day duties you would normally be responsible for as tour director. You can count on them to provide daily, written itineraries; look after all the meal planning; have activities and entertainment scheduled almost 24 hours a day; and have rooms spotless in the wink of an eye.

Because there are so many activities going on, it can be a challenge to put your own unique stamp on the voyage. An early morning (not too early though) deck walk is usually popular, and you might organize a bridge or shuffleboard tournament depending on the group's interests.

Cruising is a natural for theme tours. Many groups design an entire cruise revolving around a particular theme or special interest. To get your imagination going, here is a sampling of groups that have booked cruises:

- Alumni groups
- Bridge players
- Financial advisers (yes, even accountants like to relax once in a while)
- Fred and Martha for their 50th wedding anniversary
- Gardening clubs
- Gay/lesbian groups
- Golfers
- High school reunion classes
- Historians
- Honeymooners
- Line dancing clubs
- Magicians
- Mah jong players
- Musicians
- Orchid growers

- Over Eaters Anonymous
- Philosophers
- Quilting groups
- Religious pilgrims
- Retired bank managers (or any other profession)
- Scuba divers
- Seniors
- Singles
- Theater fanatics
- Unions of every description
- War vets

Let your creativity loose when planning special activities or presentations around the theme. One group organized a cruise around a solar eclipse. The members arranged slide presentations, lectures, and stargazing opportunities, and used the complimentary tour director berth to bring along their own astronomer!

Whether your afternoon presentation focuses on "how we were then" or features a specialist discussing the latest hothouse maintenance techniques, you will need private meeting rooms. These can sometimes be arranged on board for a spontaneous event, but they are normally booked in advance when the original cruise reservation is made. Your group will likely want to enjoy the exclusivity of two or three private functions daily. However, if certain subjects are of general interest, you may want to consider opening the event to all passengers whether they belong to your tour group or not. You should clear this idea with the cruise line well in advance as some may not allow private functions to become public. If you are thinking of charging admission to any of these presentations, check with the cruise line before departure. On board most ships, this is not acceptable.

1.6 You are still in charge

Keep visible and accessible throughout the cruise. Even though there are trained staff to look after everyone on board, you are still in charge of your group.

Like any other type of tour, as the tour director you must remain accessible to the members of your group.

2. MOTORCOACHES — ON THE BUSES

If there are roads, there will be bus tours. They will not always be in air-conditioned, fully upholstered, luxury vehicles, but you can be sure there will be opportunities for any tour guide or tour director as long as there is a pair of tire ruts heading toward a destination.

2.1 Seat rotation

Seat roation ensures everyone gets a good view.

Anyone who has attended a multiday event involving sitting will have observed the "royal chair syndrome." This is where people proclaim one seat is theirs by divine right for the entire event. The spectacle of people heading for exactly the same spot they were in before lunch or yesterday or even last week is a fascinating part of human behavior. Why it happens is a mystery, but what will happen isn't. You will soon be deluged with complaints from people who think you are allowing everyone else on the bus to have a better seat than they have. To avoid this, establish a seat rotation plan at the beginning of the trip. This will result in far less grumbling than if everyone is allowed to sit where they please.

On the first day, most directors prefer to assign seating. Not only does this set a precedent about who is in charge but it is also much easier to draw up your initial seating and rotation schedule (see Sample 4) when you are not also trying to figure out who's who and in what seat as well.

However, you may decide to let tour members arrange themselves the first time on board so friends can sit close together. One company we spoke to has passengers fill out name cards and leave them in the aisle seat pocket. While everyone is at lunch or visiting the museum, the tour guide or director moves the cards forward to the seat in front. Tour members can see where they are to sit when they reboard.

The frequency of seat rotation depends on the length of the tour and how much time has been spent in the bus that day. A good average is to change twice a day on a long-distance trip unless the group has spent most of the morning haggling in a bazaar or wandering through other attractions.

One of the most efficient and easy-to-manage rotation methods is to have everyone move forward one row at each rotation. The people at the front move to the last occupied row. You will find it easy to keep

SAMPLE 4
MOTORCOACH SEATING/ROTATION PLAN

INITIAL SEATING PLAN

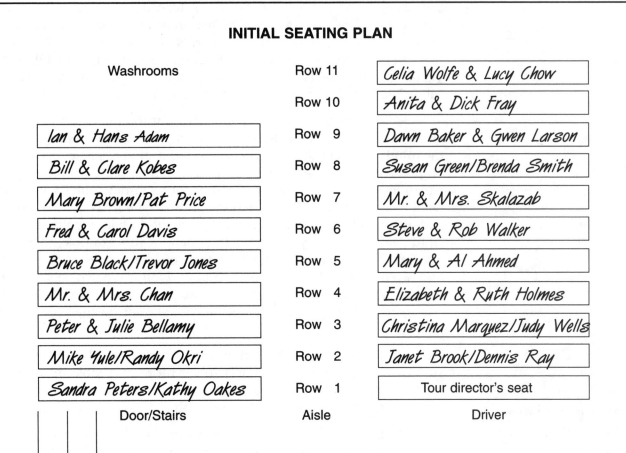

Washrooms

	Row 11	Celia Wolfe & Lucy Chow
	Row 10	Anita & Dick Fray
Ian & Hans Adam	Row 9	Dawn Baker & Gwen Larson
Bill & Clare Kobes	Row 8	Susan Green/Brenda Smith
Mary Brown/Pat Price	Row 7	Mr. & Mrs. Skalazab
Fred & Carol Davis	Row 6	Steve & Rob Walker
Bruce Black/Trevor Jones	Row 5	Mary & Al Ahmed
Mr. & Mrs. Chan	Row 4	Elizabeth & Ruth Holmes
Peter & Julie Bellamy	Row 3	Christina Marquez/Judy Wells
Mike Yule/Randy Okri	Row 2	Janet Brook/Dennis Ray
Sandra Peters/Kathy Oakes	Row 1	Tour director's seat

Door/Stairs   Aisle   Driver

SEAT ROTATION TRACKING

DAY #	1	2	3	4	5	6	7	8	9	10
A.M.		✓	✓	✓						
P.M.	✓		✓	✓						

empty seats at the back of the vehicle since most people avoid them naturally. Forward rotation is much easier than moving backwards or clockwise, because tour members can deposit their coats, bags, and other personal belongings onto the seat in front as they exit the bus — after all, they will pass that seat on their way out. Trying to deposit these items onto the seat behind usually results in a free-for-all. Moving backwards can also produce a subtle feeling of negativity. It may be "all in the head," but it can still cause irritation.

Keep track of the seat rotation on the seat-rotation chart (see Sample 4). To determine quickly who should be sitting where, simply count the number of ticks denoting rotations and move the passenger the appropriate number of rows from his or her original seat. Sample 4 shows a plan for a daily seat-rotation schedule for a ten-day tour. Each person will move forward one row when the group first boards in the morning and, depending on the amount of time spent on board, will move forward again when they reboard after lunch. In this example, there was a seat rotation after lunch on the first day, only one rotation on day two, and two rotations on each of days three and four. So when people board the bus after lunch on day four, Mary Brown, who began in Row 7, will have gone through six seat changes and will be able to enjoy a front row view for the rest of the day.

You may decide against doing a seat rotation at all. If you do, be sure to announce that you expect to see different people in the front rows as the tour progresses, and then watch for anyone displaying symptoms of "royal chair syndrome" with the best seats.

Remember to reserve the two seats directly behind the driver for yourself. You will not only need somewhere to put your traveling office (also known as a briefcase and paperwork) but you must also be able to talk with the driver and be easily visible to all your clients. You can also use this seat as a depository for front row passengers' belongings during a seat rotation. After everyone has disembarked, slip quietly back on board and move the material to the back row seats.

Here's an unusual tip: One experienced husband-and-wife tour team uses a small stuffed teddy bear to show which side of the bus gets off first at each stop. They hang the bear on alternating sides of the bus and allow this amiable character to preside over the side that gets off first. The bear is so lovable, most people don't even notice when they are last off at the hotel.

As the tour director, you will need the two seats directly behind the driver. This ensures you are visible to all members of your group and can communicate easily with the driver.

2.2 Safety

One of the most basic and important safety precautions on a bus is that everyone must remain seated as long as the bus is moving. Be fore-warned: when you are pulling slowly up the long winding driveway in front of an elegant castle, or when someone points out a window and shouts "Look at that!," most people will want to leap out of their seats. Remind everyone politely but firmly, especially at the beginning of the tour, that this is not acceptable.

Stepping off the bus seems deceptively simple. It is actually much farther to the ground than many people, especially seniors or people with mobility restrictions, realize. Helping your clients on and off is not only a professional courtesy but also a necessary safety precaution every tour guide or tour director should take at all stops.

Heavy or breakable items belong on the floor. If the bus is forced to make an emergency stop, or swerves unexpectedly, overhead racks are not designed to withstand the force of a sliding 50-pound marble statue. Neither are the heads of any passengers seated below.

At many attractions you will find yourself one of a seemingly endless stream of tour groups. Unless everyone on board is a devotee of bus manufacturers and styles (you never know — nothing is impossible as a theme for group travel), one bus tends to look identical to any other. Be sure your group knows its bus number, any markings or other visible ways to distinguish the bus easily, and the exact time of departure before they get off to visit the attraction.

Reconfirm everyone has reboarded the bus every time you stop.

Always do a head count when your group reboards the bus. It doesn't matter whether you have just had a quick stop at a roadside ice-cream stand or a three-hour tour of an ancient ruin — be sure you confirm everyone is aboard before leaving the area. For a large group, many tour guides or directors find it is easier to count the number of empty seats than the number of passengers. It makes no difference what method you use as long as you confirm your count. Never rely on someone else to do this for you, no matter how convenient it would be.

2.3 Let the games begin

Sights and attractions are a major part of the fun of group travel. But so is on-board entertainment. Music, videos, and lots of choice in reading material will go almost as far toward keeping your group happy as intriguing attractions and great dining. Some say they are hokey, but games and sing-alongs are an expected part of motorcoach travel.

Look for games that encourage group interaction and require minimal props or specialized knowledge. A great source for this type of game is the hundreds of kids' books available at any bookstore. Some may need adapting for an adult group, but with a bit of creativity and forethought you will soon have an assortment of games to suit every group.

Moderate competition is fine but is best if it pits one part of the group against another rather than one individual against everyone else. For example, you might have a wildlife spotting contest between tour members seated on the right side and those on the left.

Password is a perennial favorite. (This is the game where one person makes a simple statement, factual or not, to a neighbor, who then passes the information on to the next person, who passes it to the next, and so on. The only rule is that you must say exactly what you think you heard, no matter how nonsensical it has become. Hilarity is an inevitable outcome.) And one always-popular exception to the group competition rule is whichever version of "Guess how many miles till we reach..." or "Guess how many...(fill in the blanks)" tickles your fancy.

Lavish prizes for these games are not necessary, but simple gifts such as souvenir lapel pins from your destination or other mementos of the trip will inspire more people to join in. Just be sure everyone wins something by the time you arrive back home.

Sing-alongs should feature well-known, lively songs so everyone feels comfortable joining in. "Roll Out the Barrel," "It's a Long Way to Tipperary," and "Michael Row the Boat Ashore" are some often-used selections. Don't worry if you cannot sing well. As long as you choose the right songs, your tour members will be far too busy enjoying themselves to notice.

2.4 Your driver and you

The person behind the wheel is a professional, too. It is his or her skill that will allow you to continue your job of pointing out sights and answering questions in spite of traffic jams or adverse road conditions. It makes no difference whether it is a four-hour city tour or a three-week adventure through a dozen countries, the driver deserves the courtesy and respect of a formal introduction to the group and should be included in activities whenever appropriate.

2.5 Washroom and pit stops

Washrooms on a motorcoach are small and usually uncomfortable. A stop every two hours allows people to make use of more comfortable facilities and will give any smokers who may be on board a chance to light up where they will not bother others. **Note:** There are almost no buses that still allow smoking.

Be aware that while they are usually more comfortable, toilets at any given stop are probably not numerous enough to accommodate the whole group at once. It may sound indelicate, but you would be wise to encourage group members to stagger their visits to the washrooms when you pull into a rest area. If 30 people suddenly rush to use five stalls a couple of minutes before the bus leaves, there are sure to be some people left crossing their legs till the next stop. One guide we spoke to said she asks some people to go on arrival, some during the stop, and the rest five minutes before departure.

3. ADVENTURE/ECO TOURING

Taking a group of urbanites into the wilderness can be as much of an adventure for the tour director as for the participants. This is a highly specialized type of group travel requiring many skills no other touring does. For this reason, we will give you only some basic points to consider. People interested in this type of tour directing will need to discuss it with, and train under, a qualified wilderness guide before setting up tours on their own.

Without exception, the adventure/eco guides we spoke to all felt a need to share the unspoiled wonders of nature or ancient civilizations. There was a common reverence for the outdoors and a simpler, less-frenzied way of life. "We discover just how unimportant so many of the things that we place enormous significance on really are," says one adventure guide. "Being able to share the journey of self-discovery [with our clients] is a great gift."

Even though wilderness guides repeatedly say they are amazed how often people exceed their own expectations, it is vital to stress the need for some form of pretrip physical conditioning. Someone who has spent the last five years staring at a computer screen and who considers a walk to the fridge for a slice of cold pizza and a beer to be heavy exercise is not going to manage well on a two-week canoe trip into the depths of the Amazon.

Adventure and eco tourism is increasingly popular but needs many extra skills. Be sure you have the appropriate training before taking a group into the wilderness.

Remain constantly alert to the needs of any tour member who may be overextending themselves physically.

You must constantly monitor the physical state of your clients, and adapt your tour to their abilities. Adventure/eco participants will look after their own minor problems (such as blisters, cuts, and bee stings), but you must be aware of the way factors such as altitude, weather conditions, and dehydration are affecting your group. In the wilderness, these can be potentially life threatening, and when "help is on the way" becomes "help may be here in a couple of days if we're lucky," you cannot afford to take chances.

8
PROBLEMS COME IN ALL SIZES

Problem-solving skills are essential to any tour guide or tour director. You must have the self-confidence to assess any problem situation, make a decision promptly, and then act on your decision.

1. LOST OR STOLEN PROPERTY

If a member of the group loses something or believes it has been stolen, find out when and where the owner last remembers having the item. Mental backtracking can often uncover the lost article. If it doesn't, get a complete description, including the value of the item, and report it to the front desk of the hotel where you are staying or the purser's office, if you are on a ship.

If you believe a theft occurred, you will also need to contact the police or other local authority, and help the tour member fill out the claims forms and notify the appropriate authorities. Be sure to document each step you take, using Sample 5 as a guideline. While it is neither

SAMPLE 5
LOST/STOLEN ARTICLE REPORT FORM

Tour name: _____ Date: _____

Tour director: _____

Client: _____

Address: _____

_____

_____

Home phone: _____

Complete description of missing item(s) including size, color, distinguishing features.

_____

_____

_____

_____

_____

Approximate value: _____

First noticed missing on: _____ at_____a.m./p.m.

Last seen on: _____ at_____a.m./p.m.

Last place seen: _____

LOSS/THEFT REPORTED TO:

Tour director on:_____at _____a.m./p.m.

    Action taken: _____

    _____

Hotel/cruise staff on:_____at _____a.m./p.m.

    Contact: _____Title:_____

    Action taken: _____

    _____

Insurance agency on: _____at _____a.m./p.m.

    Contact: _____Title:_____

    Action taken: _____

    _____

IN CASE OF THEFT OR POSSIBLE THEFT:

Did client notice anyone loitering or other suspicious behavior?	Yes	No
Did client see theft occur?	Yes	No
If yes, is client's report signed and attached?	Yes	No
Were there any other witnesses?	Yes	No
If yes, total number of witnesses?	_____	
List of witnesses' names and addresses attached?	Yes	No
Are all reports signed and attached?	Yes	No

REPORTED TO:

Police on: _____ at _____ a.m./p.m.

    Contact: _____ Title: _____

    Action taken: _____

_____

Tour operator on: _____ at _____ a.m./p.m.

    Contact: _____ Title: _____

    Action taken: _____

_____

Consulate/Embassy on: _____ at _____ a.m./p.m.

    Contact: _____ Title: _____

    Action taken: _____

_____

Others (specify): _____ on: _____ at _____ a.m./p.m.

    Contact: _____ Title: _____

    Action taken: _____

_____

Follow-up action required: _____

_____

Forwarding address left with:

    ☐ Hotel   ☐ Police   ☐ Embassy

    ☐ Others (specify): _____

expected nor advisable for you to replace missing articles out of your personal funds, helping your client shop for emergency supplies is a courtesy many will appreciate and remember.

1.1 Credit cards

Most credit card companies have a toll-free line specifically for reporting lost or stolen cards. Check with the hotel or local bank affiliate for the number.

1.2 Passport

Although the black market in stolen passports is not quite as extensive as the movies would have people believe, passport theft is a more common occurrence than it should be. Travelers should keep a copy of their passport (and a list of credit card numbers and traveler's check numbers) separate from the original and should leave a third copy at home. Report missing passports to the issuing country's embassy immediately.

When travelling abroad, always keep a copy of passport, credit card, and traveller's check numbers in a different place than the originals and leave another complete list with someone trusted at home.

1.3 Driver's license

Notify the motor vehicle department of the province or state that issued the stolen driver's license.

1.4 Traveler's checks

The major companies that issue traveler's checks will have an office in all but the most remote locations. Contact the local office or call the company's toll-free number. Replacement checks should be delivered to your client within a couple of days at the most.

2. HEALTH ISSUES

No one is immune to injury or illness, so you must be prepared to handle medical emergencies of all types.

2.1 Look after your own health

Being a tour director or tour guide is a high-stress, high-demand job, physically and emotionally. Have regular checkups, especially before and after the season, and make sure any immunizations are current. You need to be in good health yourself to handle medical emergencies on a tour.

Don't neglect your own health. Stay in shape, eat properly, and get regular checkups.

2.2 Carry first-aid basics

Carry a small supply of basics such as aspirin, throat lozenges, bandages, antibacterial lotions, diarrhea treatment, and sunburn ointments. Never give prescription drugs to anyone and do not allow another member of the tour to do so. People can have severe reactions to the wrong medication; it can even kill them. Do not set yourself up for a legal suit. Even over-the-counter medication should be used with caution. Be sure to check for allergies and side effects before handing out medication.

2.3 Illness or injury

If a client is injured or becomes ill, make him or her as comfortable as possible and, if the person is conscious, encourage him or her to get medical attention. You must resist the urge to arrange medical care without the individual's permission except in life-and-death situations. If the patient decides not to pay the bill, you may be the one left holding the invoice. When an individual needs professional medical aid but stoically continues to refuse it, insist he or she sign a release form (see Sample 6). This will help protect you and your company in the event there are further, potentially serious complications. You may wish to seek the advice of a lawyer when creating waivers for your clients to sign.

Notify the person the invalid is traveling with, or the emergency contact if he or she is traveling alone, and inform the tour operator. If it looks like the member will not be well enough to catch up to the tour later, arrange for his or her luggage to be delivered to the hospital or returned home, and make arrangements for a return flight. Tickets should always be left with someone competent enough to get the injured person to the airport. Once your client is in the care of a doctor, your responsibility is to the rest of the group. You cannot stay behind.

Write out a detailed report that includes the date and time of the accident or when the illness was first reported to you, authorities and medical personnel contacted, diagnosis if known, and the names of any witnesses (Sample 7). If possible, get written statements from witnesses. Depending on the nature of the injury, you may also be required to file a report with the police or hotel. Copies of these reports should be attached to the file for future reference.

SAMPLE 6
MEDICAL ASSISTANCE WAIVER

I, _____ (print name in full),

acknowledge that the tour director has suggested I seek professional medical assistance for the following reason:

_____

_____

_____

_____

It is my decision not to seek such medical aid.

I hereby release and hold blameless the tour director, tour staff, and tour operator of any consequences of this decision.

Signature: _____

Witness: _____

Date: _____Time: _____

DISCHARGE/DISMISSAL FORM

Tour name: _____ Date: _____

Tour director: _____

Client: _____

    Address: _____

    _____

    Date of discharge: _____

    Discharged in (city, country): _____

Tour operator notified on _____ at _____ a.m./p.m.

REASON FOR DISCHARGE: _____

_____

In case of illness or accident:

    Date illness first reported: _____ at _____ a.m./p.m.

    Action taken: _____

    Name and address of doctor or hospital: _____

    _____

    Doctor's prognosis: _____

    Doctor's report attached?   Yes   No

    Is client expected to rejoin the tour?   Yes   No

    If yes, give details: _____

In case of client dissatisfaction, provide details: _____

_____

    Action taken to resolve problem prior to discharge: _____

    _____

In case of disorderly conduct:

Details of client's actions: _____

_____

_____

Actions taken to resolve problem prior to discharge: _____

_____

_____

Officials contacted (e.g., police, hotel security)

1) _____

2) _____

3) _____

The following signatures indicate agreement with the tour director's decision that the client(s) is/are unduly disruptive to the entire group and should be immediately discharged from the tour for the benefit and well-being of the majority. (Attach additional sheet if necessary.)

1) _____   2) _____

3) _____   4) _____

5) _____   6) _____

7) _____   8) _____

IF CLIENT IS NOT EXPECTED TO REJOIN THE TOUR:

The following arrangements have been made:

1) Air transportation:

    Flight #:_____Date:_____

    Airline: _____Ticket #: _____

    Client's signature for receipt: _____

    If unable to sign, the following person is taking receipt:

        Name: _____

        Home address: _____

        Home tel: _____

2) Other onward transportation arrangements: _____

_____

3) Luggage arrangements: _____

_____

4) Client's signature verifies he/she refuses/does not need onward reservations:

      _____

CANCELLATION AND REFUND REQUESTS FOR UNUSED PORTIONS OF TOUR:

1) Date: _____Hotel/Attraction: _____

    Tel: _____Contact: _____

    Arrangements: _____

2) Date: _____Hotel/Attraction: _____

    Tel: _____Contact: _____

    Arrangements: _____

2.4 Death

Death is a concern not only for organizers of seniors' tours. Heart attack, accident, or complications from chronic health problems can kill a person of any age. If someone dies on tour, you must immediately contact —

(a) The hotel manager or chief medical officer on a cruise ship (if appropriate),

(b) The local authorities such as police, hospital, and coroner,

(c) The deceased's consulate or embassy,

(d) The tour operator or the local representative, and

(e) The deceased's emergency contact (if requested to do so by the tour operator).

Collect and itemize the deceased's belongings with a witness present. Some countries will require you to turn these over to the local police. If not, you should arrange to have them shipped either to the deceased's home or to the emergency contact. Be sure to get copies of the bill of lading for shipment. You may also have to arrange the funeral or provide for transportation of the body. Fill out whatever forms are required by local authorities, and write up your own report as you would for illness or injury.

How you tell the rest of the group of the death is up to you and depends on what you are most comfortable with. It is common courtesy to acknowledge what has happened, since people will notice if one of their companions is missing. Console the group, then get the tour going again as soon as possible. Your challenge will be to keep everyone's spirits up for the rest of the tour.

Be aware of local regulations and proceedures and always write a full report should someone die during the tour.

3. DISMISSING SOMEONE FROM THE TOUR

Occasionally (if you're lucky, never) a tour member's behavior is so disruptive you must consider dismissing him or her from the tour. Perhaps the person is constantly drunk or harassing other members of the tour, or making racist or sexually abusive remarks about the country you are visiting and its people. Sometimes a tourist is even caught stealing or otherwise breaking the law.

No matter how ugly or rude the problem person is, dismissal is a radical step. Before you take it, ensure you have made every effort possible to rectify the situation. It is important to your reputation and credibility to do this as discreetly as you can. Turning a reprimand into a spectacle in front of the group makes you look unprofessional and can ultimately lead to others testing your limits with similar behavior. Instead, take the person aside and calmly explain why the behavior is unacceptable. Back up what you are saying by quoting company policy. If the action continues, repeat the warning. If there is still no result, take whatever action is necessary.

Documentation is vital in this unpleasant situation. The discharge form you use if a tour member is too sick to continue (Sample 7) can also be used as a dismissal form. The person in question will likely be unwilling to sign anything — in fact, it is almost a given that he or she will refuse to sign a statement and then will attempt to sue you, your tour operator, or both. Tour operators have insurance to cover such suits, but if you can get as many of the other tour members as possible to sign a statement testifying to the disruptive behavior, you will have a certain amount of added protection.

Arrange tickets for the person's return home, and be sure to cancel reservations for that individual for the balance of the tour.

4. BUMPING

Occasionally one or two members, or even your entire group, may be bumped off an airline flight. This does not happen as often as people swear it does, but it *is* one of the most irritating, frustrating problems a traveler can face.

If your group is bumped, your job is to negotiate the best compensation you can for the tour members involved. Try for upgrades, complimentary meals, a refund, or free flights/accommodations to be used at a later date. Even though it is your job to keep clients informed, the supplier should have a representative explain what caused the situation and what is being done to correct it. It is also worth following up to make sure the supplier sends a letter of apology to your affected clients. Receiving an official "we're sorry" may mean the difference between a repeat client and some very poor word of mouth.

If only one or two tour members are bumped, you should make alternate arrangements for them at the airport or meet with an airline official who will take responsibility for doing so. The tour director should never give up his or her seat or leave the tour. If necessary, phone the tour operator or travel agency and leave it in their hands.

5. MISSING MEMBER

If one of your tour members goes missing at an airport or other terminal, have the person paged. Sometimes people become engrossed in their book or the comings and goings of other arrivals and simply lose track of time. Also call the hotel in case the member decided to make his or her own way there.

In any case of a lost traveler, ask other clients how long it has been since anyone saw the missing person. Check the areas where he or she was last seen and give a full description, including details of clothing, to any staff who could help in the search. If you are forced to leave the area without locating the missing person, you must inform:

(a) the police,

(b) any other officials such as park rangers, the hotel manager, or security personnel,

(c) the tour operator, and

(d) the embassy or consulate, if appropriate.

Be sure to provide an itinerary to all of the above so you can be contacted when the person is discovered, and call at every stop for a progress report. If the missing tour member shows up at a later stop, let the authorities know immediately. Document each step as you take it and, if possible, have several witnesses sign a statement. This is to protect you if there is legal action later. (You can use the discharge form (see Sample 7) to document your actions.)

At some point you will need to contend with some of the catastrophes described above. Preparation and planning will help you weather any that do come your way. When disaster strikes, have a plan prepared in your mind, think things through as they occur, and remember that at some point in the future you will be able to laugh and tell stories about your "Nightmare in..."

If a tour member goes missing, document all steps you take to locate them, notify the appropriate authorities, and leave a number where you can be contacted, but your responsibility is to go on with your group.

9
SEE YOU AGAIN SOON
— FOLLOWING UP

We all have a little gremlin that sits on our shoulder whispering doubts in our ear after we have completed a job. "You weren't good enough," it says. "You should have done this differently. You should have done that better, faster, slower..." Too often, these whispers stop tour directors and guides from completing the last step of a successful, professional tour — the follow-up. Here are some great excuses to avoid doing a follow-up:

- ⊕ I'm swamped with work at the office. I don't have time to listen to a client tell me stories about the trip or complain.

- ⊕ I'm scheduled out on another trip in two days. I have to catch up on my paperwork.

- ⊕ I need to find out more information about a great new attraction for my next tour.

Don't neglect to follow up with your clients after a tour is over.

It doesn't take much effort to come up with dozens more. But before you design your own list, here is a statistic you need to know: A 1993 market study by Cruise Lines International Association shows that 25 percent of the people who said they would book their next cruise through a different agency would do so because the agent they originally booked through did not follow up to see how their trip went.

Following up is critical to your continued success as a tour guide or tour director. It is your final opportunity to show courtesy and genuine consideration for your clients. First-time clients who feel you truly care will become repeat clients and the best PR department imaginable. The feedback you receive is also invaluable for improving yourself and your tour package for next time (ask a successful salesperson in any field). Clients may tell you about something you need to change or accentuate in yourself and your presentation. They may complain about an attraction that is so seedy it is no longer worth visiting, or rave about a hotel that has been transformed by recent renovations into a palace you absolutely must add to the itinerary, even if it is only for Sunday brunch. And if everyone comments on your enthusiasm, you will know you are on the right track.

1. SHORT-TERM FOLLOW-UP

Short-term follow-up happens at the end of the trip or within a short time after your clients return home.

An "end of the tour" evaluation form (see Sample 8) is the standard and most efficient way of getting direct, prompt feedback while impressions are still fresh. Be sure to pay close attention to the "liked most" and "liked least" sections, as these are the shortcuts to building better tours in the future. And don't flinch about asking what people would like to see added or deleted from your tour.

A few days before returning home, or the day you arrive, mail everyone a thank-you note or welcome home card. Some tour directors prefer to include the evaluation form with their thank-you rather than have it filled out on the spot at the end of the trip. The major drawback with this approach is that you have less control over how many people will respond, even if you include a prepaid envelope. It can also make your thank-you look slightly less sincere because you are asking for something at the same time — thank you for your business but please do this for me now.

TOUR EVALUATION FORM

Please take a few minutes before you leave to fill out this evaluation and hand it back to your tour guide/director. Your comments and impressions are our best sources of information about how to improve our tours, options, and services in the future. There is no obligation to sign your name, so please be frank and honest.

Tour name: _____ Date: _____

Tour guide/Director: _____

Please rate using the follow scale:

1) Excellent — exceptional in every detail; far exceeded all my expectations

2) Above average — better than I expected

3) Average — about what I expected or have experienced before; adequate and acceptable

4) Below average — I was disappointed; the tour did not live up to my expectations

5) Unsatisfactory — needs improvement

THE TOUR DIRECTOR WAS:

Courteous:	1	2	3	4	5
Well organized:	1	2	3	4	5
Well groomed:	1	2	3	4	5
Punctual:	1	2	3	4	5
Made me feel welcome:	1	2	3	4	5
Made sure I knew where I should be:	1	2	3	4	5
Provided interesting, useful commentary:	1	2	3	4	5

THE DRIVER WAS:

Courteous:	1	2	3	4	5
Punctual:	1	2	3	4	5
Well groomed:	1	2	3	4	5
Safe and conscientious on the road:	1	2	3	4	5

THE BUS WAS:

Clean:	1	2	3	4	5
Had comfortable seats:	1	2	3	4	5
Had an easy-to-hear PA system:	1	2	3	4	5
Was easy to see out of:	1	2	3	4	5
Was easy to board and disembark:	1	2	3	4	5

THE MEALS WERE:

Good quality:	1	2	3	4	5
Prepared well:	1	2	3	4	5
Served and presented well:	1	2	3	4	5
Offered good variety:	1	2	3	4	5
Served at a good time of day:	1	2	3	4	5
Served promptly when ordered:	1	2	3	4	5

THE HOTEL(S) (or cruise ship) WAS/WERE:

Comfortable:	1	2	3	4	5
Clean:	1	2	3	4	5
Conveniently located:	1	2	3	4	5
Had courteous, efficient staff:	1	2	3	4	5
Had good recreational facilities:	1	2	3	4	5
Provided quality entertainment:	1	2	3	4	5
Provided useful amenities:	1	2	3	4	5

THE ATTRACTIONS VISITED:

Lived up to the brochure's description:	1	2	3	4	5
Were interesting:	1	2	3	4	5
Were well maintained:	1	2	3	4	5

Length of time allowed to see them was usually:

☐ Too long   ☐ Too short   ☐ Just right

Number of attractions visited per day was usually:

☐ Too many ☐ Too few   ☐ Just right

What I liked best about the tour was: _____

_____

_____

What I liked least about the tour was: _____

_____

_____

I would recommend this tour to a friend: ☐ Yes   ☐ No

Other comments or suggestions
(please use the back of this sheet if you need more room):

_____

_____

_____

_____

_____

Thank you for joining us and we hope to see you again soon!

A small gift or personal thank you note encourages repeat business and new referrals.

A small gift such as a photo album of the trip, a souvenir someone mentioned during the tour, or a video of one or more of the destinations makes an effective memento which will keep your name in people's minds for next time.

It has become a tradition on cruises to deliver a fruit basket or bottle of champagne to each person's room. Some tour directors try to avoid the cliché — and achieve more impact — by sending such a gift to their clients' homes as a thank-you gift after the trip. Just be careful your clients don't end up feeling they are the only people who did not receive an on-board gift, as happened in one case, to the tour director's consternation.

A phone call extending an invitation to share vacation photos is also a personal touch. Although not many people will take you up on the invitation, almost everyone will remember you made it.

2. LONG-TERM FOLLOW-UP

Newsletters are a relatively inexpensive way of keeping in touch with your past clients.

Long-term follow-up reinforces customer loyalty. A classic example is the Christmas cards that many firms send their valued customers. If you send birthday or anniversary cards instead, you may stand out from the multitude vying for repeat business. Or you could write and produce a quarterly or semi-annual newsletter reporting on recent trips and describing upcoming tours. The increasing availability of easy-to-use desktop publishing programs makes this an attractive option for many tour professionals. Producing a small newsletter takes very little time, but it will remind people of the wonderful trip they had with you. If you include useful travel tips and general travel information, people will soon be waiting to hear from you again — or calling you up to arrange their next trip.

10
ORGANIZING YOUR OWN TOUR

Many dedicated world travelers and virtually all tour guides or tour directors who have run tours on contract for an operator dream about running their own tours at some point. If you are one of these entrepreneurs, this chapter will help you make your dream a reality. Tours are as unique as the individuals who create them, so we cannot give you every minute detail you will need to prepare an itinerary; however, we can give you practical, general suggestions and questions you need to ask so you can be sure you have considered and planned for the basics common to all tours.

As you develop your own style and personal flare in putting together tours, you will find yourself adding, modifying, and even consciously omitting certain items we have listed below. When you do, congratulate yourself on your increasing confidence and ability to make your tours stand out from the rest. If you find yourself asking a question not included here, don't dismiss it as unimportant — recognize that you have spotted an opportunity to improve your specific tour even more.

Tours are not created from a cookie cutter mould. They can, and should, be as unique as you and your clients are.

105

1. THE BIG STEP — BRANCHING OUT ON YOUR OWN

Tour guides and tour directors who branch out into running their own tours share several characteristics. Usually they have special expertise (such as a passion for spelunking or an infatuation with the artwork of medieval European cathedrals) which they want to share with others. If they have been working as a tour director for a larger tour operator, they might feel their experiences will give them some insider breaks as they take a new direction in this exciting world.

Some guides and directors simply want to be in business for themselves and do not care where they travel — as long as they are on the go. Many have contacts, such as a friend who works "behind the scenes" at Disneyland or a relative — however distant — on staff at NASA, who can give their tours special insight or access.

Surprisingly, most of the guides we spoke to said they were leading tours because of an intense feeling of personal and almost spiritual connection with the destination. They were entranced by the culture, heritage, people, architecture, and natural grandeur of a destination and felt compelled to share this love with others. This desire to share is felt as much by local step-on guides working in the well-loved, well-known hometown where they were born and raised as it is by a person organizing a three-week tour of a distant country. One Hawaiian guide we spoke to explained how he had left a growing career in social research in order to share his love of the islands with international visitors. He showed the same exuberance as the Oxford professor who sold all his possessions, bought a sailboat, and now makes a living running intimate, week-long cruises through the islands of Greece.

As you make your first decision of where to take the people who will join you on a tour, the most important question you need to ask is, "What area of the world do I find impossible to resist?" The answer may be "Right here where I live" or "Antarctica, where I can be penguin watching." Once you have your answer you are ready to move on to the second step of designing a winning tour.

2. THE THEME — WHY YOUR TOUR WILL BE DIFFERENT

The concept or theme is, very simply, the reason your tour exists. Why do you want to take people there in the first place? And perhaps even more important, why do your potential clients want to go there? Here are some pointers to help you discover an area's unexpected treasures.

(a) What books and videos about your destination are available at your local library? Read every one you can find. Imagine yourself at the site as you read and pay particular attention to anything you find yourself wanting to know more about. These questions will give you clues about what may appeal to your potential clients and indicate an outline of the additional research you need to do.

(b) Who do you know who has been there and would be willing to share experiences and knowledge? Neighbors, friends, family, and business associates are all potential sources of invaluable information.

(c) In your hometown, is there a local association or club for natives of the area you want to visit? You can often find a wealth of information here because people join such a club to preserve their heritage.

(d) Does your local university, community college, or other educational institution have information?

(e) Have you contacted the chamber of commerce or tourist bureau at your destination? They can provide you with information and, in many cases, personal contacts for popular attractions, transportation, accommodations, and eating establishments. They may also be able to supply videos and publicity photographs you can use to plan and promote your tour.

(f) Have you visited a travel agency or other travel supplier close to you who may have useful information?

(g) If you love wandering through cyberspace, you will likely find a wealth of information about your destination on the Internet. There may be so much information that unless you are as passionate about sitting in front of your computer as you are about travel, it may be too much to sift through easily.

(h) Have you been there yourself? While this may seem obvious, nothing beats on-the-spot reconnaissance.

As you do your research, think about how you can enhance the theme of your trip throughout the time you are traveling. Consider inviting one of the contacts you have made to be a guest speaker, or plan to visit related attractions in the general vicinity or partake in special meals or events.

The key to making your tours unique is simple: research, research, research.

Variety truly is the spice of life. Make sure you arrange an assortment of activities and sights.

3. WE'RE HERE! NOW WHAT?

Most people take a tour because they want to see it all! For many, this will be the only time they are able to visit the destination and you had better believe they will want to see everything possible while they are there. Even if your tour's theme is "Cuisine of New Orleans' French Quarter," you will need to round out your adventure with a variety of activities. The city's antebellum mansions and, yes, even the surrounding swamps are more than worthy of a day-long exploration for your New Orleans tour participants.

There are a number of questions that need to be answered to ensure your tour members have a chance to appreciate every attraction fully. For each attraction be sure you consider these points:

⊕ What are the hours of operation?

⊕ Is the attraction open seven days a week?

⊕ Are there seasonal closures?

⊕ Is the attraction currently closed or partially closed for renovations or repairs? Are there any anticipated closures in the near future?

⊕ How many people can it accommodate?

⊕ Is an on-site guide available? If not, can (and should) you arrange one on your own?

⊕ Do you need to schedule a specific arrival time or can the attraction accommodate groups without advance notice?

⊕ What are the most popular, and therefore the most crowded, times?

⊕ Are there other tours that regularly arrive at a certain time? Can you schedule your group so you do not have to compete for space and assistance from the staff?

⊕ May you pay on the spot or is advance payment required? Will the admissions office take credit cards, bill you or your company direct, accept checks, or insist on cash only?

⊕ Is the attraction wheelchair accessible?

⊕ Are hearing aids available?

- ⊕ Will presentations be in English only? in the local language only? in any language you request?

- ⊕ How long will it take to see and enjoy the attraction thoroughly? (Be sure to allow some leeway here — you never know who will have to be dragged away from the display on antique TV equipment or the mating habits of bottom-feeding fish. This is one area where the unexpected is the norm.)

- ⊕ Is there sufficient bus parking?

- ⊕ Do you know enough about the attraction (through research or personal experience) to answer the most probable questions yourself?

4. TIMING

Holidays and special events tend to drive the price of everything up. Make sure you calculate these increases when pricing your tours.

Timing is extremely important and deceptively complex. Major sporting events, cultural festivals, and local religious customs need to be considered just as much as weather patterns and North American holidays. For example, Super Bowl Sunday and the Thanksgiving weekend are not good departure dates in the United States, and attempting to book flights to the Far East just before Chinese New Year is next to impossible. On the other hand, if you are gearing your tour to showcase these events, start planning early and expect to pay more for almost everything. Here are some points to ponder when you ask yourself "When is the best time to run my tour?"

(a) Does the timing of my tour conflict with —

- ⊕ A seasonal holiday (e.g., Christmas, Easter, fourth of July)?
- ⊕ A large sporting event?
- ⊕ A major religious festival?
- ⊕ A cultural event (e.g., theater opening, art exhibit)?
- ⊕ A school holiday either at the departure point or the destination?
- ⊕ An annual local celebration (e.g., city birthday)?
- ⊕ An election? In many places, election campaigns go on for months.

(b) Can I take advantage of any of the above by incorporating them into the concept of my tour?

(c) What will the weather be like?

- Will temperatures be hot, temperate, cool, or cold?
- Will the climate be dry, humid, or varied?
- Is the local season spring, summer, fall, or winter?
- Will it be the rainy season?
- Is the season prone to hurricanes, monsoons, blizzards, or other natural phenomena?

5. SHELTERING YOUR GUESTS

Dorothy said it best in *The Wizard of Oz*: "There's no place like home." As a tour director, part of your challenge is to make your guests feel as much at home as possible whether they are in a five-star hotel or in a pup tent on a remote island. Review the following list as you plan how to make your guests comfortable wherever you lead them.

(a) Are your tour members expecting —

- Five-star luxury throughout?
- Clean, functional comfort at affordable prices?
- Accommodations with "atmosphere"?
- Modern architecture?
- Historical architecture?
- A reasonably accurate reflection of local culture and conditions?

(b) What are the alternatives to conventional hotels?

- Bed and breakfast (check if other meals can be arranged)
- Historical inns
- All-inclusive luxury resorts
- Farms or working ranches
- University dorms

(c) What amenities and conveniences are available?

- Private washrooms
- Elevators
- Room service
- Hair dryers
- Pool/hot tub/spa
- Gym/workout area

- Porters (for those unable to carry their own bags)
- Wheelchair accessibility
- 24-hour restaurants
- Lounge/pub
- Laundry facilities
- On-site entertainment
- Shops
- Money exchange/check cashing service

If you are planning a tour to a nonWestern country, be sure you and your guests are aware of any cultural differences accepted as normal by local residents. For example, one tourist in Yugoslavia was horrified to discover only a bare light bulb hanging from the ceiling in his room. The front desk clerk, however, could not understand his complaint. Having lived with bare light bulbs in the ceiling for his entire life, the clerk believed this was the way things were everywhere.

Not all parts of the world enjoy the same standard of living. Make your group aware of the differences they can expect at your destination.

6. NOURISHING YOUR GUESTS

Holidays and grand cuisine are inextricably intertwined. The trouble arises when one person expects "grand cuisine" to include a ten-course dinner every night of the tour while another considers it to mean an open-air barbecue. While cost will always be a factor in your planning, here are some culinary considerations when developing menus for your group. Will your tour participants expect —

- Three sit-down, gourmet meals a day?
- Casual breakfast and lunch with a formal dinner?
- Ethnic food reflecting the local style of cooking?
- Western-style meals at all stops?
- Vegetarian or kosher cuisine?
- Meals that are an experience?
- Meals that are a necessity?

As well, do they want to fend for themselves for any (or none) of the meals during the tour or to participate in the preparation of meals? (If your tour's theme revolves around food and fine dining, you may want to include a lesson from the head chef of a well-known restaurant, or other hands-on experience, as part of the activities.)

6.1 Restaurants

Hunger strikes 24 hours a day; to ensure this does not become a problem, you must have answers to the following questions about restaurants in the areas you will be visiting:

- ⊕ When are the restaurants you plan to visit open?

- ⊕ When are the busy periods when service may be slow?

- ⊕ How long will it take, on average, to be served?

- ⊕ Will restaurants be closed for holidays or on certain days of the week?

- ⊕ Do you need to schedule an exact arrival time?

- ⊕ What happens if your tour is late?

- ⊕ If not all meals are included in the tour itinerary, are there places close at hand where meals can be found at all hours of the day and night?

You should also figure out the logistics of eating at the restaurants you plan to visit:

- ⊕ How many people can the restaurant accommodate at one sitting?

- ⊕ Is there room for the bus to park?

- ⊕ Are there enough washroom facilities?

- ⊕ Will a buffet setup mean some people have less time to eat than others?

- ⊕ Will there be an adequate selection of food for both the adventurous and the conservative diners?

And finally, how can you make dining an event for your tour members?

- ⊕ Is the restaurant well known for something other than its food (perhaps it was the site of an Old West shoot-out or the home of a famous movie star)?

- ⊕ What is the house specialty? Is there anything historic or unique about it? (One Arizona restaurant provides a certificate of bravery to every patron who tries its deep-fried rattlesnake!)

* Does the restaurant offer entertainment (e.g., dancing, live theater, cooking classes) as part of the meal?

6.2 What about alcohol?

There are also a number of considerations for alcohol:

* Will all restaurants have liquor licenses?

* Do they offer a varied selection of beverages?

* Will there be wine/beer tasting available? (This is especially important if the tour focuses on wineries or breweries — e.g., Oktoberfest or the Napa Valley.)

* What alcohol (if any) will be included in the tour price?

* If alcohol purchases are at the participants' own expense, how will they be billed?

6.3 Food on adventure/wilderness tours

Tours that take you away from cities and towns bring up special problems related to food. Think about the following points and decide how you will deal with them:

* How will food be carried?

* How will food be preserved?

* Can food be purchased or found en route (e.g., local fruit or wild vegetables)?

* Can food be delivered to a series of drop points along the route?

* What kind of cooking facilities and utensils are needed?

* Will there be places where modern cooking facilities are available?

* Are cooking fire permits required?

* How will you extinguish cooking fires safely?

7. MISCELLANEOUS CONCERNS

While there will always be unexpected emergencies, here are some of the most commonly overlooked and easily avoidable problems. If you are aware of them in the planning stages, you will be prepared should you encounter them during a trip.

Advance planning will help you cope with all types of surprises, from medical emergency to insurance or security concerns.

7.1 Medical

- Where are the medical facilities in each location?

- How sophisticated, sanitary, and competent are local medical facilities?

- Are conventional Western medicines readily available? If so, are they at a reasonable cost?

- Can transport to North America or another country be arranged with a minimum of trouble?

- What are the payment policies in the countries you will visit? Some may be strictly cash only.

- On a wilderness, remote area, or third-world tour, how can you get medical aid in an emergency and how long will it take to arrive?

- Is at least one staff person certified in first aid (this is especially important on wilderness trips where help may be hours or even days away)?

- Are all participants in good health?

- If there are people with special needs (e.g., mobility restrictions, medication, breathing problems), are you equipped to handle a possible crisis?

- Has everyone received the necessary inoculations and vaccinations?

- Have all forms and waivers been correctly and completely filled out?

7.2 Security

- Will you be passing through any high-crime areas? If so, what special measures will be necessary to keep your guests safe?

- Is there a history of terrorist activities? While this should not automatically dissuade you from planning a tour, you will need to take extra precautions.

- Is the local government politically stable? (**Note:** This is not the same as being of the same political belief as your guests.)

- Where are the embassies/consulates in each location?

- ⊕ Are there any tour members without embassies/consulates in any of the destinations you will be visiting?

- ⊕ Where are the police stations in each location?

- ⊕ Is bribery a way of life with government/security officials in any of the places you will visit? If it is, be prepared in case you do need assistance.

- ⊕ If there are children on the tour, what special measures are necessary for their safety?

- ⊕ Are there natural hazards (e.g., cliffs, dangerous tides, predatory animals, volcanoes) which must be safeguarded against?

7.3 Insurance

Does every member of the tour have —

(a) Medical insurance,

(b) Baggage insurance, and

(c) Cancellation insurance?

Does your group require special insurance for dangerous activities (e.g., hang gliding, mountain climbing, scuba diving)? Have appropriate waivers been signed by all affected participants?

8. COSTING OUT YOUR TRIP

Unless you are independently wealthy, you will need to ensure that what you charge each participant actually covers your costs per person. The catch is, you must also be in line with your competitors' rates for an equivalent tour. If you offer an Alaska Cruising Experience for $2,000 when the tour company two blocks up offers one for $1,500, you will need to have some solid reasons why yours is worth the extra $500, or get set to sharpen your pencil.

To ensure you provide value to your clients and an income for yourself, here are some items to look at closely before you finalize the rate you put on your tour.

8.1 Getting there

- ⊕ What are the alternatives: air, bus, rail, ship, other?

- ⊕ What is the cost of ground transfer from arrival terminal to hotel?

Make sure your clients understand exactly what extra values and services you are providing if you plan to charge more than your competitors.

- Will you be paying porters or baggage handlers? How much?

- Does the agency you work with have special deals with transportation companies that might save you money?

- Can you get cheaper rates from a consolidator?

- Are there departure or other taxes?

8.2 Food

- What is the approximate cost for each day's breakfast, lunch, dinner, and snacks? Since each day's costs will vary, you will need to calculate individual days as well as the average cost per day.

- Will you be having any special banquets or special events (e.g., a get-acquainted party, wine tasting)?

- Don't forget to figure in tips and gratuities.

8.3 Accommodations

- What is the cost per day based on double occupancy?

- What is the cost of the single supplement (if available)?

- Are group discounts available? If so, what is the number of guests required to qualify for the discount?

- Are there seasonal discounts or surcharges you should be aware of?

- Are there any alternative accommodations (e.g., bed and breakfast or university dorms)?

- Again, don't forget tips and gratuities.

8.4 Attractions

Be sure to include the cost for each attraction.

- Are group discounts available for any site you will be visiting? What is the number of people required for a group discount?

- Is there a discount for advance bookings?

- Are there seasonal discounts or surcharges?

- Can you buy tickets direct from the attraction at a cheaper rate?

- Will there be a charge for any special equipment needed (e.g., headphones, snorkeling gear, canoes)?

- Will you be paying for local guides? How much will that cost?

- Include the cost of transportation to the attractions. Will you be expected to pay tips or gratuities?

Do not forget to inquire about seniors' rates. Many attractions and even some hotels and restaurants offer discounts for people over a certain age. However, the age limit tends to vary widely — some places consider a "senior" to be anyone over the age of 50, while at other places your tour members must have celebrated their 65th birthdays before they get cheaper rates.

Always ask about senior discounts and clarify what age qualifies as a senior.

Remember, incidental costs add up surprisingly quickly. We recommend building in an extra 20 percent to cover the many small items such as postage, faxes, and stationery which are often overlooked and are notoriously hard to pin down as you cost out your tour. You will probably want to use a computer spreadsheet program such as Lotus 1-2-3 or Microsoft Excel to do your costing. Because you will constantly be revising your figures, the ability to adjust totals automatically will save you many gray hairs.

We also recommend you make the trip yourself before you begin designing a tour. Be sure to carry a journal and write down every detail and your first impressions of everything as you go — where the baggage carousels are, whether you need local currency to get a baggage cart, how far it was from the airport to the hotel, what the restaurants were like, whether the locals are friendly or stand-offish. Knowing these small details in advance will be an invaluable aid when you bring a group and will make you look more professional and reliable.

Nothing beats first hand experience. Always check a destination out in person before you take a tour group there.

If you are working with a travel agency (see information on this arrangement in chapter 11), the agency may be able to help defray the cost of the trip with special travel agent rates. Even if this is not possible, be sure to tap the agency manager's knowledge and expertise.

Once you have mapped out the details of your tour, you must start concentrating on finding clients to fill your tour. That is what the next chapters are about.

11
RUNNING YOUR OWN TOURS

1. WORKING AS AN OUTSIDE AGENT

Before you get started on your first tour, you need to consider how you will let travelers know that your tour is available and how you will sell it to interested clients. Say you want to run a tour to Africa in six months. You could set up your own company with its own office and phone number. You would probably have to get a lawyer involved, apply for a municipal license, check out insurance...

A far easier way is to work under the auspices of a travel agency. This arrangement is common and easy to do. It means you can concentrate on your tour instead of learning a whole new set of skills. Once you start marketing the tour, a professional sales staff of experienced travel agents will be in place to sell your clients the tour, travel insurance, extra side visits, the air flights (with extended stay before or after the tour), and a host of extras. They will collect the money and do all the paperwork. At the end, the agency will hand you a check for your

Working under the auspices of a travel agency means you can concentrate on your tour instead of learning a whole new set of skills.

share of the commission. The agency takes care of all the legal stuff and provides a professional front for your business. Sound easy? It is.

Tour guides and directors who work with travel agencies in this manner are called outside agents or outside consultants. Usually they direct new business to the agency by sending friends and colleagues there. The agency's staff — inside travel agents — then sells the agency's products as well as the tour, and the outside agent gets a percentage of the money the customer spends.

The travel agency wins because it gets new customers without having to spend time and money finding them. Marketing is a big expense for travel agencies, so if an agency can earn commission — from the airlines, hotels, and other travel suppliers you will be using for your tours — without spending money on advertising, it will be thrilled. You win because you can concentrate on the tour arrangements and marketing instead of spending your time on all the details of booking flights and purchasing insurance. If something goes wrong, there are people backing you up who have a stake in sorting out the problem as quickly as possible. When you are in a remote location and one of your clients gets sick, or the pickup bus never arrives, it is comforting to know there is someone back at head office who can burn up the phone lines on your behalf.

If you make a connection with a travel agency, you also have a great source of revenue. There are very few travel suppliers who will pay you directly for the services your tour customers purchase. Airlines definitely will not pay you a commission. Their policy is to pay commissions only to IATA-appointed agencies. You might be lucky and find a hotel or two that say they will pay a commission, but our experience is that actually collecting the money is rare.

By working with a travel agency you are fitting into an already established system for selling services.

By working with a travel agency, you are fitting into the established system for selling services and paying invoices. Within this framework, airlines and cruise lines generally pay very promptly. Most hotels, car rental agencies, or bus services are somewhat slower but do pay eventually.

Working with an agency also means you do not need to worry about registering as a travel business, a necessity in some states and provinces where selling travel without a license is a crime. If you are running only a few tours a year, it is probably not worth the effort and expense to get a license.

1.1 Choosing a travel agency to work with

Selecting the agency you will work with is one of the crucial choices you must make. Ideally, you want to choose an agency with a fine reputation, an established and well-supported outside consultant program, and staff who are willing to spend some time helping an outside consultant. You are unlikely to find such a perfect company, so here are some of the things to watch for when choosing an agency.

(a) Small versus large agencies

There are a few large agencies with formal, structured, outside agent programs designed to field an army of part-time consultants. At the other end of the scale are hundreds of agencies that have a person or two working part time from home. Each type of company has its advantages.

One advantage of an agency with a program in place is that it already has experience with outside consultants and will have corporate policies stating how the program should be run. This will make your work go smoothly and give you little extras such as contests (with trips as the prize, of course!) and seminars specifically for outside consultants, not open to inside staff. You will meet other people who are running tours through the agency and will be able to compare notes. Just as important, the inside staff will know what to expect so you will not be treated as a nuisance. The company may also run a short orientation course and give you business cards at the outset. Probably the biggest advantage of working through a company with a well-developed program is that you can begin booking tours and sending clients to them immediately, so you will receive your first check from them much sooner.

The bad news is that, as with any large organization, there is some limit to the flexibility allowed. For instance, many agencies do not give reduced rate travel to their outside consultants until certain high-volume sales targets are met. As well, training programs, seminars, and product launches may not be available to you until you have reached a certain sales volume or worked for the company a set length of time. These requirements are set by corporate policies which may be difficult to circumvent.

Smaller independent agencies, where the owner works in the office, may be more flexible about reduced rate travel and other perks such as higher commissions. This is especially helpful if you need to get overseas to explore your tour area. The same flexibility could extend to training programs, seminars, and product launches. The more tours you are planning, the more training you will want. With a small independent agency, you may be able to take advantage of these offerings much sooner.

It is much easier for you to be noticed if you can produce a significant increase in the firm's revenue, and it is certainly easier to increase a small agency's sales by 10 percent than it is to increase a large agency's. Since even a 2 percent or 3 percent rise in sales can be cause for celebration, you may find it is easier to get good travel deals for yourself and your tours in a small agency, where you can shine more easily. Also, if you are the only outside consultant for a small firm, you are more likely to be treated as someone special. This will give you a better chance at free trips or at least put you on an equal footing with inside agents. This is rarely the case with larger firms.

If it sounds like small agencies are the only way to go, they aren't. There are some real advantages to working with a large firm. Because of their higher volume with the airlines, large agencies probably have more reduced rate trips for their staff than a small agency has. Small agencies may not receive perks from some travel suppliers at all, while a volume-producing agency may be able to make all kinds of special requests on your behalf.

(b) IATA/ARC and non-IATA/ARC agencies

As you learned in chapter 4, there are two governing bodies in the airline industry. The Airlines Reporting Corporation (ARC) operates in the United States, while the International Air Transport Association (IATA) sets the standards in the rest of the world. IATA/ARC regulations are the only worldwide standards in the travel industry.

⊕ Although non-ARC or non-IATA agencies are sometimes viewed as disreputable by others in the industry, they are not. They must still register with the correct civil authorities and comply with their requirements, just as any other agency must. They may have simply chosen not to join ARC or IATA. If an agency specializes in a certain kind of travel — for example, a cruise-only agency — it may not do enough airline ticket business to justify the fees and paperwork involved, so it is worth their while to forgo the formal stamp of IATA/ARC approval.

⊕ However, there are implications you need to be aware of. Lack of certification can mean these agencies do not comply with the IATA/ARC regulations concerning experience, finances, or a number of other requirements. As well, non-IATA/ARC agencies are excluded from many industry perks. Worse, some suppliers, particularly airlines, may not pay a commission to these agencies. Reduced rate airline tickets are seldom available to non-IATA/ARC agencies, and they are often denied reduced rates by other suppliers such as car rental companies and hotels. Our advice to you is to work with an ARC- or IATA-appointed agency unless you have a very good reason to do otherwise.

(c) Choose an agency that can sell travel insurance

Do not forget about travel insurance. Most travel agencies have a working relationship with a particular insurance company that supplies travel insurance for its clients. A few do not, and it is important that you steer clear of them.

There are two governing bodies in the airline industry. ARC operates in the United States and IATA sets the standards in the rest of the world.

Not only is insurance very profitable because of its high rate of commission, but it will also help you avoid trouble. The medical insurance your tour members buy does not give you any direct insurance protection. However, if uninsured members get sick and cannot pay for hospitalization, you will be faced with the choice of leaving them on the street in a foreign land or abandoning your tour to make sure they receive care.

Likewise, if a client has no trip cancellation insurance, misses your tour due to illness, and loses the nonrefundable $1,500 payment for the tour, guess who he or she will turn to for a refund? Some people, faced with the loss of their vacation money, will try just about anything to get it back. You may be legally in the right, but the law will not protect you from moaning customers. If the fee for the tour is nonrefundable but your customers have cancellation insurance, they will be reimbursed if they cannot go because of a medical emergency, a death in the family, and a host of other nonvoluntary reasons. (There is no insurance that will reimburse a traveler for voluntarily deciding not to go on a trip.)

Strongly encourage everyone to get medical and cancellation insurance. You may want to follow the lead of many tour operators and make them mandatory for your tour.

Lost baggage insurance is not quite as critical as medical and cancellation insurance — you can learn to ignore nearly naked people on your tour if you put them at the back of the bus. They are usually quieter than the sick. But if tour members have insured their luggage, they will be reimbursed for their missing possessions (up to a predetermined

Travel insurance provides a very necessary safety net for you and your group and also generates income for you.

policy limit) and, more importantly, will receive money immediately to tide them over until the bags turn up or are proved to be lost or stolen.

In summary, travel insurance not only provides a very necessary safety net for you and your group but it also generates income. Push insurance hard.

(d) Using multiple agencies

We do not recommend using several different agencies at the same time because it spreads your clients out. Since your negotiating power comes from sales volume, you may find you do not qualify for travel benefits or a higher commission rate with any of your agencies. Of course, you may have a special reason to direct customers for different tours to different agencies. Tours with a tightly focused theme, such as Cordon Bleu cooking or Danish ice fishing, may require agencies with a specialized focus. You will have to weigh each particular circumstance.

1.2 How to find an agency to work with

You must actively seek an agency to work with. Here are the three main ways to track them down.

Find an agency to work with by:
1. checking employment ads
2. calling agencies in your area
3. asking your friends

(a) *Check employment ads in your local paper.* In larger cities it is as easy as that. Many agencies advertise in the "Salespeople wanted" column for outside agents.

(b) *Call agencies in your area.* Ask if they will take you on. Explain you are looking for a commission only and that you have a few regular customers you would like to steer their way. If the agency does not have something for you, ask if it knows of another agency that might help you. This is probably the best approach for small towns.

(c) *Ask your friends.* You are almost guaranteed to know someone who has been in some part of the travel industry and can point you in the right direction.

2. COMPENSATION — TRIPS AND CASH

Many tour directors start out because they want to get a free trip or two. Enthusiasm and the challenge of the task are great motivators in the beginning, but eventually most people want some kind of cash remuneration to compensate for all the hard work.

2.1 Free trips and tour director seats

All travel suppliers have free tour director tickets, rooms, or cruise ship cabins for tour directors if they are leading a large enough group. Some airlines, for instance, give one free seat for every 15 paying passengers. Some require a much larger group. If you are planning a tour to Las Vegas or some other very popular destination, you may have to have 25 paying passengers before the airline will give you a free seat. Cruise lines generally require a booking of 15 to 20 cabins, while hotels may require from 10 to as many as 20 rooms before they provide a freebie. Car rental companies almost never give free cars regardless of how much business you bring them. However, you will likely be able to negotiate a much better rental price for the group.

If you are going to a popular destination at peak season and have only a small group, you might still be able to get a free trip, but not with tour director seats. Read on to find out how.

2.2 Getting paid cash

Another way to travel "free" is to earn enough cash from your venture to pay for the trip. Most outside agents are paid at least 20 percent of the agency's commission from the travel supplier. On average, travel agencies get from 5 percent to 10 percent of the trip's selling price. Some airlines, especially for domestic tickets, pay as little as 6 percent commission. A few international hotels and airlines pay as much as 15 percent, although this is rare. Consolidators may pay a higher commission, but if an agency is making more than 15 percent it will likely pass the excess on to its clients via a discounted ticket price or a rebate. After the discount is deducted, the agency is probably making the average 10 percent commission.

For example, say the air tickets for your tour to Egypt cost $1,000. The travel agency may earn 10 percent or $100 for each ticket sold. Once the agency is paid its commission for the tickets, it will pay you 20 percent of what it made on the transaction, or $20. If the agency uses a consolidator or gets override (extra) commissions, it might receive 15 percent or $150 on each ticket. In most cases, the agency will pass this extra commission along to the client by reducing the price it charges for the ticket. In this example, if the agency earned 15 percent or $150, it could give the passengers a break by charging only $950 for the tickets. In this case, the agency still earns only $100 after the discount ($1,000 x 15 percent = $150 less a $50 rebate to the passengers = $100 net commission). Your commission remains at $20. (Rebate details vary from agency to agency, and all you really need to know is that it is legal and quite common.)

One last point. Travel suppliers are always trying to figure out how to pay retail agents less. Over the years, commission rates will fluctuate depending on how much the suppliers feel they need the agencies to sell their product. In recent years, not only have commission rates decreased, but a cap or ceiling has been put on the amount of commission that can be earned, regardless of the price of the ticket.

2.3 Other ways to get paid

Ask the manager at your travel agency for help the first couple of times you negotiate prices with travel suppliers.

Another variation of the same idea is to put together a package of special prices from the airlines and hotels, then charge members of your group a slightly higher total price. For example, say you are buying airline seats from San Francisco to Frankfurt for an Oktoberfest tour. The going rate for the seats is $700. A consolidator offers the same flight to your agency for $580 as a wholesale price. Even if you give your group a break by charging only $650 per ticket, the agency still makes $70 per person. If you get 20 percent of that, you make $14 per person off the top. You will find that, with the commissions you might get from hotels, tourist attractions, hotel-airport transfers, insurance, and other commissionable things your group might need, your portion adds up quickly.

You will need the help of the manager at your travel agency the first couple of times you negotiate prices directly with the airlines and other travel suppliers, but it is a straightforward process, and you should get the hang of it quickly.

2.4 Getting more commission

If you conduct tours several times a year, the higher volume of sales you are bringing in should enable you to negotiate a better rate of commission with the travel agency. The top rate we know of is about 60 percent, which means on the airline tickets in the Frankfurt example above, you would get 60 percent of $70 or $42 per ticket. With 15 people in the group (15 x $42 = $630), you have more than paid for your own airfare.

Use Table 4 as a guide in negotiating your commission split with the agency. (Note that these are just guidelines and are not hard rules.) Occasionally you can find an agency willing to pay more, even at the beginning. It is always worth asking for more, just to see what happens. Also be aware that if you want more commission, you will need to do more of the arranging. If all you do is steer your clients to the agency and the inside agents do all the work, you will never get the top rate on the commission scale.

TABLE 4
COMMISSION CHART

Total gross sales volume	Total annual commission you earn for agency (10% of total gross sales)	Your commission rate
occasional sales		20%
$ 5,000 to 30,000	500 to 3,000	30%
30,000 to 40,000	3,000 to 4,000	35%
40,000 to 60,000	4,000 to 6,000	40%
60,000 to 100,000	6,000 to 10,000	50%
100,000 +	10,000 +	60%

3. ARRANGING THE TOUR YOURSELF

Many tour directors and guides would not dream of letting anyone else do the booking and insist on taking care of the details themselves. If you fit this category, here are some hints to keep you on the right track when signing up your tour.

(a) *Identify yourself.* When you call a travel supplier, state your name, agency (if you are working with one), and what you are looking for. It is unlikely you will speak to the correct person right off the bat, so be prepared to repeat this information many times as you are passed from person to person within the organization. A good starting point is to ask for the supplier's sales representative or the sales office.

(b) *Be prepared.* Have your own or your travel agency's address, telephone number, and, if applicable, IATA or ARC number handy.

(c) *Repeat back everything.* Always confirm and reconfirm what was said. It is all too easy, on either side, to hear a "B" as a "V" or to transpose two digits. It is also helpful to learn the international phonetic alphabet (see Table 5). Your friends may kid you about it, but the people on the other end of a reservation line will thank you.

TABLE 5
INTERNATIONAL PHONETIC ALPHABET

A - Alpha	H - Hotel	O - Oscar	V - Victor
B - Bravo	I - India	P - Papa	W - Whisky
C - Charlie	J - Juliet	Q - Québec	X - X-ray
D - Delta	K - Kilo	R - Romeo	Y - Yankee
E - Echo	L - Lima	S - Sierra	Z - Zulu
F - Foxtrot	M - Mike	T - Tango	
G - Golf	N - November	U - Uniform	

(d) *Know who you are talking to.* Always get the first name of the person you are dealing with and a locator (also called a confirmation, booking, or reservation number) for any booking you make. Most companies do not require reservation personnel to give out their last name, but a first name and locator will go a long way toward proving your credibility and resolving the problem if things go awry.

(e) *Confirm both the amount and method of payment.*

(f) *Write everything down.* Start a separate file for everyone you book. Color-code each booking file with bright colors so you can quickly find the one you want on your messy desk or kitchen table.

(g) *Do not miss deadlines.* Not only is missing a deadline unprofessional but it can also be very costly. If you are lucky, you may only have to pay a higher price. If you are not lucky, missing a deadline may mean you are unable to book certain hotels or attractions. In a worst case scenario, you could be forced to cancel the entire trip.

(h) *Cancel anything you are not going to use.* You may find that because you forgot to cancel a booking, you are now the proud owner of a ticket to Barcelona, Spain, and the agency you are working with was automatically debited the amount owing through the Bank Settlement Plan (BSP) or the Airlines Reporting Corporation (ARC). The agency is obligated to pay this amount or lose its license. Your agency's manager will not want to hear excuses; he or she will just want to know how you are going to pay — now.

(i) *Have alternatives.* To save time and to look professional, know the exact itinerary of your tour (including the preferred times you want to travel) and have second choices ready. There are times when nothing goes right and you end up changing everything over and over. Be warned: every change is kept with the record in the airline file, so you begin to look like a scatterbrain to anyone who has to deal with your very long file. Careful planning will save you this embarrassment.

(j) *Remember visas and passports.* Make sure you know what documents your tour members must bring, including visas for the countries you are traveling to.

(k) *Use the right phone numbers.* Every agency has a huge book listing hotel phone numbers for just about every destination. These are the phone numbers the hotels want agents to use. Most car rental companies have toll-free numbers you may use for reservations.

(l) *Shop around.* Comparison shopping is a must. Be sure to ask for both weekly and daily rates, as well as any specials the travel supplier may have.

(m) *Always dress neatly.* Image counts. The more you look like a professional doing business, the more smoothly things will go.

(n) *Always smile.* Charm, patience, and a smile go a long way in this industry. Also, grace and poise under pressure can get you out of many tight situations.

(o) *Thank everyone.* Thank-you notes will make you memorable. If you can, mention names of specific people in the organization who were particularly helpful. If your contact at the supplier's office receives praise from the boss because of your note, he or she will be pleased to help you again.

4. PRICING YOUR TOUR

Once you have worked out the cost of the tour (e.g., airfares, accommodation costs, bus and driver fees), you must set the price. Pricing is an art. Clearly you do not want to sell your tour for less than it will cost you, nor do you want to charge so much you scare potential customers away. Although there are pricing guidelines to follow, ultimately you must make an educated guess to set the right price for your tour.

First you should figure out what your personal travel costs will be. Add up the total charges for your hotel, airfare, transfers, insurance, and commission for the agency, then divide it by the number of people going on the tour. This figure should be added to the price. Depending on how extensive your marketing campaign is, you will also have costs for printing, postage, couriers, long-distance telephone calls, and a host of other charges. Beware of dismissing these costs because they are so small. They add up with amazing speed. For many tours, these sundry costs can make the difference between a profit and a loss. Estimate what the total costs will be, divide that figure by the number of people on the tour, and add that figure to the price.

Now look at how much your competitor charges for a comparable tour. If your tour costs more, you must reduce the price or make sure your tour has some extra benefits that are worth the additional charge. Stress these extras in any promotional material you produce. The easiest way to make your tour worth more than your competitor's is to make it unique. Instead of calling it "Touring Atlanta," for example, add several heritage houses to the itinerary and offer a tour of the "Antebellum South's Finest Mansions." If you are an aficionado of pre Civil War mansions, your knowledge and stories might be that extra something which will get you an extraordinary price for your tour.

It is equally important to know your customers so you do not undercharge. If people would willingly pay more for your tour, you have undercharged and cut down your hard-earned profit. As an extreme example, any time before the 1996 Olympics you could get a room in Atlanta for less than $50 per person per day. By that summer, demand was such that rooms, if you were lucky enough to find a vacant one, ran more than double that rate. Atlanta's hoteliers clearly read their market

Don't forget to:

1. confirm amount of payment
2. write everything down
3. meet all deadlines
4. cancel what you're not going to use
5. have alternatives
6. have visas and passports

correctly and charged accordingly. It might even be argued that since all rooms were sold out, they undercharged. They probably could have charged even more and still sold out.

If you build up the perception of value by giving your customers something no one else has (such as the Olympics), you are justified in charging premium prices.

Build up the perception of value by giving your customers something no one else has.

12
MARKETING YOUR TOURS

Marketing is the key to staying in business, making a profit, and having your dreams come true. No business will survive a lackadaisical marketing effort for long, and tour guiding is no exception. There are a thousand other tours vying for the same customers. Every one of your clients is a jewel you must fight for.

1. MARKETING IS NOT JUST ADVERTISING

Most people think marketing is advertising. Although advertising may be a very important piece of your marketing plan, it is not all of it. Marketing is the total effort you make to get clients to buy from you and continue to deal with you. It is the series of decisions you make concerning what products you will sell, what price you will charge for them, how you want your tours to be perceived, and what things you will do to promote awareness of the package you put together. To induce the public to buy from you the first time, you will need to use clever advertising, great pricing, personal contacts, and catchy promotions. To make sure people continue to buy from you, you must ensure you have the right products at the right price combined with efficient service.

Our experience shows a multipronged marketing strategy works best. By trying several ideas at once you will quickly discover the profitable tactics and discard the unprofitable. Working your way through the various options one at a time may seem like a less expensive and sensible approach, but if you rely on only one approach, you may be in trouble if it does not pan out.

What follows is not an exhaustive survey of options and alternatives, nor a generic marketing plan that will work for all tour operators. We will give you a few ideas to think about, but a winning strategy is the result of a creative process; you must tailor it to your situation by assessing different tactics, observing how they work in your area with the mix of people living there. We suggest that you take courses, read as much as you can about marketing, and watch your competition for helpful approaches.

Marketing is the total effort you make to get clients to buy from you.

Marketing thrives on imagination and optimism. This is your chance to tell the world about your dream tour. Enthusiasm is infectious; it will make potential clients sign up for your tour. If you have people working with you, your enthusiasm will allow them to see a successful business even if the financial picture is not all that great in the beginning.

2. YOUR BROCHURE

Your brochure is one of your most important marketing tools. If you are thinking of putting together a tour more complex than simply some air flights and hotel reservations, you should be prepared to invest time and money to make the brochure the very best you can.

Collect a sampling of brochures put out by other tour operators and see what they are doing. Then sketch out an initial design for your own brochure. Be sure to have the manager of the agency you are working with take a look at what you are doing. His or her experience will be invaluable.

One of the blessings of the last ten years has been the advent of desktop publishing for the masses. When we first started marketing, we either had to hire someone to design and execute a project — which was expensive and required weeks of lead time — or do an amateur job ourselves, which meant a heavy investment of time for a not-so-great result. Now we can do a reasonable brochure in a day and have complete control over the process. If there are price changes or late-breaking information, we can produce an eye-catching announcement, complete with illustrations, in an hour.

All you need is a Macintosh or an IBM-compatible computer with Windows and a cheap desktop publishing program (some easy-to-learn software is as cheap as $10). If you want a real boost, take a quick night school course in desktop publishing to learn all you need to know to turn out simple black-and-white brochures.

Color brochures are a different matter. The skills required to effectively put together a good product are much more difficult to master Also, because the cost of four-color printing is so high, you cannot afford to make any mistakes. While a botched black-and-white printing job might cost you a few hundred dollars, the same mistake in four colors can easily cost in excess of a thousand dollars. At these prices you want every picture to be the best it can be, and the copy should be perfect. Hire a professional for your color brochures.

2.1 Legal fine print

Use the legal fine print on your competitors' brochures as a guide when you set your own policies for refunds, cancellations, payment terms, schedule changes, and the like. The agency you work with should be consulted here. It will have final say on policies because these could affect the agency's license.

2.2 Photos

Professional-quality photos can be expensive but are absolutely essential. A less expensive alternative to hiring a professional photographer is to contact tourist boards at your tour destination and ask if you can use their stock photos. Be sure you get permission in writing before you go to print. You don't want to have to abandon your brochure because a new tourism director will not honor a predecessor's verbal agreement.

2.3 Printing

Have the brochure professionally printed. Even though color laser copiers are becoming more refined, they still can't match the quality of a professional press. Ask for printing quotes from print shops in other states and provinces as well as in your own area. Sometimes the cost elsewhere is half what you would pay at home, even after you have added shipping charges.

Spend the money to have your brochure professionally printed.

2.4 Keep words to a minimum

Punchy descriptions are the key. Let a series of striking pictures tell most of the story.

3. USE YOUR PERSONAL CONTACTS

You may not want to deal with close friends when you first start out, but you have dozens of acquaintances who could turn into great sources of business. Get a head start by drawing up a list of all the clubs and organizations you belong to. Then make a point of going to meetings, lunches, or other events that will put you in contact with members.

Your business card should be with you wherever you go. Even if you are too shy to offer it voluntarily, just mentioning travel and your new tour business should elicit requests for your card. Some of these will ultimately lead to sales. No high pressure selling; just get out there and meet people in social situations. And it does not cost a thing. In your list of organizations don't forget to include:

- Associations — fraternal, health, environmental
- Book clubs
- Car rally groups
- Cardplaying clubs — bridge, poker
- Church groups — choir, study groups
- Fund-raising groups
- Hobby clubs — model airplane or train clubs
- Professional associations
- Recreational clubs — tennis, golf, hiking
- School or university alumni
- Social clubs — dinner, dancing
- Sports teams — hockey, swimming, aerobics, skiing, diving
- Unions
- Volunteer organizations

If any of the organizations you belong to have a periodic newsletter, see if you can get a congratulatory paragraph about your new tour business included. The editor may even want to interview you!

Your business card
should always be
with you.

4. THE ULTIMATE MARKETING TOOL — WORD OF MOUTH

Nothing works better than word of mouth. It is believable, costs nothing, and has a multiplying effect that cannot be duplicated. The ultimate goal of your marketing campaign is to have all your clients coming to you because of the superb recommendations your tours get. To accomplish this you must make sure the clients who try your services are so impressed with how you fulfilled their expectations that they not only come back again but they also tell their friends about you. You will get only one chance to impress most people. To benefit from each opportunity it is essential to set the stage before the client ever contacts you. Make sure your tours are organized, efficient, and the very best you can make them.

You will get only one chance to impress most people.

5. KNOW YOUR COMPETITION

Whether or not you are able to discover a profitable niche you can service depends, to a large degree, on what the competition is doing. Contrary to what you might expect, your competitors are not necessarily in your hometown. Your closest competitor may be in the next city or the next state, or may be one of the big multinational tour operators. What defines a competitor is whether it offers the same products and markets to the same people as you do.

Once you have identified which tour operators are your competitors, watch them carefully. If your competition suddenly undercuts your prices, it may be a tip that there are new airline deals or new consolidators available. Keep a close eye on your competitors' marketing strategy, too. The techniques they use might work equally well for you.

Competitors may even be a source of solutions for mutual problems. Get to know other tour directors and management. Undoubtedly, you will meet these people at trade shows and seminars, and as in most businesses, a cordial acquaintance may help you later.

6. FREE PUBLICITY

Media coverage has two advantages: it is free and it gives your business great credibility because the information is presented as news rather than promotional filler.

Unless you are an experienced writer who knows how to market your material, it is unlikely you will get an article published in a major daily since most have staff writers or favored freelance writers who write these, but it may be possible to get a reporter to interview you about your tour. Alternatively, the paper may be interested in a short article about your tour destination. If your tour is unique, write about it — what people will see, hear, and learn about. Offer the story to as many newspapers and magazines as you think might be interested in it. Create a catchy angle by emphasizing the most unique part of your trip. Be warned that this will require a fair amount of effort on your part and audiences are small, but the experience you gain will be useful. Small local newspapers are always hungry for material.

If you feel comfortable in front of a camera or on the radio, arrange an interview. Like local newspapers, local stations and cable networks often jump at the chance to have a "homegrown celebrity" on their program.

Another possibility for free publicity is to arrange a spot on a regular weekly newscast to talk about the best airline deals of the week or to comment on changes making news in the travel industry. Weekly appearances get easier the more you do them, but they are still a major commitment of time and energy. In return for all this hard work, the station should let you be the sponsor of that segment or at least put a plug for your tours into every show. This tactic takes a prodigious amount of effort. You must first interest a station in your ideas, then research your topics, script each week's message, and finally record the program. Keep your eye on the prize, though: an apparent endorsement from a major media source is a terrific boost to your business.

Since radio and TV stations do not want to seem to be giving away free advertising time (after all, this is news!), you may have to fight to have your telephone number aired. From our own experience, we can tell you that if a station refuses to air your telephone number, the exercise is not worthwhile. When stations refused to give out our telephone number during the program, we devised a free mail-out which provided more information on the topic of the day (e.g., the tour or destination we talked about, senior citizen's discounts, travel contests). The station announced our number at the end of the show, and the listener or viewer could call us for the mail-out. Radio and TV stations loved the idea that their audience was getting something for free — and we got to build our mailing list!

If you are willing to make the commitment to a long-term campaign and have an imaginative approach to a topic, here are the steps to getting an interview or becoming a program sponsor.

Media coverage has

two advantages:

1. it's free

2. it gives your business great credibility

(a) Produce a press release. Write a snappy headline and a concise paragraph about the topic you are interested in talking about. Make sure it is a newsworthy item, something new or exotic and not just a commercial for your tour. Put your name, address, phone number, and the date in the upper right-hand corner of each page. There are many books on how to write a scintillating press release. Refer to one for tips.

(b) Research the stations you are interested in approaching based on the audience they reach and the format or topics they use. Once you have selected the most promising station or stations, call them to find the name of the news director or, even better, the person who produces a news format travel show. Mail him or her a copy of your news release.

(c) Follow up about a week later with a phone call to make sure your contact received the release and to find out if he or she is interested in talking to you further. At this point you will get either an invitation or a refusal.

(d) Three to six months after an interview, go back to the same station and suggest an update you can do for them. Stations that receive dozens of calls for your number after a show will want you back.

As you might guess, TV interviews generate the most response while radio programs aired during the drive to or from work run a close second. Interviews in major newspapers about current travel industry events are great if they include your phone number. Interviews in magazines are not terrific traffic generators, but they don't take much time either. Some can even be done over the phone. It takes an amazing amount of perseverance and luck to earn free media coverage. Be prepared to give a lot to get a lot. It may be time-consuming but will be well worth it in the end, especially if you are cash shy.

It takes an amazing amount of perseverance to earn free media coverage, but the payoff is worth it.

7. CONDUCTING INFORMATIONAL SEMINARS

Some tour operators attract customers by putting on seminars. Usually there is a destination theme — South Pacific beaches, for example, or English castles. Of course, the tour or tours the company runs are highlighted as the best way to see these marvelous sights. At the end of the seminar the company's staff is on hand, ready to answer questions about the company's products and to sign people up for tours. Like arranging free publicity, setting up a seminar can be time-consuming and expensive, but, done correctly, seminars can bring you paying customers.

When setting up your seminar:

1. check the calendar
2. pick an accessible location
3. keep it under two hours
4. find and advertise door prizes

Market your seminar aggressively. Make it the focus of your life for a month beforehand. Advertise, tell existing clients about it, and notify every single one of your contacts and acquaintances (remember the list earlier in this chapter?). Be sure to take advantage of free public service announcements offered by some radio and TV stations. Push suppliers hard to announce the seminar to everyone they know by pointing out that it is in their best interest to do so. If the turnout for the seminar is low, you will at least know your marketing effort was not the culprit. (If turnout is low, you might also want to reexamine your tour concept. Maybe no one is interested in your destination.)

It is easy to do your own seminar, so do not pay someone else to put it on for you. You may feel overwhelmed by the thought of PA systems and slide shows, but usually the staff at the auditorium or hotel where you have rented space will have lots of helpful suggestions. They will also provide (at a cost) all the hardware and audiovisual equipment you may need, as well as some light refreshments. You can save money on rent by focusing on groups that already have a meeting place, such as seniors and volunteer organizations, but look carefully at the types of prospects this may bring you. General advertising and a public location, though more expensive, may yield more appropriate prospects.

You can save on expenses by getting the suppliers you work with to help out. Many suppliers will have a public relations department or someone in the sales department who is responsible for helping their customers — and that is you! Take full advantage of any assistance they can give you. Here are some other thoughts to keep in mind as you set up your seminar.

- Check the calendar. Absolutely do not schedule your seminar during Christmas, Easter, or Thanksgiving holidays, when a major sporting event is being run, over a long weekend, or during spring break for schools in your area.

- Pick a central, accessible location with lots of parking.

- Keep the presentation under two hours in length, with a question-and-answer period to follow.

- You might think about charging admission if you have an extraordinary guest speaker or a unique slide show, but most informational seminars are free.

- Seminars require a lot of preparation and evening work. You will not want to do very many of them if there is not a clear indication that they work for you. Make the first one count.

- Try to convince your suppliers to donate door prizes such as free trips, T-shirts, or luggage. If they agree, stress the prizes in all marketing because they will dramatically increase attendance.

- Free advance tickets and reservations can work for you by making the seminar seem more valuable, but they can also discourage last-minute participants who think they will not be allowed in without a reservation. Many people will decide to attend at the last minute. Even with reservations, only 60 percent of the people who call about a free seminar will actually show up.

8. SELLING THROUGH TRAVEL AGENTS

If you are working as an outside agent for one travel agency, that agency can in turn act as a tour operator and sell your tour to the public through other agencies. Your agency would continue to book flights and accommodation for tour members, and would collect a commission from the airlines, even for tour spots booked by other agencies. Your agency would also be paying the other agency a commission of five to 15 percent. Be sure your agency's manager knows exactly what you are doing and supports you if you are going to offer your tour this way.

Selling your tours through travel agents seems like a wonderful way to have a huge sales force without carrying the expense. In theory it is. You pay the travel agents their commission only after they sell one of your tours and have given your agency the client's cash. But because this commission is coming out of your agency's take, you will want a terrific deal with the airlines to make sure you are receiving more than a negligible amount of money when you get your 20 percent. The key is to do a large volume of business or to drop your up-front marketing costs because you have so many outlets working for you.

Selling through travel agents will bring in some business, but it will not be the mainstay of your sales effort. If you are selling the same kind of tour as a major, established operator, most agents will deal with the bigger firm because they feel large operators are less likely to go bankrupt. In reality, size does not equate with financial stability, but the perception is that bigger is better.

As well, agents fear that new tour operators could take the money and disappear. No one looks forward to telling clients that their money has vanished and they will not be getting the vacation they paid for — in fact, they may not be getting any vacation at all.

Travel agents are also bombarded with hundreds of deals each day. How are you going to get their attention? Strategies employed by larger tour operators are usually expensive and often do not work well for a small operator. Many agents expect to be wooed with incentive contests for the highest selling agent, free food at product launches, and personal visits from you. All this costs a lot of money, and you must expend constant effort to refresh agents' memories about your products. Our experience in the retail end of the chain is that small, unknown tour operators are ignored.

Finally, most travel agents do not have time to read and learn about tours suited only to a small number of their clients. There are exceptions to this rule, of course, but not many.

We recommend you market directly to the public in the beginning. Later, you can experiment with travel agents. Of course, if the tours you run lend themselves to some cheap, creative blitz that will grab the attention of the travel trade, do it. If you have a truly unique tour, many travel agents will refer their clients to you even if they don't get paid. As an example, we know of some small operators who have become known for shopping tours of New York City and Hong Kong. Through great publicity, these people have made a name for themselves and travel agents are willing to sell their tours without compensation as a service to their own clients.

Market directly to the public in the beginning.

9. DIRECT MAIL

You should develop a mailing list of past customers and people who contact you about your tours. Purchase and learn one of the data-base programs and use it for your mailing list. This makes it easy for you to select only the people interested in a certain kind of tour for a targeted mail campaign. For small tour operators, this is one of the most cost-effective ways to get business, but it does take perseverance. You will not have a data-base mailing list when you start out, but if you make the effort to collect this information you will have a cheap and effective marketing tool within a couple of years.

Make an effort from the beginning to collect information for your data-base mailing list. It will eventually be a cheap and effective marketing tool.

10. ADVERTISING AS A SMALL TOUR OPERATOR

Advertising is very expensive. As a small tour operator you probably do not have the budget for a sustained campaign. Advertising agencies will tell you that a potential customer has to see your ad three or four times before it sinks in. We agree. One-shot advertising is probably wasteful and a campaign is often too expensive to make sense. Focus your efforts on free media coverage, word-of-mouth promotion, and the other marketing strategies outlined in this chapter.

13
USING THE INTERNET

The information super highway is here and it has been a boon to tour guides, making research and communication easier and less expensive. Marketing has taken on a whole new dimension. But there are some pitfalls which can threaten your enterprise, and with all the hype about the Internet, it is difficult to get proven information. We would venture to say that there have been few comparable times in history when zealot's opinions have been sold as fact to the extent that they are now.

1. RESEARCH

As more companies put information online, the opportunities for research have expanded.

It's now possible to look at hotel rooms, get city maps, make reservations, see what kinds of attractions are nearby, book airline tickets, look at restaurant menus, and accomplish a host of other time consuming tasks in a fraction of the time without ever leaving your office.

But be aware, one of the major pitfalls we found while doing research is that some companies do not update their information frequently. It's important to get into the habit of looking for some indication of when the site was last updated. Prices and availability should still be checked verbally or in writing. Even very large companies sometimes abandon their sites or cut their Internet budgets so severely that stale information is all that's left on their Web site. A few big companies have even been sued successfully for not honouring old out of date prices that Internet customers relied on.

2. BOOKING AIRLINE SEATS, CARS, AND HOTELS

We believe the Internet will never totally replace a good travel agent to work with. The information is certainly available on the Internet, but it is often difficult to find what you need when you need it.

Travel agents have access to consolidators and wholesalers who can sell you the same airline seats for much less than the airlines will directly. These wholesalers do have Web sites but there are thousands of them. Your travel agent's experience about who has which products is something that cannot be duplicated by a search engine. In fact, in almost all tests we have done, our agent was able to get better rates for airline flight reservations than anything we could find on the Internet.

In addition, your travel agent knows many of the pitfalls that are not apparent when you book through the Internet. We have heard more than one story of someone who purchased a ticket through the Internet only to arrive at the wrong airport in a city, thereby missing their connecting flight. Travel is complex with lots of hidden problems just waiting to bite the unwary.

Lastly, the whole process of searching for and booking a ticket online is still very cumbersome. A travel agent will do all the work for you, get a better price, possibly provide accounting services or tickets dropoff, and smile while doing it. We also keep hearing the same story over and over — it is possible to book seats, cars, and hotel rooms over the Internet, but it can easily take many hours. Our conclusion is that it is still way too early to do bookings yourself unless you must. Even then, skip the Internet and use a more direct connection.

3. E-MAIL

We have found e-mail is one of the best communication tools to come along in a long time. Among other advantages:

(a) it is free to connect from anywhere in the world

(b) you have a written confirmation of your communication

(c) you don't have to worry about waking someone in the middle of the night because of different time zones, or staying up half the night to connect with someone on the other side of the world

(d) you don't have to chit chat as you would over the telephone so your messages can be precise and succinct

(e) you can send drawings, photographs, maps, or huge documents at no extra cost

E-mail accounts like Hotmail (www.hotmail.com) are free, the software to use e-mail is given away for free, and if you have troubled figuring out how to use any if it, there is sure to be someone nearby who can help — for free.

4. MARKETING USING THE WORLD WIDE WEB

Whole books have been written on this subject, and it is still a subject of hot debate. A Web presence is becoming almost essential as people come to rely on the World Wide Web as a giant, global Yellow Pages. However, don't become so enamored with this new technology that you put all your marketing dollars into this one basket. Remember, not everyone is connected to the World Wide Web. Are your customers?

When you are ready to venture into the world of cyber advertising, here are some of the common pitfalls we have seen:

(a) Not having a clear objective about what your Web site or your Web marketing campaign is supposed to achieve

(b) Setting up a Web site and not updating it

(c) Underestimating of the amount of money required to set up a Web site

(d) Not hiring professional help to design the Web site

(e) Not hiring professional help to implement the Web site

(f) Not allocating enough time, effort, and money to the project

Although there are thousands of "Web masters," all industries are crying for Web designers, people who can conceptualize and layout the Web site before any computer code is written. If your site is too complicated, not interesting, or too cumbersome for your customer to use, you are wasting your money. Do not underestimate the amount of time, frustration, and effort necessary for you to get up on the Web.

No matter how terrific your Web site is, you must promote it as if it were a product, and the means to promote it are virtually the same for any product. Only the tools have changed. The process of finding people to review your site, or enticing people to write about your Web site, or encouraging visitors to your site would be familiar to any public relations, marketing, or advertising person. Discovering the right person to do this job is as difficult as finding the right person to hire as your regular marketing or public relations specialist.

Our own experience has been that there are lots of people out there who think that they can do this job on the World Wide Web solely because they know computers. This can't be further from the truth. To make matters worse, we hear the same complaint all over the high tech industry — after you spend all the time to hire someone who you think is perfect, someone else offers them more and they're gone.

This leaves you or a trusted employee as the only consistent marketing force for your company on the Web. In close questioning of several Web marketers, there seems to be a consensus that it requires to at least three hours each day to make a marketing program succeed. The question you have to ask yourself is whether you can afford to spend up to three hours each day shopping the World Wide Web for opportunities to promote your company or whether you can afford not to.

5. YOUR BROCHURE

Use smaller file formats such as JPEG to keep the size of your e-mail brochure manageable.

One of the simplest ways to use the Web for marketing and cut printing costs is to put up your brochure. By then putting your Web site address on all of the material that leaves your office, you give potential customers a conduit to one of your best selling tools. Every piece of paper and every e-mail that goes out of your office should have your Web site address on it. In addition, it is now possible to send your full color brochure by e-mail to anyone who requests information. Those savings will really make your mouth water.

6. SPAM

Some businesses use e-mail to attract business by sending out thousands of unwanted advertising e-mails called spam. In a very limited number of cases it does work, however, be prepared for a huge negative reaction. While spamming is legal at present, you could find that your service provider will cut you off for spamming.

Putting aside the moral problem, it will cost you a fair amount of money and time to set this up and the chances of actually getting a return on all your expenditures is tiny. What's worse, the negative feeling you engendered will affect all your other marketing endeavors.

It is almost as if you must choose between spam as your only marketing tool or using the more usual methods of marketing. Money spent on publicity, promotion, advertising, and a terrific sales force may well be valueless because you have already irritated your potential customer.

7. COLLECTING MONEY OVER THE INTERNET

Collecting money securely over the Internet using credit cards and even cheques is becoming easier. There are now companies out there who will set up your entire e-commerce system for a reasonable fee. Still, it will require that you put a fair amount of research into finding the right company and integrating its product into your marketing.

At least for now it appears that most customers still want to deal directly with a person at your company. Bed and breakfasts and hotels have been using the World Wide Web for many years now and their experience is instructive. Bed and breakfasts typically report that many of their customers find them on the Web and then call directly to confirm details and make bookings. One hotel chain said the time and money they had put into their Web site had resulted in so few direct bookings that it basically cost them five hundred dollars per reservation.

8. KEEPING IN TOUCH

With the advent of small hand-held computers with internal modems, it is possible to set up a worldwide communications network very cheaply. Not only that but computer prices are still in a nose dive. The hand-held computer Rick bought last year for $800 has a cheaper competitor this year for under $150.

In conclusion, do not abandon your normal channels of marketing and distribution but do keep up with changes happening in the high tech arena. Give a fair amount of thought to each move you make and do not embrace the World Wide Web as a be-all-and-end-all answer to all your marketing needs. It is not, but it is proving to be a marketing tool worth watching.

14
BUILDING A TOUR COMPANY

1. AM I READY TO GET BIGGER?

You have run a few tours to Europe and they have been a resounding success. You have got some cash in your pockets, your name is becoming well known from the publicity you have been working on, and a few travel agents have begun referring people to you on a semiregular basis. Your house is now overrun with paper; you have several people who work with you doing bits and pieces: bookkeeping, running an occasional tour you don't have time to do yourself, basic secretarial, and answering the phone when it starts ringing off the hook. Your neighbors can't figure out why all these people are coming and going from your house, and parking is becoming an irritation, but you are enjoying every minute of it.

And, as much as you hate it, you are still working for someone else part time to make ends meet. You dream of having your own office to go to each day, your own staff to help you plan the next few tours, and enough flexibility to pick which tours you want to lead. You want everything in one place. The irritations of running a growing but decentralized business are becoming a real problem.

You may be ready to make the big jump to become a full-time tour operator. But being an independent tour guide and running a company with employees to take your clients on tours are worlds apart. The biggest transition will be that your focus will shift from travel to the business of travel. As the owner of a tour company, you will spend most of your time supervising the company's day-to-day affairs. The stress will be much greater but the rewards will be greater too.

You will probably never get rich as an independent tour director or guide. In fact, it is more likely you will always hold down another job of some sort. As the owner of a tour company, however, you not only call the shots but you may also end up with a multimillion dollar company. We know people who started off running tours and later sold out for huge amounts of money. It can be done.

2. DAY-TO-DAY LIFE OF A TOUR OPERATOR

Unless you have the cash to hire a professional manager for your new company, you will be the day-to-day manager. In the beginning, your day will consist mainly of supervising staff, paying bills, making sure the office is adequately staffed during your employees' vacations, complying with regulatory authorities, speaking with your accountant and bookkeeper, doing the banking, and answering the phone when the office is busy. You must be familiar with office systems for handling paperwork, and a capacity for details is a necessity. If you hate detail, find a partner who thrives on orderliness. Ignoring deadlines, forms, and filing will cost you credibility, time, and money.

The travel industry sells dreams and convenience, and it runs on paperwork. Think of it this way: Your clients are going to give you thousands of dollars in exchange for a piece of paper that promises a service of unknown quality to be delivered sometime in the future. Your credibility and reputation will become the keys to repeat business.

Once you start running your own tour business, you will soon discover there are always a few fires smoking in the background. Perhaps one of your staff gave an incorrect quote to a travel agent. You know the error will cost you money, but you also know the agent is a valuable spokesperson for your business who has sold several of your tours before. The travel agent's clients will not understand why they suddenly have to pay a higher price, and the agent will not be pleased to lose a finished sale. The agent has asked you to help smooth things out.

Or perhaps a check to one of your suppliers did not arrive on time. The supplier is in a huff and threatening to cancel the client's arrangements. Or tickets have not been delivered to the home of a client who is leaving tomorrow. It goes on and on.

In return for all this effort and aggravation, you get to keep whatever money is left after everyone else has been paid. Some months are great, others are dismal. Even after you give yourself a paycheck, you may have to give it back because you know that several extraordinary bills are due next month.

In the first couple of years of any new business, most owners take very little time off. Even when a company is well established, it still requires constant supervision to be profitable. There are not many absentee owners of small tour operations because there is just not enough money to hire competent management early on.

Much of this description is the same for all new business ventures. But added to the normal stress of opening a company, owners of travel businesses must contend with a host of difficulties peculiar to the industry. For one thing, selling a service of unknown quality to be enjoyed at some future date but with payment required up front is tough. For another, everything is time sensitive. Deadlines mean stress, and arranging travel is deadline after deadline after deadline. Travel is a high-priced item and the cost of a mistake can be exorbitant. Travel arrangements involve an incredible amount of detail — a one-minute error in connection times between two flights, or a supplier who does not show up to serve your tour, can result in missed flights and ruined vacations. You might be held responsible.

Your credibility and reputation will become the keys to repeat business.

3. REWARDS

High stress, low pay, and long hours do not fit with the travel mystique, but take heart because there are some wonderful compensations to balance all this hard work.

(a) *Self-fulfillment.* Many people never dare to venture after their dreams. Your first accountant's report may be discouraging. Just remember to add all the positive, intangible things you have achieved to the profit and loss statement. The currency you will be paid in is not all money.

(b) *Good feedback.* Sure, clients can sometimes be a real nuisance. They can also be excited, enthusiastic, and bubbling with stories about their trips. In few other businesses will you get the consistent stroking from your clients for a job well done. Give yourself a well-deserved pat on the back when all your hard work bears fruit.

(c) *Control.* Owning your own company means you have control over certain aspects of your life that an independent or contract tour guide does not. You are your own boss, with the luxury of making some choices about how to spend your day. The only person who can stop you from going fishing early on Friday is you!

(d) *Satisfaction.* Owning a growing business you have created is a great satisfaction. Owning a business many people only dream about is even better.

(e) *Reasonable hours.* After the first year or two in business, the hours should be reasonable — sometimes as low as 40 hours per week. There is very little weekend or evening work you cannot skip if you choose.

4. STATISTICS ABOUT TRAVEL BUSINESSES

Just because you are working hard and giving up your social life does not mean you are making money. Watch the bottom line.

On the other hand, just because you are working hard and giving up your social life does not mean you are making money. It is hard to make a good living in the travel industry, with its low margins and price-cutting competition. No less a financial wizard than Warren Buffet, arguably the richest man in the United States, claimed that, taken as a whole, the airline industry has not earned its owners a dime on their investment since commercial aircraft first took to the skies.

Statistics on tour operations are not as comprehensive or readily available as those for many other industries, but there are very good numbers about their close cousins, retail travel agencies. Since it is quite possible your business will be a combination of retail, wholesale, and your own packaged tours, these numbers may give you an approximate picture of what is in store.

A survey conducted by Louis Harris and Associates for *Travel Weekly*, one of the premier industry magazines, showed that 41 percent of retail travel agencies in the United States operated at a loss in 1991. Granted, this was a year of recession and of war in the Persian Gulf, but even in 1990, 24 percent reported average losses of $16,910. In 1991 the average loss per agency increased to $24,800. Between 1989 and 1991 there was an 8 percent increase in the total dollar volume, but with a 6 percent rise in the number of agencies, the average agency increase for the two-year period was only 3 percent. Before the recession and the Gulf War, dollar sales volume for all agencies increased 343 percent between 1978 (the year of deregulation in the United States) and 1991. Whether growth in the industry will return to that prewar pace over the long term is anyone's guess. Here are some of the other highlights from the Harris and Associates' study:

(a) Ninety-eight percent of all agencies book some form of tour package and 44 percent of the $18 billion leisure-market sales volume was generated from tour packages.

(b) Domestic travel accounted for 69 percent of sales while 31 percent was international travel. This is approximately what the split has been since 1985.

(c) Airline tickets accounted for 56 percent of the total revenue agencies generated. This is a decrease from 63 percent in 1981.

(d) Only 69 percent of agencies had a computerized reservation system (CRS) in 1981. 96 percent are now automated.

(e) Profitable locations averaged $59,600 profit in 1991 and an estimated $66,300 in 1992.

And according to a study by the American Society of Travel Agents, more than 90 percent of nationally marketed tours are sold through travel agencies.

If you love statistics, we recommend you look up a copy of the August 1992 issue of *Travel Weekly* (Vol. 51, No. 65), which includes excerpts from the survey. A more comprehensive analysis of the survey costs around $200 and can be obtained by writing to:

Travel Weekly
500 Plaza Drive
Secaucus, NJ 07096
Tel: (201) 902-1500

5. WHAT ARE YOUR GOALS?

Before you invest your money, time, and future in this challenging business, you must answer the question "What do you want to achieve?" Clearly defining your objective is the first step. Becoming a tour operator is a serious undertaking and there is no room for muddled thinking.

Before you invest your money, time, and future make sure you know what you want to achieve.

Write your ideas down, then think about how realistic they are. In our years of consulting, we often asked our clients what they hoped to achieve. Following are some of the most common objectives we heard expressed.

5.1 Cheap travel

Most people with little or no travel industry experience say their primary objective is to be able to wander the globe for free or very little money. While this is a definite perk of owning your own business, don't forget that the same benefits can be gained working as a contractor for a tour company or travel agency. Granted, your cheap travel is always limited by someone else's dictates, but so is your stress, risk, and capital outlay.

5.2 Owning your own business or changing careers

You know you want to run your own business, but why do you think it should be a travel business? Many people who have traveled and led tours assume their travel experiences mean they have the skills necessary to run a successful tour business. This is not automatically true. Some would-be owners are very social and feel their excellent people skills will bring them clients and success. Although it helps to have a pleasant personality, it is not a prerequisite to managing a tour business. Others believe they have a sure scheme for selling a particular destination because of their contacts there. Destination contacts are easy to find and are eager to sell you their product.

Acquiring clients is the hard part. Many people have an "in" with the local church or sports league that they believe will bring them an instant clientele. Having potential groups of clients lined up will help, but it will not get you through the winter. Even assuming you have a huge number of clients who express interest in your tour programs, you are likely to find most of the interest evaporates when it comes time to sign up and put some money down. The competition, with all its experience and contacts, is fierce. Unless you can match its prices and service, your "clients" will book elsewhere.

5.3 Travel professionals looking for a new career

Travel agents, airline reservation personnel, hotel managers, and other travel professionals who are looking for another career in the hospitality industry do have the advantage, one assumes, of starting with an established clientele and/or a fund of knowledge. They have the advantage of knowing the industry and, as problems come up, they will already know where and how hard to push to get solutions.

But beware! The transition from frontline personnel to manager and owner of a business is not simply a matter of switching offices. Being a good travel agent or front desk clerk does not necessarily mean you will be a good manager. Experience can also be an obstacle. You may have certain perceptions from your years as an employee that cause you to institute unprofitable policies for the best of reasons. A travel agent we knew opened her own travel business and, as owner, made sure her employees were treated just the way she wanted to be treated when she worked for someone else. After a year of mounting losses (real out-of-her-own-pocket cash losses!), she lowered salaries back to the industry average, tied the number of trips employees could take to an informal quota system, and increased the work load for everyone.

The only rationale for starting a business is to make money.

5.4 Tax savings

There are many travel businesses that lose money regularly while their owners are off traveling all the time. The theory is that even though the business loses money, there is a tax savings to offset some of the loss. At the end of the year, the owners hope they have saved more on travel than they lost on the business. Many couples with one high-income earner and one person who wants to work only part time can benefit from the tax advantages. Setting up a tour operation provides the part-time employment, their travel is cheaper, and they save on taxes.

Tax savings by themselves are never a good reason to start a business. There are too many risks for what you gain in tax savings. However, combined with other reasons it can make sense. See your accountant if you are considering this. You will need professional help to make it work.

5.5 Making money

The only rationale for starting a business that truly makes sense is that you see a genuine opportunity to make money. Careful and realistic planning and research will tell you if you can be a success.

5.6 Nothing else will do

Finally, there are those persons for whom the idea of a tour guiding business is really attractive. No matter how much hardship or how many obstacles they face, nothing seems to dim their fascination. The

Take an extensive and objective personal inventory of your skills and qualities before you start your own business.

idea pulls them onward. If you are one of these people, do your homework, work hard, and you will eventually succeed.

6. ASSESSING YOURSELF

Owning a business is not for everyone. To be a success in any business you must have the right personal qualities combined with experience or education. Before you spend a penny, take an extensive and objective personal inventory of your skills and qualities.

6.1 Your personal qualities

Assessing personal qualities requires you to be scrupulously honest with yourself. No one else needs to know anything about your self-assessment. Base your answers on your past behavior, not your resolutions for the future, and suspend for a moment any preconceived notions you may have about yourself. Look at yourself afresh. Worksheet 2 gives you a sampling of the kinds of questions you should think deeply about.

There are dozens of good books that will help you assess whether owning your own business is for you. Self-Counsel Press has published one called *Have You Got What It Takes?* Do not skip this self-examination. It may alert you to areas needing to be improved or underscore the sacrifices you will have to make.

6.2 Your experience and education

Ideally, you should have some general business or office experience, preferably in the travel, retail, or service sector. The general business principles necessary to make a success of a tour operation are fairly straightforward and common to other businesses. If you already know what a balance sheet is, how overnight couriers work, or what marketing does for a business, your life will be much easier.

If you are working in someone else's office, many of the principles and details of how to run a business may have rubbed off on you, but you will still need to take stock of what you can do by yourself and what you need to bone up on. Even in professional offices where you may be more insulated from buying and selling, having a general overview of how a business works will give you a head start. In the months before you quit your current job, pay close attention to details of how the business is run. Look at the people you know who are in business for themselves. What kinds of skills do they have that you do not?

WORKSHEET 2
AM I READY TO OWN MY OWN BUSINESS?

(a) In the past have you exhibited perseverance and commitment?

(b) Do you take a realistic, commonsense approach to problems?

(c) Are you innovative, creative, and flexible?

(d) Are you optimistic?

(e) Are you self-reliant and a self-starter?

(f) Do you enjoy solving problems?

(g) Are you in good health?

(h) Can you live well with uncertainty and risk? Can your family?

(i) Can you be organized and logical when the situation demands?

(j) Are you a good communicator who enjoys people?

(k) Do you see mistakes as an opportunity to learn?

(l) Can you accept responsibility and make decisions quickly?

(m) Is your family supportive of your venture?

(n) Can you accept advice?

(o) Are you detail oriented?

(p) Can you handle pressure to perform?

(q) Do you enjoy working hard for long hours?

If you have never been in business for yourself or have been out of the work force for a number of years, go back to school. There are hundreds of books, courses, and seminars available that will teach you the rudiments of business. Everything you can learn before you get involved in the day-to-day frustrations of a travel business will save you time and money.

7. PRESCRIPTIONS FOR SUCCESS

We recommend you work through the following tasks to evaluate whether the travel industry is for you. Each task will alert you to problem areas you may be able to remedy before you open your doors.

7.1 Explore the industry

Before you commit yourself to opening a tour guiding business, talk to everyone you know in the industry about what they do on a daily basis. Take travel agency managers to lunch and pepper them with questions. Ask other tour guides and operators about their experiences. This will give you a reasonable idea of what to expect.

7.2 Develop your skills

Figure out exactly what skills you have that fit the tasks to be done in your tour guiding business. Can you learn or improve on other skills before you open? Your business cards may say you are the president of the company, but you can be sure you will also be janitor, delivery person, window washer, and general "gopher." Owners who don't want to get dirty must pay someone else or take staff away from sales to do maintenance. Initially, your time may be the least valuable. As part of your preparations to open your business, here are some skills and knowledge you should brush up on — or acquire.

(a) General skills
- math
- business writing
- the art of negotiation
- lease negotiation
- public speaking

(b) Office management skills
- math
- interviewing techniques

- ⊕ staff motivation
- ⊕ how to do payroll deductions
- ⊕ office security (e.g., safes, alarm systems)

(c) Financial skills
- ⊕ bookkeeping
- ⊕ how to read financial statements
- ⊕ how to do a cash flow projection
- ⊕ balancing a check book
- ⊕ how letters of credit work
- ⊕ the rudiments of tax law (depreciation, write-offs, exemptions, personal versus corporate tax rates)
- ⊕ how to file your business income tax return

(d) Machine skills
- ⊕ fax machine
- ⊕ small business telephone systems
- ⊕ photocopiers (including minor maintenance)

(e) Computer skills
- ⊕ basic operation and maintenance
- ⊕ word processing
- ⊕ spread sheets
- ⊕ accounting packages
- ⊕ modems and e-mail
- ⊕ creating a Web page for advertising

(f) Travel agent skills
- ⊕ math
- ⊕ using a computer reservation system
- ⊕ booking travel
- ⊕ filling out invoices and various forms

Your business cards may say president, but you'll also be janitor, delivery person, window washer, and gopher.

7.3 Planning

Plan everything on paper first. Planning now will save you hours of grief. From the layout of your office to the intricacies of a marketing campaign, no detail is too small. Plan the color and look of your stationery as well as how many pens and pencils you will need. This is

Planning everything on paper first will save you hours of grief.

harder than you think since you need to know how many employees you will have. Plot out what the opening schedule and other crucial timelines will be. This task may seem endless, but as you work on it you will gain confidence, and problems will begin to resolve themselves.

One caveat: Planning is not an end in itself. You may find that by planning and replanning you are actually avoiding the final commitment. If this describes your behavior, look carefully at whether running your own business is really for you.

7.4 Take on a knowledgeable partner

Never choose a partner who has the same skills you do. Pick someone with complementary skills. Not only can you save cash with more skills between you to draw on but you also always have someone to confer with on big decisions. Even though you must share the rewards when the venture is successful, it may be more important to share the risk in the beginning.

The search for a compatible partner can be frustrating and lengthy, but the effort often brings issues to the fore that you had not considered, such as differences in personal work style or general knowledge. To reduce any friction between you and your partner as you work, each partner should be responsible for particular areas of the business. Partnership is not for everyone. You must carefully assess whether you work better with shared decisions and responsibility or whether you prefer to go it alone.

7.5 Educate yourself

Education should be an ongoing part of your effort.

Being in business for yourself means being an expert in many areas. Education should be an ongoing part of your effort. Formal education and practical courses will markedly improve your chances of success. Also learn by reading. Order subscriptions to every industry magazine you can. A list of some of the more popular ones can be found in Appendix 3. Alternatively, see if your library has a subscription, or find a travel agent who is willing to give you back issues.

7.6 Learn how to market your business

The one area of your business you must constantly pay close attention to is marketing. Without a plan to generate sales, it is unlikely you will succeed. Before you commit yourself to starting a business, have a clear idea of how you will do your pricing, what kind of promotion and advertising you need to generate sales, and the image you want to project to your prospective clients. You should not need to engage in high pressure tactics to make sales — after all, a good tour product sells itself. However, you will need to be aggressive and persistent to keep your tours in the public eye. There are dozens of courses, seminars, and books that can help you. An excellent guide to researching your market is the Self-Counsel Press book *Marketing Your Service*.

8. PREPARE FOR FAILURE, THEN CONCENTRATE ON SUCCESS

Every year, thousands of people go out of business and lose everything. None of these people decided to lose money. Some were very well prepared, but unforeseen circumstances destroyed their dreams of making a new life for themselves. It could happen to you.

Prepare for failure and then forget about it.

Thoughts of failure have a tendency to worm their way into your consciousness at three o'clock in the morning. They rob you of the optimism you must have to succeed and stop you from taking the risks you need to take. It is important to get rid of this crippling influence. The best way to do that is to prepare for failure and then forget about it. As long as you have ensured that your family will not end up penniless, homeless, and without medical care because of a failure, you will get more enjoyment out of your new business.

The following tips will help ensure your financial base is not eroded. Each of these prescriptions must be evaluated carefully to make sure it fits with your legal and financial situation. Your lawyer and accountant will be able to tell you which of these ideas will work in your situation.

8.1 Put all your major assets in someone else's name

While putting all your major assets in someone else's name is a fairly common practice, it is not one to be taken lightly. You must have absolute trust in the other person's integrity and reliability. You are signing over most of your wealth; if you have a falling out with that person, there will be little you can do to get your assets back, should that person be uncooperative. Remember, too, that there are transfer costs, and you will certainly need legal advice. Also, if you wait until you are in trouble before you try to transfer assets, you will find yourself in extremely hot legal water. Definitely see a lawyer before taking this step.

8.2 Incorporate your company

Forming a limited company will limit the assets creditors can take from you if there is a failure. Banks and landlords tend to look closely at corporations with no assets, so you may still have to sign personally or give a personal guarantee for some things, but the more you can limit the damage a dispute may do, the better. Your accountant will have some words of advice about the tax implications of this.

8.3 Sign everything in the company's name

Sign everything in the company's name. Your lawyer can instruct you on how to sign documents on behalf of your corporation. Careful attention to this small detail may save you later. If landlords or lenders require your personal pledge, so be it. But make the choice consciously, not by default by inadvertently signing documents in your own name.

8.4 Set limits on the risk you will take

Carefully assess what a failure would do to your lifestyle and set a dollar limit on how much you are willing to lose. Once you set this limit, you can choose to disregard it, but at the very least it should serve as a reminder to re-evaluate carefully before you go on. Be sure you define your risk-taking comfort level long before you open the doors of your business. Trying to set this limit during the emotional storm of a failure is impossible. Your objectivity is gone as you try to avoid the immediate consequences. This can lead to a real catastrophe.

Once you have done all you can to prepare for the worst, forget failure. Concentrate instead on visualizing your success. Take a high energy, optimistic stance and get ready to enjoy your achievements.

9. DO YOUR HOMEWORK

We cannot stress enough the importance of doing your homework. It is not unusual for all the items in this list to take a year of hard work. But the more thorough you are, the less chance there is that you will find nasty surprises waiting for you. A disregard for planning and evaluating is like playing Russian roulette with five of the six chambers full.

The most important point to remember is: Do your homework.

15
MAKING YOUR BUSINESS LEGAL

Three levels of government affect any business, and each level has jurisdiction over specific areas of law. Among other things, the federal government requires you to pay taxes, comply with labor standards, and pay taxes on behalf of your employees. State and provincial governments have their own tax and labor laws, as well as laws on how to set up your business. Municipal laws govern where, when, and how you can operate your business. The most common regulations you must be concerned with are outlined in this chapter.

You could fill out all the forms and registrations, and fulfill all the requirements to comply with the various laws yourself. It will require a fair amount of research on your part to understand the implications of the regulations affecting your business, but it can be done. However, we recommend you spend the money to hire an accountant and lawyer to do most of the work for you, especially if you have not owned a small business before. It is vital that you understand what they are doing. Ask lots of questions. Part of what you are paying for is an education so that later you can make intelligent decisions yourself.

1. SET UP YOUR BUSINESS LEGALLY

There are several ways you can set up a business: as a sole proprietorship, a partnership, a limited partnership, a limited company, or, in the United States, a subchapter "S" corporation. The brief overview provided here is meant to give you an idea of what options are available to you and what postponing the decision to incorporate or form a partnership can mean. Remember, it is not how much money you make but how much you keep that is important, and there are tax implications for each form of business that will affect what taxes you pay and what tax breaks you get. It is important that you understand what these are, so speak to your accountant or lawyer and read some of the many books on the subject. This is an education that will save you thousands of dollars.

1.1 Sole proprietorship

If you choose to do nothing about forming a company, you will, by default, be engaging in what is called a sole proprietorship. The big advantage of a sole proprietorship is that there are no legal fees or paperwork involved in getting started. You are in business because you say you are. You are the only owner and decision maker and do not need to answer to anyone else. Should you decide to quit, you do not have to tell anyone you have ceased business.

If you choose, you can still register your business. Most provincial and state governments have a registrar of companies where you can register your company for a modest fee. Call and ask the registrar to send you a sole proprietor form. By registering as a sole proprietorship under whatever name you choose, you have some reassurance that the name will not be used by anyone else. Of course, if the name (or one similar to it) has already been registered, you will need to decide on a second choice for your business. Name protection is a sticky subject with many exceptions, but registration provides a degree of protection that may well be worth the cost and effort involved, especially if you have a distinctive company identity.

The second advantage to registering your business is that you will occasionally be asked for your registration. For instance, a registration certificate is sometimes needed to prove you are in business before you can open accounts with some banks and financial institutions. There may also be tax advantages. All expenditures and income you make

It's not how much money you make, but how much you keep.

from the business are reported on your personal income tax form. In the beginning, when cash going out usually exceeds cash coming in, you can probably write off your excess losses against other income you earned and get a refund (or at least pay less tax). Talk to your accountant about how best to take advantage of the tax laws when you start.

The most important implication of a sole proprietorship is that if you incur debts, you are personally responsible for them. Should your business go under, your home, car, and other personal assets may be seized to satisfy the claims against you. You should also realize that it is harder to raise capital as a sole proprietorship. You cannot sell shares since you are not a corporation, and most silent investors will not want the liability that goes along with a partnership.

1.2 Partnership

When two or more people enter into business together, it is called a partnership. You can have silent partners who contribute only cash, or working partners who get involved with the day-to-day workings of the company. There is no restriction on how many partners of either type you may have.

Partnerships are easy to put together but are harder to dissolve without losing money. It is wise to have a lawyer draw up a partnership agreement to outline each partner's obligations, even if your partner is your spouse or best friend. It is a fact of life that people change, and money can be a great motivator for a bad change. A handshake deal gives you no protection if a dispute arises between you and your partners. A legal agreement, while it cannot prevent the unpleasantness, gives you some legal protection and recourse.

You are also responsible for any debts your partner incurs on behalf of the business. Even if you are a frugal, competent businessperson, you will have to pay for the mounting losses caused by your cavalier partner's extravagant spending. And if your partner decides to skip the country to live in luxury on a tropical island, guess who will be obligated to pay and pay and pay. You! Some businesses become so preoccupied with internal feuds between the owners that an otherwise successful company fails.

However, on the plus side, partners share the business risks with you. If times are tough, a partner should be as willing to forgo a paycheck as you are. A partner generally works harder and brings more enthusiasm to the business than an employee because a partner has more of a stake

Set up your business one of the following ways:

1. sole proprietorship
2. partnership
3. limited partnership
4. corporation or limited company
5. subchapter "s"

in the business's success. He or she can be a welcome help in sharing the responsibilities of the business and can also bring much-needed skills to supplement your strengths and weaknesses.

1.3 Limited partnership

Limited partnerships are usually used for real estate deals involving one or more general partners with unlimited liability plus silent investors who have limited personal liability. A limited partnership is not commonly used for small businesses. It is expensive to set up and you will need a lawyer to help you.

1.4 The corporation or limited company

The most complicated form of business is the corporation. When you form an incorporated company, you create a separate and distinct entity. The corporation has a life of its own; it is the corporation that is taxed, assumes debt, sues, and is sued.

Incorporation can be done on a provincial or state, or a federal level. In some jurisdictions you can do this easily yourself; in others it is more advisable to go to a lawyer. As a ballpark figure, lawyers charge about $600 to $1,000 for a simple incorporation. If you live in an area where you can incorporate without using a lawyer, you can save approximately half the cost, sometimes more. The rest of the expense is unavoidable registration fees, notary costs, and the like.

The big advantage of incorporation is that your creditors can take only the company's assets if you are sued and lose. This protects your personal assets, such as your house, should your company incur any debts you cannot pay. There are exceptions to this generality, though, and if you are not familiar with the legal aspects of a corporation you should buy an hour of your lawyer's time to have it explained to you.

One other advantage worth noting is that incorporation makes it easy to transfer your business or part of your business to someone else when you sell it or take on investors. You can do most of the required legal work yourself, whether the shareholders are silent investors or active in the business. As with partners, a legal agreement should be prepared. At a minimum, we recommend that a shareholders' agreement be drafted, laying out exactly how one shareholder can buy out another if there are problems later.

The biggest disadvantage of a corporation is that there is much more recordkeeping. Corporate records must be completely separate from personal records, so you must have a company bank account as well as your personal one. This means twice as much accounting and bookkeeping. Governments have more regulations and forms for corporations than for sole proprietorships or partnerships. There are also important tax implications for corporations. It is wise to have an accountant explain exactly how this will affect your taxes.

We recommend you incorporate when you first start up your business to protect your personal assets and to make it easy to transfer part ownership to investors or new owners. Admittedly, incorporating later makes it easier to get the first-year tax advantages, but your accountant should be able to structure the firm in such a way that you can get some or all of the tax benefits anyway. Another consideration if you wait to incorporate is that the registrations required by travel regulatory associations may have to be done over again. For example, IATA requires you to reregister when you change from a sole proprietorship or partnership to a corporation. This is an unnecessary headache and expense.

Incorporate to protect your personal assets and to make it easy to transfer part ownership to investors or new owners.

1.5 Subchapter "S"

In the United States there is a special corporation with tax advantages called a "subchapter S." The corporation itself pays no taxes. Any profit or loss flows through to the shareholders. This is the best of both worlds, as you get the write-offs when the business starts up and is losing money, but you also get the personal asset protection of a corporation. Subchapter "S" is a complicated form of business and you will need a tax accountant to explain the advantages and restrictions to you.

2. OTHER REGISTRATIONS

You need to be aware of other government regulatory organizations when you start. Contact each one regardless of whether you think you need to register or not. They will let you know.

2.1 Workers' compensation

Check with your local workers' compensation board about whether you must register. In certain locations, travel businesses are considered offices and registration is voluntary. In others it is mandatory. You may have to fill out the forms so the authorities can assess whether you need to sign up.

Find out about:

1. workers' compensation
2. employee registration with the government
3. goods and services tax
4. provincial and state taxes
5. municipal license
6. better business bureau

2.2 Register with the government for your employees

All money collected on behalf of the government for employees (unemployment, social security, and income tax in the United States; employment insurance, Canada Pension Plan payments, and income tax in Canada) must be remitted to the government promptly. In Canada, register for an Employer's Account Remittance number by contacting any Revenue Canada office for the correct forms. In the United States, register for an Employer Identification Number (EIN) through any Internal Revenue office. The forms can usually be obtained by mail, but it can take up to two months to get registered, so do this early. There are stiff penalties for not complying.

2.3 Goods and services tax (Canada)

In Canada, the commission you earn from selling travel is subject to the Goods and Services Tax (GST). Your travel business must register for GST unless you earn less than $30,000 annually in sales. Since GST must be paid quarterly, you can start doing business before you register. Registration usually takes about a month.

2.4 Remitting provincial and state sales tax

In most locales this is not something a tour operator needs to worry about, as travel services are not generally subject to state and provincial sales tax, but check with the appropriate government to make sure.

2.5 Municipal license

A business license gives proof of how long you have been in business. In some people's eyes, a license lends a certain amount of legitimacy to your operation, especially if you are a sole proprietor. In all our years of business, we have had only one person check us out at city hall, but you never know when that one person will be important to you and your future plans.

Business licenses are generally issued by city hall in the municipality where you are doing business. They cost between $15 and $100. In some locations you may also need an occupancy permit before you can get a business license, even if you are not doing any renovations. Check with your local municipal hall engineering office.

2.6 Better Business Bureau

We are great fans of the Better Business Bureau (BBB). Membership in this nonprofit organization lends a certain credibility to your business venture. There is a small fee for membership which, in most areas, entitles you to benefits such as group insurance rates, discounts on credit card merchant charges, and discounts on fuel. You can request information or an application from the BBB directly. It takes about a month and a half to get registered. Be aware that there are restrictions on the use of the BBB logo and name. The Bureau limits your use so you cannot use its name to endorse your business.

3. REGULATIONS CONCERNING TRAVEL BUSINESSES

There are no federal regulations or standards in Canada or the United States governing tour guides or tour/travel businesses specifically. Anyone can legally set up as a tour guide in most jurisdictions.

Some states and provinces require some form of registration or certification for travel businesses.

Most states and provinces have little or nothing to say about who can offer travel services to the public or how travel businesses must do business. Instead, individual travelers are left to pursue matters in the courts if they have a problem with how a business treats them. Where laws do exist, they arose partly to help prevent con artists from setting up, taking consumers' money, and then skipping town before delivering the product. These laws also ensure the consumer does not bear the risk of a risky industry. In some places, if a travel company goes under and the services a traveler paid for have not been provided, the traveler will be reimbursed by the government.

Each province or state has specific regulations which change constantly as legislatures and administrators fine-tune existing laws. The most detailed laws have been patterned after the IATA/ARC regulations in that they require applicants to prove both their financial capacity and experience to carry on a travel business. If you are contemplating an IATA/ARC appointment, you should not have much problem with state or provincial regulations.

More jurisdictions are considering laws, so it is imperative that you contact your state or provincial government early to determine what you need to do. If your government is considering legislation, find out if there is a grandfather clause allowing those already in business to avoid the expense of conforming with the new laws. It may be worth your while to speed up your plans to escape the burden of extra regulations.

4. SHORT CUTS AND REGULATIONS

When a business opportunity opens, it seldom stays open long. Jump at the chance. Do not be so afraid of doing something that you lose a golden opportunity requiring immediate action. You do have some flexibility with government regulations while you concentrate on reeling in the business. Few things you do cannot be undone or redressed later, although it will usually cost you money and headaches. As a rule of thumb, the longer you go without complying, the worse the headaches get.

While it is hardly a smart idea, general accounting and federal income tax matters can be put off for as long as 15 months before the first deadline rolls around. Under NO circumstances can you skip or delay any employee-related payments. Remit all withheld taxes, unemployment insurance, and pension amounts without fail. Government penalties are heavy and noncompliance can have serious and long-lasting ramifications — jail being one of them. If you are going to have employees, contact the government before you open.

In some states and provinces, government regulations require you to set up a trust account that holds your clients' payments. A trust account needs constant attention from the day it is opened. Bad record-keeping can bring your company to grief and the consequences could follow you personally for the rest of your life.

5. IATA, BSP, IATAN, AND ARC

If you will be working with only one commercial or charter airline to run your tours, skip this section. Try to set up an agreement directly with the airline or a consolidator that will give you satisfactory booking procedures and a commission structure.

If you will be using several airlines and you want to earn a commission from them, you can work out an independent agreement with each, but that may be cumbersome depending on how many airlines you work with. At this point you should seriously consider an IATA or ARC appointment, particularly if you plan to run any kind of a retail travel business in addition to your tour operations.

It is not a legal requirement to be IATA-, ARC-, or IATAN-appointed, but there are some big advantages. An appointment gives people doing

Don't be so afraid of doing something that you lose a golden opportunity requiring immediate action.

business with you a certain amount of comfort. After all, an independent organization has looked at your agency, inspected your premises, and continues to monitor your business. If you are not accredited, some travel suppliers could delay your payments or require you to do extra paperwork. There are hotels, many airlines, and a variety of other suppliers that will not pay you at all. Nonaccredited agencies are also excluded from many of the industry perks. Certain reduced-rate airline tickets, car rentals, hotel accommodations, cruises, and in some cases, FAM trips (see chapter 4 for a discussion of FAM trips) are not available to nonappointed agencies.

A travel company receives an appointment from IATA, ARC, or IATAN only after it has undergone a series of checks and investigations designed to identify companies that might cause losses for the airlines through ineptness or fraud. Appointment does not prevent bankruptcy or dishonesty, but it does indicate at least a modicum of financial depth and ability. In their application procedure, these organizations ask questions about the experience and reliability of the agency's owners and managers, its financial status, even who its potential customers are. The agency is also expected to meet certain physical security requirements to protect blank ticket stock and the airline plates used to make them valid.

Regulatory bodies:

1. International Air Transport Association

2. Bank Settlement Plan

3. International Airlines Travel Agent Network

4. Airlines Reporting Corporation

5.1 International Air Transport Association (Canada and elsewhere)

IATA (pronounced *eye at ah*) is the International Air Transport Association. The 206 members, primarily airlines, of this worldwide trade organization use IATA to speak with one voice about issues affecting them. The membership includes almost all the world's largest airlines. There are non-IATA airlines, but they do a small percentage of the world's business. If you do not have an IATA appointment, an airline will usually not allow you to act as its agent and will not give your agency ticket stock and plates to write valid tickets. In all countries except the United States, IATA administers the Bank Settlement Plan (the BSP).

There is no required length of time an agency must be open before applying for an IATA appointment. We recommend you apply within the first week or two of opening your travel company. IATA will accept financial statements up to three months old. If you apply as soon as you open, you can normally use the same financial statements for IATA that the governing body in your state or province required for your agency to be licensed. This can save you accounting costs. Opening financial statements, usually just a balance sheet, are less complex than statements at any other time in an agency's lifetime. Waiting longer than three months means you must do new statements, which means more effort and expense.

To order an application package, write or phone IATA at this address:

IATA
2000 Peel Street
Montréal, Québec H3A 2R4
Canada
Tel: (514) 844-6311

5.2 The Bank Settlement Plan (Canada)

The Bank Settlement Plan (BSP) is the clearance facility responsible for collecting money from IATA-accredited agencies and distributing each payment to the proper IATA-member airlines throughout the world.

BSP's second important function is to report to the airlines on each travel agency's sales. BSP's reports can give an individual airline a timely picture of how its marketing techniques are affecting the sale of its product. Acceptance by IATA means your agency can use the BSP; agencies do not apply directly to the BSP.

5.3 International Airlines Travel Agent Network (United States)

The International Airlines Travel Agent Network (IATAN) and ARC represent some of the same airlines. However, since some airlines (mainly international ones) are not covered by ARC, it might be to your advantage to apply to both IATAN and ARC, especially if you are doing a lot of international business. You must apply to IATAN separately and comply with its specific accreditation policies. To request an information kit or an application (known as an endorsement kit), contact IATAN at this address:

IATAN
#342 - 300 Garden City Plaza
Garden City, NY 11530
USA
Tel: (516) 747-4716

5.4 Airlines Reporting Corporation (United States)

The Airlines Reporting Corporation (ARC) fulfills basically the same functions in the United States as IATA does elsewhere. It maintains similar personnel, agency public access, and security requirements. US travel agencies wishing to be ARC accredited must apply to and be approved by ARC. Prior to approval, applicants must provide a bond or letter of credit to ARC. Your bank can explain exactly what you need to do so that it can issue an irrevocable letter of credit. The *Federal Register,* a publication printed by the US Treasury Department, lists bonding companies that issue bonds acceptable to ARC. The ARC kit can be ordered from:

Airlines Reporting Corporation
P.O. Box 96194
Washington, DC 20090-6194
USA

Since requirements change from time to time, contact ARC by phone at (703) 816-8085, Monday to Friday, to get the latest details before you order your kit.

6. IS AN APPOINTMENT FOR YOU?

Not all tour businesses need to be accredited by one of these organizations. If you are going to offer your clients a full-service tour agency and use general airline tickets, you must be able to issue tickets on behalf of many airlines and you will want to collect commissions from hotels and other travel suppliers. In that case, IATA/BSP or IATAN/ARC are the only way to go.

If, however, you plan to specialize in only one or two or three destinations, you may elect to avoid all the paperwork an appointment requires. The amount of airline ticket business you plan to do may not justify the fees and time involved to get the stamp of approval. (On the other hand, in many states and provinces you must go through so much licensing in any case, that it will take very little extra effort to get your appointment.) Also, consider some of the side effects of an appointment. Will it cost you more to hire staff who know how to ticket and do the required paperwork if you become endorsed, or is the reverse true? Will you have trouble hiring the quality of personnel you need because you are not appointed? Will suppliers such as car rental companies and hotels refuse to pay you commissions because you are not appointed? These nonmonetary issues can be extremely important.

In many states and provinces you must go through so much licensing that it will take little extra effort to get your appointment.

7. AIRLINE PLATES AND APPOINTMENTS

Your agency is not appointed until you receive your number in writing from the accrediting body. This may take as little as a few weeks to as long as six months if you have not answered all the questions on the application satisfactorily. You will be required to sign a passenger sales agreement, set up with the appropriate settlement plan, come up with a validator (similar to a credit card imprinter), and get your ticket stock before you can actually issue your own tickets.

After you have received your appointment, there is one final chore. You must contact every airline and ask them to send you their carrier identification plates (CIP). Tickets cannot be issued until you receive these. Usually all you need to do is fax a letter requesting the CIP to the airline sales office, accompanied by a photocopy of your IATA, IATAN, or ARC appointment. Some require that you mail the letter and photocopy.

16
WHAT WILL MY BUSINESS LOOK LIKE?

If you have a good supply of customers already and the only thing you need to handle your growing business is an office, your bigger business will look like a more organized version of your current tour guiding operation. You will not need to hire more people right away, offer new products in order to attract customers, or change any of the legal bits of your business. You may even have the financing or capital in place to buy more equipment or raise your working capital. Just move the phone lines out of your home, let everyone know what your new address is, and you are back in business.

If this is your scenario, count yourself very lucky! Most tour guides who expand into commercial office space are going to need a lot more income to cover the expense of an office and, possibly, extra staff.

The least risky way to increase your revenue and make the jump to a larger organization is to expand what you are already doing successfully. If the market for your present tours is large and you are always

turning people away, then you can skip this chapter. Just keep doing what you are doing and expanding what you know works.

If there is not quite enough business to justify opening an office but too much business not to, you may need to supplement your income by selling other travel products such as retail air tickets or travel insurance. Ultimately, many tour companies end up with a full retail agency and a tour wholesale business, too.

1. SELLING RETAIL PRODUCTS

Selling retail airline tickets and cruises in addition to your own tours makes sense in many ways:

(a) You can provide your clients with a one-stop shop by offering airfare and travel insurance as well as the tour.

(b) You can earn extra cash in the form of commissions from other tour operators, car rental agencies, hotels, and airlines.

(c) A retail travel agency gives you a cash flow while you expand your existing tour business.

(d) You can fill in downtime between your own tours with off-the-street retail travel business.

(e) A retail travel agency allows you to diversify. If the government in your favorite tour destination closes the country's borders, you can stay afloat with the cash from your retail business.

The disadvantages of a retail travel business include:

(a) You will need to hire, and pay, more qualified staff.

(b) There is more paperwork.

(c) You will be dealing with the general public — not just people interested in your tour — which requires a certain amount of forbearance that not everyone has.

(d) You will need a nicer office.

2. SELLING COMPLEMENTARY TOURS

You may decide that since you are going to invest the time and money marketing your own tours, you might as well market some noncompeting tours to round out what you have to offer and make a bit of commission for yourself as well. Try to have tours that complement your own, perhaps a tour that goes to a nearby destination (for example,

If the market for your present tours is large and you are always turning people away, just keep doing what you are doing.

Italy rather than your tour of the Greek isles) or that contains a similar component or theme (bicycling in the Napa Valley instead of Utah).

Selling other companies' tours has a number of attractive features and benefits. You can start immediately without spending time on research, preparatory groundwork, or cultivating contacts at your tour's destination. Even better, you get paid right away for every tour you sell, with no hassles. You also get to find out how easy or hard it is to sell certain destinations, and how much interest there is in them, before you commit your own time and capital. For instance, when marketing another company's tour to your clients, you may find a lot of interest in a destination you never considered to be popular. Knowing ahead of time that a market exists makes it much less risky to set up your own tour. You can be confident that once you have done your own research, set up the contacts, and arranged for local handlers, you will show a profit.

3. HOW TO CHOOSE YOUR PRODUCTS

Regardless of whether you choose to sell only other tours or a full complement of travel products, these are some factors you should consider when choosing the product line you will concentrate on.

Marketing several disparate products simultaneously may cause some confusion in the consumer's mind about what you are really good at.

(a) *Staff and training.* If you offer a wide range of products you must have a more qualified staff and better training. This may cost you more.

(b) *Product focus.* Do not spread yourself too thin. Selling treks in Nepal requires a different marketing thrust than selling cruises. To sell both requires that you devote time, attention, and money to both.

   Marketing several disparate products simultaneously may cause some confusion in the consumer's mind about what you are really good at. You will have difficulty convincing the public that you are a tour operator, a retail cruise specialist, and a corporate travel agency with only three staff and a small office.

(c) *Equipment.* Consider what equipment you need. It may differ depending on your product line. If you plan to sell high volumes of domestic airline tickets, you will need at least a computerized reservation system and ticket printer. Kayaking tours will require life jackets, paddles, and kayaks — hardly necessary items for cruises.

Have your staff fully trained in the products.

(d) *Competition.* Look at the competition. An aggressive competitor may make it unprofitable to sell certain products. However, a less aggressive competitor, even one with better prices, often has little or no effect on your ability to make money.

(e) *Contacts and personal knowledge.* Are there particular destinations you know well or have extraordinary contacts in? They may form the basis for your product specialization.

(f) *Unpopular products.* Steer away from products that will not be popular in your location. People in Las Vegas or Palm Springs rarely want to tour desert hot spots.

(g) *Clientele.* Tailor your offerings to the people you think will be your clients. Young families often want adventure tours. People in retirement communities generally tend more toward sun and cruises.

(h) *Your travel agent's knowledge.* Ask the agents you hire what they think will sell. Experienced agents will be able to give you some idea of what sells and how hard it might be to develop a market for specific products. Be aware that agents' views on what constitutes a profitable product may be wishful thinking; you need to track carefully the results of any marketing based on their suggestions.

Whatever your final choice, do it well. Have your staff thoroughly trained in the products. If you are the best you can be in that particular area, word of mouth will eventually bring you success.

4. HOW TO SELECT SUPPLIERS

When comparing products, your choice is easy if you are comparing suppliers with two identical products. All things being equal, you want the one that pays the highest commission.

The choice is slightly more difficult if one supplier is a long distance from you. Calculate the commission that you would be paid and subtract what you might expect to pay for long-distance phone calls and faxes, couriers for overnight rush deliveries, and mail. This can add up to a substantial amount of money. As time goes on, you will get more efficient at containing these costs.

Now compare a potential supplier's price for a product and the price your competition charges for the identical trip. Even with additional inconvenience and communication costs, a higher commission may force you to use an out-of-town supplier in order to undercut your competitor.

Keep the following in mind:

(a) Is the service you get exceptional? Is the supplier's staff responsive when you have problems? No matter what the commission, if the supplier abandons you at a crucial moment or makes it difficult to remedy problems, do not deal with that company.

(b) Does the supplier have a good reputation? If you don't know the supplier, you may still want to sell the products, but do so carefully by limiting the exposure your firm has to them.

(c) What chance do you have of getting an override commission in the near future? Will this allow you to offer the product at a preferred price? Is it worth temporarily giving up another supplier's higher commission to get this override?

(d) You should always be the final decision maker about who your company deals with and what products it offers. Before one of your staff embarks on selling a supplier's product, set a policy that it be cleared with you first — no exceptions!

If a supplier abandons you at a crucial moment or makes it difficult to remedy problems, do not deal with that company.

17
LOCATION

If you have decided to run a retail agency along with your tour operation, location may be the linchpin of your marketing effort. The proper location will be essential to getting clients in the door. However, if you decide to devote more time and money to other forms of marketing, your task is much easier. A wide range of locations will be available to you. The trick is to find a less popular and less expensive location that does not scare away potential clients, and use the savings to mount an effective marketing campaign.

For information on what is available in your area, contact a real estate office or leasing agent. You should also look through the classified sections of the newspaper and drive around areas you are interested in.

Location may be the linchpin of your marketing effort.

1. TYPES OF LOCATIONS

1.1 Enclosed malls (retail only)

Malls have several advantages over other types of locations, but you pay for them. Here are some of the benefits malls offer:

(a) There is plentiful free parking.

(b) Security is probably provided, even if it is only in the form of mall management occasionally making the rounds.

(c) Malls are recognizable and accessible.

(d) Other mall businesses draw customers who may become your clients.

(e) The mall may have a program of shared advertising.

(f) Competition within the mall is often restricted, so you do not need to worry about a major chain opening beside you. Check to ensure your lease contains this important provision.

(g) The mall management may have statistics about the demographics of the mall's customers and a very accurate walk-by count. Do your own count anyway. It is a great way to see for yourself what it would be like in that location. Be sure to do counts at various times and on different days of the week.

There are disadvantages to locating in a mall:

(a) There are almost certainly rules you must follow. Many of these, such as the type and amount of insurance you must carry or the kind of leasehold improvements you must make, may cost you money.

(b) A mall will dictate the hours its merchants must stay open. If the mall is open seven days a week, you will need to staff your office for the entire time even if people do not shop for travel on Sundays and late evenings.

(c) Larger malls may not let you in unless you are part of a chain or have an established credit history.

(d) The price per square foot is relatively high.

1.2 Retail street level and small strip malls

Although street location prices vary widely, you can usually find something less expensive at street level than in an enclosed mall. As well, you should have fewer rules to comply with and you will be able to set your own hours.

Street offices often suffer from chronic parking shortages, which can affect the accessibility of your business. You can partially alleviate this problem by personally delivering or mailing some of your tickets, but you will need to take time to ensure foot traffic patterns are going

Be sure to factor the cost of installing alarm systems or steel shutters, or hiring security patrols, into your monthly expenses.

to be adequate. Capitalize on the hours when traffic is at a maximum by having a full staff available. You can always cut back during slower periods.

Security is more of a problem at street level, especially if you have alleys and possible entry points through skylights or back doors. You may incur expenses installing alarm systems or steel shutters, or hiring security patrols to thwart would-be burglars. Be sure to factor the costs into your monthly expenses.

1.3 Downtown versus suburban

There is a higher concentration of customers in a downtown area than in the suburbs. There is also more active competition for those clients, and the result is a high turnover of businesses, with new travel agencies opening as old ones close down. Parking and accessibility can be a major headache. Downtown locations are often abandoned Sundays and evenings, when suburban shopping areas bustle with activity.

1.4 Office buildings

Office tower space is ideal for tour operators. It is cheaper and usually more secure than retail space. In many cases, your leasehold improvements will be negligible.

For retail agencies, however, office buildings have little walk-in traffic. Many office buildings do not allow display material in their windows, except possibly on the ground floor, so many potential clients will not be aware of your presence. Unless you already have an established clientele or your marketing campaign is geared toward potential customers telephoning in, do not be tempted by the cheaper price of upper-floor office space.

2. POINTS TO CONSIDER

When selecting your location, consider these important points:

(a) Does the location you are contemplating satisfy the needs of your customers?

(b) Again, parking is a major consideration for all retail clients. Is there sufficient parking available within walking distance?

(c) Is your office accessible to the public? IATA and ARC require public accessibility and will not accept access through someone else's office or noncommercial premises.

(d) Is the rent competitive? Is there something cheaper in a similar neighborhood? Check with a leasing agent and survey other locations.

(e) What will be the essential leasehold expenses? Essential leasehold improvements are those that add to the security and visibility, or improve the layout, of the office. Be sure you have a very clear idea what it will cost you to secure your ticket stock. Installing steel bars on a back door can be a hefty expense.

(f) How close is your real competition? Will customers simply cross the street and start a bidding war? Would you welcome the competition or not? Remember that not all travel agencies are your competition. Many specialize in completely different things. A concentration of agencies may work to your advantage because people will be drawn to that particular area to shop for travel. Earls Court Road in London, England, is a prime example of an area where dozens of agencies operate side by side, all drawing people and encouraging sales. If there is a large number of agencies in one place, can you do a better job than your competitor or offer a unique product?

(g) What is the neighborhood like? Is it on the way up or the way down? How much new construction is there? Do people show pride in their neighborhood by keeping it clean and in good repair?

(h) What is the crime rate for the area? Is it a hangout for undesirables in the evenings or on weekends?

(i) Was there a travel agency in the location before? If so, why is it gone?

(j) Will you be able to sell the agency in this location? Although this may seem a minor point if you are not planning to sell or share your business in the beginning, at some point in the future you might want to sell your operation, either outright or to a potential partner. A ground-level location will be easier to sell.

(k) What are the extra staffing costs? A mall location can mean higher staffing expenses because of the longer business hours dictated in your lease. At street level you must be prepared for unpredictable rushes of clients and may end up carrying higher staffing levels during all hours. In an office tower, however, you can staff the office alone if much of your business comes over

A concentration of agencies may work to your advantage because people will be drawn to that particular area to shop for travel.

the phone. And since you will rarely have to worry about walk-in customers, you can use a "back in five minutes" notice instead of hiring another person to cover for you when you step out of the office.

(l) How much space do you need? Offices come in every possible configuration and size. We have seen some as small as 200 square feet (19 square meters)! The customary arrangement of an agent's seat, a desk, and two chairs for clients takes up about 50 square feet (7 square meters). You will want a small reception area even if it is only a space in front of the first desk. Consider how complicated it will be to acquire a larger space if you need it in the future. The building manager may be willing to let you swap your space for a larger office if one becomes vacant later.

(m) Can you negotiate a month-to-month agreement while you try a spot out? Moving any office is expensive, disruptive, and time-consuming, but it is cheaper than remaining in the wrong location.

3. WILL YOU GET ENOUGH WALK-IN TRAFFIC?

Few walk-in agencies survive a terrible location. Be prepared to spend extra time and money researching your target location to maximize your chances of success. While there is no easy formula to guarantee you will get walk-in traffic, these points may help you make your decision:

(a) The most important question to ask yourself is whether the extra rent you will pay in a popular spot could be better spent on a concentrated advertising campaign. Paying big bucks for the privilege of sitting and waiting for customers who never walk in the door is not the way to go.

(b) Count the number of adults passing your proposed location and compare that to the number passing prosperous-looking agencies in other parts of town. Try the exercise at several different times of day. When comparing, remember that other agencies might not be as prosperous as they appear or they may not depend on walk-in traffic for their profit. Traffic counts give you some basis for comparing the rent you would pay in different locations. Within reason, it may be a more useful comparison than using cost per square foot (or square meter).

(c) Is the location visible to people passing by? If no one can see your storefront, it does not matter how much foot traffic there is.

(d) Is the nature of the foot traffic appropriate to support your marketing plan? Seasonal tourists do not buy trips — they are on one already! A high traffic count in a tourist area is useless. Likewise, an area frequented by young people or students may show a high traffic count and still have low potential for sales.

(e) Use a map to chart where your competition is and also to work out how many residents of the area are actually your potential customers. For example, perhaps an entire subdivision is made up of first-time homeowners with young families. Many of these people will be staying home for the next few years. A retirement community, on the other hand, could be filled with people who have both the time and the money to spend on tours and travel in general.

4. NEGOTIATING THE LEASE

Great care must be taken when negotiating a lease. It could easily commit you to paying as much to the landlord as you pay to set up your agency. Rent of $1,000 a month for five years is $60,000! This could turn your projected and manageable $30,000 budget for a new agency into a $90,000 bombshell.

Read the lease over several times and have your lawyer and accountant read it. Confirm each and every detail in the contract.

Take as much time as you need to understand the lease before you sign it. Read it over several times. Have your lawyer and accountant read it. Confirm each and every detail in the contract no matter how fussy and time-consuming this may seem. The last lease we signed committed us to pay for utilities on the basis of the square footage. The measurements in the contract were wrong and we ended up paying for the error over five years. A small item, but we would rather have had the money ourselves than have had to give it to the landlord.

Before you sign the lease, ask these questions:

(a) Is there enough parking for you, your staff, and clients? Is it included in the lease or extra?

(b) Do the heating and air conditioning work?

(c) Is the office correctly zoned?

(d) Are there any health department restrictions you need to know about?

(e) Is there a washroom for you and your staff?

(f) What kind of signs are allowed? Are there restrictions on what you can put in the window?

(g) Are your plate glass windows open to the street? Are they covered by the landlord's insurance or yours?

(h) Must you have a certain color scheme and does that fit with what you want?

(i) How secure is the building? Are there any entry points easily accessible to intruders?

(j) Where are the fire exits? Will the landlord pay to upgrade these?

(k) Can you alter the premises to your specifications?

(l) Is there enough electrical power to run your computers and lighting? Check every switch and plug to make sure they all work. Are there sufficient plugs to give you flexibility when you set up your office?

(m) Are there any businesses nearby that create loud noises or foul smells?

(n) Will the lease allow directory listings in the lobby? Can your office be easily found?

(o) Does the roof leak? Look for water stains.

(p) What will your insurance premiums be like in this location? Get several quotes.

(q) When it is dark before closing time, will your employees be safe when they walk to the bus stop or parking lot?

(r) Is there enough room for a small storage area where you can stash undisplayed brochures or the coffeemaker?

(s) Is major construction going to start next door?

(t) Is there a demolition clause? Demolition clauses are a way for the landlord to terminate the lease with only a few months' notice to allow for property development. If the landlord wants this clause, it can be a great deal for you if you are willing to face the chance of a forced move later. Push extremely hard to have the lease cost reduced and use the savings to build your business when you relocate. If you are cash poor in the beginning, a property like this might be perfect.

18
EQUIPPING YOUR OFFICE

The problem with setting up an office is that it can be fun if you like to shop. It is amazing what you can justify buying if it is for business. And the best part is that you can write it all off on your tax return. The government is helping you pay for all these things!

If you feel this way, you are headed for trouble. We highly recommend you act as if there will be no business coming through the door to pay for your purchases for the next year. We have seen far too many bankrupt companies that started with hand-crafted import furniture, the best computer system, and custom interior decorating. Unless you are catering to the rich and famous, settle for functional furniture and equipment bought secondhand. The money you save may be your rent payment six months from now. When you show a profit, reward yourself by upgrading over time with furniture you really like or timesaving conveniences.

A bare bones office is all you really need to get started (see Table 6). Depending on what kind of tours you are offering, you may not need ticket stock or an IATA/ARC appointment, so you can eliminate office

A bare bones office is all you really need to get started.

189

TABLE 6
BASIC OFFICE EQUIPMENT

- One desk per person and a couple of extra small tables or desks for fax machines and other equipment
- Desk chairs for the employees
- Chairs for clients (approximately two per desk)
- A good light source for each desk
- One telephone per person
- Stand-up desk or wall calendar for each person
- Daily appointment calendar for each person
- Shelving for each sales agent to hold client files and reference books
- Computer and printer with desk
- Fax machine
- A small table for coffee, etc.
- A file cabinet (If you are to be accredited, you will need a locking one)
- A safe (You will need a safe weighing 1,400 pounds (635 kg) or more to comply with accreditation standards)
- Shelving for brochures
- Stationery: pens, paper, envelopes, paper clips, stapler, file folders, a three-ring binder or two, Post-it notes, message pads, fax paper, invoices, booking forms, hotel and transfer vouchers
- Phone books and lists of suppliers
- Maps or atlases
- Accounting journals and books
- A clock
- Window display material if you are at a ground floor location (contact the airlines for posters)

items they require. And if your plans do not include retail trade, you can eliminate even more items — client chairs, for example.

1. TELEPHONE SYSTEMS

Your single most important piece of equipment is the telephone. You can use one just like the one at home if you wish, but we recommend you start with at least a two-line, touch-tone phone with hold, redial, line-in-use indicator, and hands-free speaker features. The speaker option is essential. You should pay no more than $160 for phones with these features, and it is possible to get them on sale or at discount stores for under $100.

When you are ready to upgrade, we recommend you add another two-line phone for each staffperson. Although that will put two phones on each desk, it is a great convenience to be able to use both at the same time. While you are on interminable hold with one supplier, you can continue to make or take calls on the other phone. You will be able to monitor your first call (or the elevator music that office plays) on the speaker phone.

Total cost per desk should be around $220 for four telephone lines connected to two telephones (assuming you got the phones for $110 each), not including the telephone company's line installation charges. Four lines should serve two agents easily and three agents well, except in exceptionally busy periods. Remember that a dedicated fax line can also be used for outgoing calls in a pinch.

Another piece of equipment that we swear by is a telephone headset. You can get them with single or double lines and they are a life saver for people who spend the day on the phone.

In our offices, we always designate our telephone lines as either incoming or outgoing lines. The phone numbers of the incoming lines are published in our brochures and other marketing material, and these lines carry most of our incoming client calls. We try to keep them as clear as possible so clients don't have to put up with a busy signal. Outgoing lines have unpublished numbers and are used by staff to call suppliers or to return calls to clients. When you are spending long hours on the phone organizing every detail of your tours, you do not want to tie up the same lines your sales come in on.

You do not need any special electronic knowledge to install numerous multiline phones after the telephone company has installed the telephone lines. With creative wiring, we have hooked up as many as

Try not to tie up the same lines your sales come in on while you are organizing every detail of your tours.

five desks with four lines each. You will need telephone extension wire and splitters, which can be purchased at any department or electronics store for an additional $20 to $40 at most.

1.1 Expanding your telephone service

Keep your telephone system simple to cut down on expense and staff training time.

When your busy periods start causing you and your staff excessive frustration, or if you start getting complaints from suppliers and clients about busy signals, it may be time to move to more lines and more telephones. If you already have two two-line phones in full use, your only option is to expand to a more complicated phone system. Most telephone companies have their own telephone equipment dealerships that will be happy to quote on a system for you, or you can check the Yellow Pages for commercial suppliers of new and used phone equipment, or watch in your newspaper for notice of private sales of used equipment. Keep a close watch on the price, as even secondhand systems can be expensive. Worse, you often must pay someone to install and repair them. If the cheaper two-line phones break after warranty, you can simply buy replacements.

The other word of warning we offer is to keep it simple. The more complicated the system, the more expensive it is likely to be and the more training your staff will require. A speed-dial function for frequently called numbers will definitely be useful, but intercoms, complicated clocks, and call-forward features are expensive add-ons that seldom get used.

1.2 Reducing line charges

Since your monthly telephone bill can be one of your larger expenses, you might see if your area phone company has business measured lines. Unlike regular business lines where there is a flat monthly fee regardless of the number of calls you make, the monthly charge for a measured line is lower but you pay for each outgoing call. Usually a certain number of outgoing calls are free before the per-call charge kicks in. Incoming calls on a measured line are all free regardless of how many there are.

Consider having your advertised phone numbers (the ones calls come in on) as measured lines and the rest as regular lines. This will encourage staff not to tie up the advertised lines with outgoing calls to suppliers. The savings in a year can be substantial. Be sure to ask for specifics about where measured and unmeasured lines can be used. In some regions, a measured line must come into the office in a different room than the regular line.

1.3 Answering machine or service

Who answers the telephone while you are out? The easiest solution is to get an answering machine. You will miss a few calls because there are still people who are reluctant to leave messages, but a recorded message is preferable to an endlessly ringing telephone. If you use a machine with cassette tapes, buy new tapes frequently so the message is always crisp and clear. A garbled message does not encourage people to phone back.

Answering machines also give you an opportunity to advertise your latest tour offering and keep clients updated about general travel information. Be sure to change the message often to keep people interested.

Voice mail and call answer programs offered by most major telephone companies provide extra flexibility and have been steadily dropping in price over the past few years. They may be more expensive than an answering machine, but are often better suited to business requirements.

2. COMPUTER

A computer with laser printer and the appropriate software has become a standard in any business. In the travel industry, computers save hours when you are typing up itineraries, hotel and transfer vouchers, and other standard forms. Although most software comes with preset forms, it is well worth learning how to design your own (called templates) for these day-to-day items. By creating your own templates, you can modify each form to suit your own needs and preferences. Check out the night school courses in your area for basic software training if you feel at all uncomfortable about attempting this.

There are thousands of people who regularly discard their six-month-old computer equipment the minute something bigger, better, and faster comes on the market. This means there are some incredible deals on secondhand computers for those who are willing to spend time looking. Used computers are cheap (usually $1,000 or less), often come with software already installed, and have had all the bugs worked out by the previous owner.

New equipment with a warranty does give you peace of mind. In general, avoid service contracts. They tend to duplicate the manufacturer's warranty coverage and some are so expensive they amount to prepaying for repairs on any breakdowns you might have. Computer

Telephone answer systems give you an opportunity to advertise your latest tour offering and keep clients updated about general travel information.

repair and service has become highly competitive and unless you live in an isolated area, you should be able to get good, inexpensive service easily.

3. FAX MACHINE

Don't go overboard on the bells and whistles for your fax machine. The only extras we find consistently useful are a paper cutter, a memory for when the paper runs out, and a document feeder. We never use the rest.

You may want to get a fax installed in your computer. Computer faxes require little training and the initial cost of $100 or less per machine will give you a modem so you can get set to surf the Internet too. Computer faxes are great for saving paper, because you can preview faxes you receive and print only the ones you need. The drawback is that they are less flexible than a manual stand-alone machine. While you can receive faxes from any source, you can fax out only documents created as files in your computer, so you will not be able to fax a signed contract to a supplier or send a hot promotional brochure to a client. Even with a fax/modem installed in your computer, you will need a regular fax machine as well.

4. PHOTOCOPIER

To save money, use your fax machine as a copier and make a deal with someone else to use his or her photocopier occasionally. Most fax machines come with a copy feature which is sufficient for day-to-day copying.

Personal copiers are the next step up and run from $350. They can be slow and may handle only a limited range of paper sizes, but they will meet most of your needs. Secondhand, reconditioned, or obsolete models can also be had at substantial savings. We do not recommend buying a service contract on a secondhand photocopier, as this can almost double your costs. There are lots of telecommunication technicians out there who can help you if you have a breakdown.

Check also a combination fax, answering machine, photocopier, and laser printer. Basic models start at well under $1,000. Not only will you spend less than you would buying four separate pieces of equipment, but you will also save space.

To save money use your fax machine as a copier.

5. DECORATIONS

Spruce up your office to make it more inviting for clients and a better work environment for your employees. Inexpensive posters and plants can make a real difference.

6. COMPUTERIZED RESERVATION SYSTEMS

Whether you start a tour operation or a combination tour and retail business, at some point it makes sense to have a computer reservation system (CRS).

Having said that, and even though 96 percent of all agencies have a CRS, do not be pushed into leasing a reservation system before you need it. Some people will insist you cannot have a travel business without a reservation computer. You certainly can. Computers are a convenience, but they can also be one of the heaviest drains on your money if you do not know what to do with them. If you are geared toward certain types of travel, a CRS can and should be avoided. Few small tour operators are on a CRS. Since you will need to use the phone in any case to contact all those that are not on a CRS, there is no point in paying for a computerized system that you will not use.

There are several reservation systems in North America. These systems give your staff access to flight information including routes, prices, and times, as well as weather, visa, and state department advisories, and a host of other useful items.

Each CRS prices its service differently, but all have an incentive system that decreases the cost of the reservation system the more you use it. Some agencies pay nothing because their volume is high; if you do few airline bookings, a computer can cost you hundreds of dollars a month. On top of that there is a substantial installation fee. Negotiate with the reservation company for some kind of reduction in the installation price and monthly fees — it often works. You might be able to get your system installed more cheaply if you are in an area where several companies are competing or where one of the reservation companies wants to increase its market share.

19
FINANCING YOUR TOUR OPERATION

In this chapter, we suggest how you might get financing for your tour business. We do not intend to explain the nuances of financing a small business; there are many good books and evening courses devoted exclusively to the subject of obtaining money for start-ups. As well, we cannot tell you exactly what it will cost to open your operation. Start-up costs vary widely depending on the location you choose, what part of the continent you are on, and the kind of business you are going after. We *will* tell you about the special aspects of financing a tour guiding business and give you an outline of the items you need to include in costing your start-up.

Start-up costs vary widely depending on the location and the kind of business you are going after.

1. SOURCES OF FUNDS AND FREE FINANCING

1.1 Banks

Banks are unlikely to finance much of a new tour operator's cash needs. From a bank's point of view, travel businesses are not good risks. Banks know most of the start-up money will be used for brochures, salaries, and leasehold improvements — things that cannot be repossessed if business goes sour. Unless you have a rich cosigner or enough collateral to secure the loan, you will probably have difficulty convincing a bank to play a large part in your financing.

If you have most of the money or some form of collateral already, you will need to do a loan proposal, including a business plan, and prepare for a thorough briefing with the loans officer. For more information on this subject see *Preparing a Successful Business Plan,* another title in the Self-Counsel Series.

Banks can help you by arranging letters of credit to comply with government or accreditation requirements. Usually they require you to deposit the full amount of money needed to back the letter of credit and then charge you a fee to do the paperwork.

1.2 Government guaranteed loans

In the United States and Canada, a number of programs are in place to help small businesses obtain financing. The Small Business Administration in the United States and the Business Development Bank of Canada are federal government organizations that might put up the cash if you have been denied financing by other financial institutions. You must still come up with a reasonable business plan and the standards used to assess your venture are only marginally less stringent than those of the major banks.

Canada also has a Small Businesses Loans Act which enables chartered banks to loan money to businesses at preferred interest rates. Loans may be used for equipment and leasehold improvements only. Check with any bank for details. The equivalent US Small Business Administration loans can be used for both equipment and working capital.

1.3 Venture capital

Venture capitalists are unlikely to be interested in a travel business because the returns in a mature, highly competitive industry are too small to be attractive.

1.4 Family and friends

The age-old solution of borrowing from friends and relatives is attractive but has some nasty hazards, though these investors are more likely to call to see where they can travel for free than to find out how their money is doing. No matter what business you start, taking on "silent" partners can lead to excessive meddling. With relatives and friends, you may find nonbusiness issues getting in the way of operations. We recommend you avoid the pressure of safeguarding your grandmother's retirement fund or your own lifelong friendships, if at all possible.

1.5 Personal lines of credit, personal loans, and credit cards

While banks ask a lot of questions for business loans, they require comparatively little information from you for personal loans. Small amounts of money can usually be had on the basis of your credit and job history. Banks and credit card companies charge high interest for personal loans, but they can be helpful if you are in a hurry. If you are employed now, apply for a personal line of credit with your bank before you quit the job to start your tour operation.

Personal lines of credit and credit cards are deadly as a main financing option.

Be warned, though. While it is certainly possible to use several credit cards combined with personal loans and vendor financing to fund your business, the interest you pay will sap the life from your company. Personal lines of credit and credit cards are great to hold in reserve for special circumstances, but as a main financing option they are deadly. These loans should be the first to be paid off.

1.6 Other private investors

If you decide to get your IATA/ARC appointment, your tour operation will have one huge financing advantage (see chapter 15). There are hundreds of people who want to own a travel business so they can take advantage of the discounts travel agents are entitled to or be part of the glamourous image associated with travel. Many of these potential investors already have good jobs and do not want to change careers. The key to making this work is to make these potential investors working members of the company as independent contractors. Their job will be to send you business from among their contacts, friends, and colleagues.

Even if these investors produce no new business for you, there are some discounts they are entitled to. If they become good producers, sending you business on a regular basis, they will have earned just about all the privileges of an inside travel agent. In return, they will make either an interest-free or low-interest investment in your business. You get added business and some funding; they get discounted travel as well as the thrill of sending friends down to "their" travel business. Sample 9 shows a contract for exchanging travel benefits for an investment, while Sample 10 shows the letter your supplier will need to offer reduced rates to your investors and staff.

As consultants, we occasionally run ads to find partners for agencies needing capital. For the cost of a two-line ad, we can usually generate more than 20 leads in a week or so. This does not mean you can skimp on your homework, only that you will have more potential sources of money than almost any other new business we can think of. You must still have a solid business plan and a background that will give investors confidence they will not be throwing their money away. Though it is possible to fully fund your business with borrowed money, you will probably need to put up some money of your own as a sign of your commitment.

It does take time. Most investors need to feel a gut sense of trust as well as a positive, rational assessment of your potential before they will give you money. Repeated contacts with an interested investor are usually necessary. We find it takes about six months from the time we first talk to an investor to the time he or she signs a check. We spoke with one investor about once a year for three years on different projects before he finally decided to meet us. (He eventually lent us $25,000 at no interest.)

If this sounds like a lot of work, it is. You may want to use a faster form of financing to get started — maybe arrange something with your friends and family so you can reduce the amount of interest you are paying out — and take your time finding an investor. Unless you have readily available funds, you will probably use a combination of the approaches described here to open your business.

2. HOW MUCH MONEY WILL YOU NEED?

The amount of money you need to open your new business depends on a number of factors. Some factors are beyond your control. If you live in New York City, you can bet your rent, leasehold improvements, and just about everything else are going to cost more than if you live in a rural area. Some factors depend on the choices you make. If you decide to sell premium priced tours, you may have to pay out the money to impress your wealthy clientele with genuine rosewood furniture instead of inexpensive but functional simulated oak.

Your business plan is important. Check the Web for sites that offer business plan templates.

CONTRACT FOR EXCHANGING TRAVEL BENEFITS FOR AN INVESTMENT

June 3, 200-

This agreement is between Joseph Smith and Kristin Smith

and

YOUR BUSINESS INC.

Loan

Joseph and Kristin Smith will lend $25,000 to YOUR BUSINESS INC. This money will be put in a term deposit at YOUR BANK to back a letter of credit in favor of the STATE OR PROVINCIAL government and to satisfy IATA's working capital requirements. All interest will be paid to YOUR BUSINESS INC.

Either party may end this agreement on six months' notice. At the expiry of this notice period, the loan must be repaid to Joseph and Kristin Smith and all business cards and other documentation must be returned to YOUR BUSINESS INC.

Employment

A commission will be paid to Joseph and Kristin Smith on whatever business they refer to the travel business and, as part of their duties for YOUR BUSINESS INC., Joseph and Kristin Smith agree to send as much business as possible to YOUR BUSINESS INC.

Joseph and Kristin Smith acknowledge that in their capacity as outside consultants, they are independent contractors and cannot bind YOUR BUSINESS INC. in any contract or agreement nor act as agents for YOUR BUSINESS INC.

Travel benefits

Joseph and Kristin Smith will receive travel benefits under the following conditions:

1. All expenses relating to travel or the arrangement of travel, including courier charges, communication charges, special letters, business cards, industry ID cards, and the like will be paid by Joseph and Kristin Smith.

2. YOUR BUSINESS INC. will provide an employment confirmation letter and other industry-accepted documentation as required as proof of Joseph and Kristin Smith's employment with YOUR BUSINESS INC. As well, YOUR BUSINESS INC. will include Joseph and Kristin Smith on the company's IATA list when applicable.

3. Joseph and Kristin Smith may attend any industry functions, cruise ship tours, or FAM trips for which they are eligible, together with a companion if allowed. If there are restrictions on the number of people that may attend from one office, inside sales staff has the right of first refusal, and outside staff will be accommodated on a first-come-first-served basis.

4. Joseph and Kristin Smith will make their own bookings for any reduced rate travel with the advice of the staff of YOUR BUSINESS INC.

5. Joseph and Kristin Smith will be reimbursed all their commissions earned on their own or their children's travel by YOUR BUSINESS INC. except for a 3% (of the gross) administration fee. This applies to nonreduced rate travel only. Commission is never earned on reduced rate travel.

6. All reduced rate travel must comply with any supplier guidelines or IATA regulations.

If YOUR BUSINESS INC. is sold, Joseph and Kristin Smith will have these options:

1. To move their funding to any business set up by the principals and continue this agreement,

or

2. If Joseph and Kristin Smith or family have not taken advantage of any travel benefits, any interest earned by YOUR BUSINESS INC. will be paid to Joseph and Kristin Smith as salary, the principal will be repaid, and this agreement will be terminated,

or

3. The staff at YOUR BUSINESS INC. may arrange for the same agreement to be continued with the new owners, in which case the interest earned on the term deposit will be kept by YOUR BUSINESS INC.

Joseph Smith
_____
Joseph Smith

Jennifer Jones
_____
Jennifer Jones
Owner, Your Business Inc.

Kristin Smith
_____
Kristin Smith

LETTER OF EMPLOYMENT FOR OUTSIDE AGENTS

YOUR BUSINESS INC.
101 Main Street
Anytown, ZA 123 234

June 24, 200-

To whom it may concern:

This letter is to confirm the employment of those listed below as travel agents within the meaning of resolution 880 of the IATA regulations.

Name	Date of employment
Jennifer Jones	April 21, 1995
Ashley Wells	April 10, 1996
Lindsey White	September 15, 1995
Joseph Smith	June 23, 1997
Kristin Smith	June 23, 1999

Thank you.

Sincerely,

Jennifer Jones

Jennifer Jones
Owner, Manager, Agent

Your business plan is important. It gives you hard numbers to assess the amount of money you will need to open and stay in business for the first few months. The following are some of the factors you need to consider as you cost out your business.

2.1 Your market

If you will be selling only through travel agents and never expect to have a client enter your premises, you can get away with really cheap digs. One tour operator we worked with for years sold premium products out of a one-room warehouse with no reception area. One would step directly into a pandemonium of papers, brochures, and coffee cups covering every flat surface. But the rent was cheap!

If you are going to set up a retail agency, however, you will need a more businesslike look and location for your office.

2.2 Geographic area

A downtown location is more expensive than one in an outlying area, and big cities are more expensive than small towns. You might consider setting up in a cheaper area and making extensive use of the telephone, fax, and courier to service your clients and travel agencies.

2.3 Size of your telephone system

If you use a reservation system to do a significant portion of your quotations and reservations, you will still need at least one telephone line per employee. If you are doing a retail business as well as a tour business, you may need as many as two-and-a-half lines per full-time employee, since many suppliers are not in any reservation system and must be called directly. You can certainly start with fewer lines and fine-tune the number you need, but make sure the phone system you purchase or lease can handle an expansion in the foreseeable future. Adjustments to your phone system, such as installation and equipment, cost money.

2.4 Equipment

In addition to telephones and possibly a reservation system, you will need desks and chairs for yourself and chairs for your clients. The price for this varies. We used comfortable patio furniture to add a holiday air to our vacation travel office. Business office furniture is generally more expensive, but by making use of secondhand or less costly alternatives, you can save hundreds of dollars. Alternatively, you could lease office equipment. Leasing is an expensive way to purchase equipment since, in effect, you are borrowing the money at an interest rate of as high as 21 percent. Leasing does have tax advantages, though, and you do not need to put out the full price in cash right away.

As a rule of thumb, if you have the cash, purchase. If you don't have it, lease. Ask the salesperson to do a cost comparison for you. Be sure you have an exact breakdown of the cost of the equipment and the financing cost over the life of the lease.

Leasing is an expensive way to purchase equipment.

2.5 Expenses associated with your location

The expenses associated with moving into a new location fall into two categories: installation expenses and leasehold improvements.

Installation costs include security deposits, hook-up fees for utilities and telephone, moving expenses, dedicated computer line installation, and security alarm installation.

Leasehold improvements usually require construction of some sort. Since tour operators and travel agencies are simply offices, you should be able to get away with very little construction. No one needs a separate office, and a storage area can be made using shelving units and plants as dividers. Use individual desks instead of expensive custom counters. Movable furniture can be taken with you if you move later, whereas anything you add to the property is the landlord's to keep at no cost to him or her. Extensive leasehold improvements are a great way to waste money. Unless your clientele demands it, start out with inexpensive offices and build something more to your taste later, when you have funds.

2.6 Working capital

Working capital is the money you need to keep your business running. Money always seems to be needed in chunks. Several bills come in at the beginning of the month, but cash to pay them may not appear until the next week. Rather than irritate all your creditors by waiting until money comes in before paying them, use working capital to pay the bills.

In some parts of North America, the government demands that you have a certain amount of working capital on hand. IATA and ARC have their own regulations for working capital and net tangible assets (think of this as cash and the office equipment or things in your business you can physically put your hands on). If your business does not need to

If you extend credit, you will need to pay suppliers out of your working capital.

meet either of these requirements, and you do not extend credit to your clients, you might be able to use a line of credit from a bank to smooth out the cash flow. In that case, you might be able to get away with $3,000 working capital for a small business.

If you extend credit, you will need to pay suppliers out of your working capital and wait to be reimbursed by your clients. In this case, your working capital will be all the money not yet collected. It is not unusual to have $50,000 in working capital for a large business.

2.7 Other licensing fees

In addition to accreditation and government regulation licensing fees, set aside money for municipal licenses, any zoning changes you must make, and other association or consortium fees.

3. ADDING UP THE COST OF YOUR BUSINESS

It is fairly simple to figure out approximately what you will need to open your doors and stay in business for two or three months with no sales. Using the costing sheet in Sample 11, research each category for a range of prices. For example, the telephone company can give you an exact cost for the basic rental of each telephone line you install. To estimate the long-distance charges you will incur, think about where your clients are. Even if most of them are local, you will likely have a few out-of-town suppliers to contact on occasion. You might estimate an additional $40 to $50 a month. By estimating a range of costs, you can plan for the worst-case scenario and never be surprised.

Of course, costs vary from place to place, and they change. During a recession, rents may come down but your advertising costs may go up as you pump more money into bringing in new customers. Each time you examine a new location or consider a new piece of equipment, you should recalculate the costs.

4. RECOMMENDATIONS

4.1 Forget the frills

Unless you know you have a built-in clientele and an income (e.g., if you have been working as a tour guide for years and you know your clients love and adore you), be very conservative on expenses and equipment. For some people, opening a business is a license to shop till they drop. And salespeople love to help you spend: "If you just get one

SAMPLE 11
PREOPENING SET-UP COSTS

Initial installation and equipment cost range:

	Low Nonaccredited business	High Accredited business	Your business
Banking, checks	$ 50	$ 200	$ _____
Legal	500	1,000	_____
Telephone equipment	300	600	_____
Telephone, 2 lines installation + deposit	100	100	_____
Photocopier	600	2,000	_____
Fax machine	300	600	_____
Safe	500	3,000	_____
Desks and chairs	2,000	3,000	_____
Stationery, postage inventory	200	500	_____
Insurance, fire, theft, liability	200	300	_____
First month's advertising	200	600	_____
Subscriptions	30	200	_____
Leasehold	500	5,000	_____
License and permits	100	100	_____
Accreditation	0	900	_____
Government registration	500	1,000	_____
Accounting	300	1,000	_____
Salaries, preopening months	3,000	4,000	_____
Signs	100	1,000	_____
Answering machines	30	150	_____
One month's rent for setup	0	1,500	_____
Printing (business cards, invoices)	200	300	_____
Fridge, microwave, coffeemaker	200	300	_____
Security or rent deposits	0	0	_____
Totals	$ 9,910	$27,350	$ _____
Contingency fund of 20%	1,982	5,470	
Recommended working capital or IATA/ARC-required working capital	5,000	25,000	_____
Approximate cash needed	$16,892	$57,820	$ _____

model up from this phone system, your customers can listen to soft music while they wait for you." Good service and prices promote your business. Frills do not. Be skeptical of all salespeople. They have to eat too, but let someone else be the bacon in their breakfast.

4.2 Trade time for money

Conserve your cash by doing things yourself instead of paying someone or buying the latest timesaving device. For example, put up with the inconvenience of calling the airlines instead of relying on a costly reservation system until your volume can justify its use. Optimizing your cash flow requires you to reexamine your options often. Remember, too, there comes a point where saving the cash is foolish.

4.3 Do not go into debt for the long term

Interest is an avoidable business expense in the long run. You might want to use a line of credit as a cushion to smooth out the ups and downs in your cash flow, but not as a source of long-term cash. Of course, if interest rates are extremely low, you may be willing to put up with a small amount of debt and forgo the inconvenience of partners.

4.4 Hire people who care

Whether it is your lawyer, accountant, or staff, a caring attitude on their part can mean the difference between a good effort and a great effort. Great efforts save you money and bring repeat customers.

4.5 Read carefully

Read every boring phrase of every contract as if your lifestyle depended on it.

Read every boring phrase of every contract as if your lifestyle depended on it. It does.

4.6 Think small

Big successes are built on small successes. Big flops are built on big ideas that require big debt and big risks. Small ideas are easier to finance than grandiose, continent-spanning travel corporations. The journey to your dream business doesn't take any longer with small steps.

20
REVENUES AND EXPENSES

1. COMMISSIONS

If you have decided to open a full IATA/ARC agency as part of your tour business, you need to know how to get the best commissions from the airlines and other travel suppliers you will use for your tours. All travel suppliers have a standard commission rate for new customers. Airlines tend to be more rigid in the requirements you must meet to obtain higher commission rates, while tour operators tend to be a little more flexible. There are several strategies you can try to get higher commissions from suppliers when you first start up.

1.1 Ask for a higher commission

If you are completely new to the business, just asking does not usually work, but once in a while someone will sweeten an offer without your pushing too hard. You will have better success if you can give a supplier a good reason to increase your commission. For instance, if a competitor is offering higher compensation, you should point this out to the supplier. Even if the competitor is in another state or province and is not

When your volume with a particular supplier has grown substantially, discuss an increased commission rate.

one most agencies in your area deal with, the supplier might increase its offer to get your business.

If your volume with a particular supplier has grown substantially, you will want to review your new level with the supplier's sales representative. Find out when you can expect to be paid more per booking. At the very least, asking for a higher commission rate will alert the supplier to your ambitions and you can arrange for a reassessment after a three- or six-month period. Be sure to follow up. Most suppliers forget without your gentle reminder.

1.2 Override commissions

In addition to the normal commissions suppliers offer, there may be extra commissions, called override commissions, paid on tickets the agency issues itself. (Airlines never pay overrides based on the volume your agency does with any intermediary such as a wholesaler, consolidator, or other retail agency.) Override commission amounts range from a fraction of a percent to over six percent, but few companies attain the upper end of the range. Contracts must be negotiated individually and are usually subject to revision with a minimum of notice. Some override commission agreements simply add a percentage point or two to each regular commission, which you can bank once the sale is made. Under other agreements, you may be paid all your earned override commissions in a lump sum at the end of the year.

Generally, major airlines will not discuss override commissions until after your first year in business. Even if you managed to generate a significant volume with the carrier in your first year, it may be willing to pay you overrides based on your second year's volume only — and would pay those in a lump sum only at the end of the year. Smaller airlines and some international carriers may be easier to persuade, but they normally serve less popular destinations. It can be difficult to achieve high volumes with small regional carriers. Frankly, as a new agency, unless all your volume goes to a particular destination, your chances of negotiating significant overrides with the airlines are extremely slim.

Be careful not to fall into the common trap of selling tickets at cost in order to make your override quota. Some agencies do this, reasoning that even though they are losing a little money on tickets by rebating all their regular commission, the number of clients they entice to purchase tours and other travel will increase their volume to the point where they will receive a huge override check. The danger is that they may still not make the quota and end up with a heavy loss.

1.3 Use wholesalers and consolidators

Many wholesalers and consolidators will give you a higher commission rate than you can get by issuing the ticket yourself. This will bring you the same result as any override program, but without a quota.

1.4 Join a consortium

Consortiums are companies that combine the sales volumes of their member travel agencies to act as a negotiating block with the airlines, cruise lines, hotels, tour operators, and car rental companies. Consortiums also make money on override commissions they get directly from the suppliers. Members pay an initial fee and a yearly fee; with tough negotiating, the initial fee is sometimes waived.

Wholesalers and consolidators may give you a higher commission rate than you can get yourself.

When choosing a consortium (most are exclusive and require you to belong to one only), pick one with a lengthy track record, a long list of agreements with popular companies, and an easily understood manual that explains any special booking instructions for obtaining a higher commission. You should be given enough time to review the manual and figure out whether the extra commissions offered will benefit you.

Many consortiums specialize in vacation or business travel. Ask yourself if the clients you market to will use these suppliers and whether the extra commissions you will generate in a year more than offset the monetary and administrative costs of belonging to the consortium.

As well, the list of suppliers the consortium presents to you in the manual may look long and impressive, but can you get the same benefits dealing directly with the supplier? If you can, the consortium fees are money wasted.

Would you ever use the suppliers they have signed up? If there are a lot of third-world airlines you have never heard of or if you can get a higher commission only on major airline flights originating in a part of the continent far from your own, you are wasting your time. For instance, the agreement may exclude extra commission on any bookings for flights originating west of the Rockies. An agency on the West Coast will book most of its clients from the West Coast and will not collect significant extra commissions.

Another common consortium tactic is to pay you only at the end of the year, on a sliding scale. On closer examination, you will realize that your new agency will never achieve the minimum for the sliding scale. For instance, the consortium might require that you have a sales volume of $500,000 to get a 1 percent increase in your commission, $1,000,000 for a 2 percent increase in your rate, and so on. Some even require that you do a certain amount more business this year than last year to qualify for an increase.

Exclusions covering popular destinations are not uncommon either. For example, the agreement might exclude extra commissions on all bookings on a particular supplier's winter-sun destination flights. If your primary business is sun flights in the winter, you will not retire on the extra income you get from that particular supplier.

Pay special attention to the service a consortium provides to help members solve commission disputes with suppliers. You should be able to pick up the phone, call a toll-free number, and have someone in the consortium's management respond within hours with a solution to your problem. Mailing letters back and forth in order to collect extra commissions is not profitable.

Ask the consortium for references and check them.

Finally, ask for references and check them. Find other consortium members and ask them if the association has been worthwhile. If the response is no, ask for specifics about the kind of business that reference does. It may be that they are not well matched to the consortium. However, if the agency's business is similar to yours, beware.

1.5 Join forces with another agency

In a pinch, you might be able to find an agency close to you that will give you a share of its overrides in the hope that your added volume will increase its negotiating power with a particular airline. Our experience is that the extra paperwork is not worth the effort and it is better to spend the time cultivating a wholesaler or consolidator. The only exception might be if the airline serves a specific destination and no consolidator you feel comfortable with is offering those flights.

2. EXPENSES

Expenses vary widely depending on your geographic location, the kind of office you run, the experience of your staff, and numerous other details. The sample expense sheets in Sample 12 show a rough estimate of the costs for a small (two-person) office and a medium-sized office (four to ten staffpeople) in a major city. (The smaller office is about as small as an agency can be and still break even.) If you do more extensive advertising, produce color brochures for your tours, or install a computerized reservation system, you can easily double your costs.

Controlling expenses is a great way to earn money. Think of it this way. When you find a way to save money, that money goes right into your pocket. A common mistake made by first-time owners is to assume they must have the best of everything. Others believe all travel agencies require elaborate computers and fancy telephone systems. Carefully assess whether you are getting good value for the money you spend.

SAMPLE 12
EXPENSE SHEETS FOR SMALL- AND MEDIUM-SIZED OFFICES

Monthly expenses	Small office	Larger office	Your estimate
Rent	$ 800	$ 4,000	_____
Advertising	300	1,500	_____
Telephone	200	1,000	_____
Utilities	50	250	_____
Payroll	3,000	15,000	_____
Office supplies	150	400	_____
Insurance, miscellaneous	200	300	_____
Accounting, bookkeeping	100	700	_____
Courier, postage	100	300	_____
Fees, licenses	50	100	_____
	$4,950	$23,550	_____

Note: No interest on borrowed money or depreciation is included.

21
PERSONNEL

A competent staff is essential to your success. The people you choose will not only be the salespeople for your organization but they will also have a wealth of experience you can draw on as you set up your office. Choose well.

1. INSIDE AGENTS

We recommend you hire, in the beginning, experienced sales staff to do the day-to-day sales. For the few hundred dollars you might save by employing an inexperienced agent, you can ease your own burden immensely. Besides, people love opening new enterprises and even old hands at the business often become enthusiastic about getting in "on the ground level" and helping with all the chores that must be done. Let them help set up your tour operation before you open.

As in any business, inside agents can run from the bad to the truly dedicated. The daily work of a tour operation is high-pressured and requires an individual who is good with details, has excellent organizational skills, and is able to work with never-ending deadlines. An agent without these abilities will not last long.

Choose your staff carefully, they are the salespeople for your organization.

If you are an experienced travel agent or have tour sales in your background already, you might be able to get away with hiring inexperienced agents as staff. However, you may not be saving in the long run, as inexperienced agents must be supervised and trained carefully.

2. MANAGERS

It does not happen often, but owners sometimes hire managers who run a tour business into the ground. They alienate sales staff who then flee with the clients, order expensive equipment you do not need, or commit outright fraud. Be vigilant when hiring a manager, especially when checking references.

Most managers for small tour operators also work as sales agents. Usually they have some knowledge of accounting systems and know how to comply with IATA and BSP regulations. Larger tour operators may have managers who do not act as sales agents, and a few of the largest operators have managers who are business management specialists with no travel experience at all.

You would be best to start off with a manager who has experience running a tour operation or travel agency, has the background to solve both customer and supplier problems, and is willing and able to do sales as well. Bookkeeping skills are an asset but not a necessity.

There will always be people who apply for a manager's job who have been managers in name only and do not have the skills you need. Your business depends on your ability to weed out these people.

3. HOW MANY PEOPLE DO YOU NEED?

IATA/ARC, as well as some state and provincial governments, require that you have at least two experienced agents in the office, each working at least 32 hours per week. Even at the beginning when business is slow, we agree that two is the minimum to provide relief for breaks and lunch, and to give you a reserve to draw on during busy periods. In an unregulated rural area it is possible to have a smoothly running agency with one agent and one inexperienced person.

Typically, business goes in cycles. The tour business is even more seasonal than most. For example, if you have a business that runs only in the summer, you may find that between February and October you are hard pressed to find any spare time at all.

After October, however, you may need to lay off staff as the season winds down. Even if yours is one of the few agencies that runs tours year-round, end of month may be busier than the middle of the month because of payday and June will be busier than January.

As peak times overwhelm your staff more frequently, you must consider hiring more people. Training additional full-timers only to let them go when business slows is an expensive proposition that demoralizes the remaining staff. Hiring full-time people who will not be busy all year is inefficient, too. One solution is to cultivate a part-time work force which can help smooth the road for your full-time workers. As it gets busier, you increase your part-time employees' hours; as it slows down, hours can be cut back. If sales stay high, your part-time staff is a ready-made pool of trained people from which you can pick additional full-time staff.

In some cities, there are employment agencies specializing in providing the travel industry with full-time workers and temporary relief. Although these agencies are usually fairly expensive, in a real jam it is worth hiring through them for a few days. A temporary agent with experience in your area of the country probably already knows which suppliers to use for which products. With the cooperation of other workers and a minimum of training in your office procedures, a temporary agent should be productive immediately. Normal employment agencies tend to send secretarial help or receptionists; this might suffice for one or two days if you need help answering the phones, but such temps will be of little assistance working with clients or issuing tickets.

Training full-time staff only to let them go when business slows is an expensive proposition.

4. EXPERIENCE AND QUALIFICATIONS OF STAFF

Many agents who end up working with tour operators have gone through a training course offered by a commercial travel agency school or a public university or technical school with a travel agent component. Tuition for these courses ranges from $3,000 to $5,000 or more, and a course can last as long as six months of either full-time or part-time study.

The travel industry gives commercially trained students mixed reviews. It is unfortunate, but many universities and technical schools emphasize travel management even though students will be frontline salespeople for years before they become managers. In some three- to six-month courses there is not adequate training for selling to the public, telephone manner, or customer relations. When you hire graduates of one of these programs, you will still need to teach them about the suppliers you use, your particular office procedures, and how to fill out your forms. Do not be surprised if you also have to teach a few elementary lessons in courtesy to clients as well. Some students become so disillusioned by the differences between the work world and the picture painted for them in the classroom that they quit in the first month.

Often an apprenticeship or practicum is a formal part of the curriculum. Students are required to work for a tour operator or agency as part of their studies to gain some real-world experience. Many travel businesses do not accept students for practicums, however, as the owner can be faced with taking time away from earning a living to teach someone the ropes and then watch an enthusiastic student become resentful and disillusioned as all the unskilled and boring tasks fall to him or her.

In some ways it is easier to train someone from scratch than to mold new employees who think they are fully trained by virtue of the schooling they have had. We find new employees without formal training are more motivated since the industry is brand new to them and they understand that they are at an educational disadvantage. If you can harness this enthusiasm, you have a good chance of gaining an exceptional and probably very loyal employee.

Airlines have their own ticketing and sales courses that are open to travel industry employees. These are offered periodically in major urban centers; some of the more intensive ones are taught at the larger airlines' training schools. For the money, these courses are dramatically better than what is offered at most commercial schools.

In summary, formal training is a help but the attitude and experience of a potential employee are more important. While we recommend hiring at least one experienced and well-trained agent (even though experience does cost more), a bright, enthusiastic person willing to work hard often makes up for a lack of formal education. A combination of a student and senior agent may be acceptable for your new tour operation if business is slow in the beginning.

Attitude and experience are often more important than formal training.

5. WHERE TO FIND EMPLOYEES

There are four major sources for finding qualified candidates: word-of-mouth, industry publications, newspaper advertising, and employment agencies.

(a) The best source of new employees is a word-of-mouth recommendation. Many travel agency managers are willing to do a favor for agents they know who are out of work or looking for a change. Start by calling agency managers you became acquainted with during your start-up research. An active approach to this task is crucial. If you wait for leads to come to you, you will be waiting a long time.

(b) Read all the industry news. Besides reading the employment classified ads, look for news of lay-offs in related services such as airlines or other tour operators. Contact the companies involved and ask them to post your job.

(c) The local newspaper's classified employment ads are relatively inexpensive, but be prepared to spend much of your time fielding inquiries from inexperienced dreamers who want information about a career in travel. To save time, your opening question for every conversation should be "Are you an experienced travel agent?" Unless you consider requests for career counselling to be your weekly volunteer commitment, brush off any people who answer "No."

(d) We have found that employment agencies are the least productive avenue, but they are worth a try if you have had no luck with the other three sources.

6. THE INTERVIEW

There have been many good books written on how to screen candidates, including *A Small Business Guide to Employee Selection* in the Self-Counsel Series. In addition to the general selection process recommended by this book and others, there are a few questions specifically on the travel business which you should ask all prospective candidates during the job interview.

When you are hiring, be sure to check every reference and each past job.

(a) How many years have you been in the business?

(b) What formal travel education do you have?

(c) Have you taken any sales training courses?

(d) Do you know how to write tickets?

(e) What was your volume per month at your last place of employment?

(f) With which res systems are you proficient?

(g) How much time did you spend working on these systems?

(h) Have you worked with any accounting systems? Which ones?

(i) Have you worked for any other tour operators? What were your responsibilities?

Be sure to check every reference and each past job. This is not a waste of time but an absolutely essential step. At the very least it will give you a feel for the work habits and personality of the person you are thinking of hiring. Unexplained gaps in a résumé will alert you to jobs the candidate may be reluctant to disclose.

7. SALARIES

Well before you open you should be gathering information on salaries for your area. You can get a clear idea of competitive compensation and different commission schemes by collecting information from a variety of sources.

(a) Speak with working managers of tour operators and travel agencies in your area. They will have the best idea of the going wages. Many of them will be helpful and you may discover some valuable sales contacts as well as the information you are looking for. Your friends and other contacts in the industry may be able to help, too. Although your friend the airline pilot may not know the specific salary ranges you are researching, he or she is sure to know someone who does.

(b) Travel schools can give you an accurate idea of wages for the new agents in their current graduating class.

(c) Professional associations such as the Association of Canadian Travel Agents (ACTA) or the American Society of Travel Agents (ASTA) tend to err on the high side in their estimates, but this allows you to establish the upper limits of what you should pay.

(d) Ask potential candidates for a complete earnings history, but beware of exaggerations.

The upshot is that there are no rules about salaries; depending on the timing and your locale, salary ranges can vary by up to 100 percent. In British Columbia for instance, a new agent's starting salary is sometimes as low as CDN$1,200 per month (approximately US$850) with two weeks' annual vacation. Salaries are about the same in other provinces and the United States. As a rule of thumb, the larger the company, the higher the starting salary, though some full-time inside staff accept less than a living wage because they feel the travel benefits make it worthwhile.

Remember, too, as in any other job market there are ebbs and flows in the available pool of labor. Every few years we see a surge of new travel agents entering the market. When there is a glut, some people will work for almost nothing, but when the number of unemployed agents drops, salaries can zoom up by 50 percent. One common mistake is to hire someone at a ridiculously low salary when there are lots of candidates for the job. Then, when the labor market absorbs the excess and other managers are willing to pay more, your low-paid agent will move to better money. If you do not keep current about wages, you could find yourself continually training new people to replace those who leave. Replacing workers is a time-consuming and costly strategy.

Keep current about wages or you could find yourself continually training new people to replace those who leave.

7.1 The commission component

The trend in the travel industry is to a combination of salary and commission, primarily to reward and encourage top producers. Many owners find commissions provide an incentive not only to increase sales but also to encourage the sale of high-markup products such as insurance. Commission rates for combination salary and commission compensation range between 25 percent and 35 percent of the amount the agent earns for the agency. Agents on straight commission and no salary can earn as much as 60 percent of their sales.

Many different commission structures are workable. Common variations include a quota the agent must reach before commissions kick in, commissions on only certain products, or a sliding scale of some type. Sliding scale programs can work retroactively or not. For instance, agents making a certain level of sales in a month may be given the higher level of commission on all their sales for the month (retroactive commission). More commonly, the higher commission applies only to sales above a certain threshold. Commission levels may even be cumulative. In this case, once agents attain a certain level of sales during their employment with you, they will be given the new commission rate regardless of what their month-to-month volume is.

We have no favorites among the various compensation schemes. We do warn you that incentive structures must be carefully crafted to ensure they reward the actions and attitudes you want. For instance, rewards for high-volume sales may eventually result in competition rather than cooperation among staff. You might discover that paperwork is done sloppily because staff are bent on making sales rather than completing forms properly. "Service with a smile" may suffer as agents try to churn customers through as fast as possible. What you gain in sales may have to be spent on advertising just to keep the phones ringing. A less sales-oriented person may feel more secure on full salary and give you better all-round results.

To muddy matters further, some research suggests that changing your pay structure every few years does as much good as any specific compensation package. The newness of the scheme may very well be enough incentive in itself.

7.2 Benefit packages

Benefit packages are expensive and require time to explain to your employees and to administer. Most small operators cannot afford a benefits package that can compete with the ones offered by bigger companies, but take heart. Some consortiums have terrific benefits packages you can use for your employees.

7.3 Reduced rate travel

Younger agents are especially receptive to the idea of travel as compensation for their job. Older workers with family obligations usually need cash. When putting together a compensation package for young workers, ask if they would prefer a higher salary or more time off, even unpaid, and a better shot at some of the industry perks that come along. Those with other means of support will often jump at the chance for better travel benefits.

7.4 Vacation time

Most areas have laws on the minimum amount of paid vacation time a company must give its employees. Be familiar with these rules. In the travel industry, because of the opportunities for travel, vacation time can be a major issue. It does not make sense to work in the industry and never have a chance to travel. Extra time off is a good bargaining chip.

Most small agencies offer new agents the minimum vacation time dictated by law, and even senior agents may get only two or three weeks. Larger firms have better vacation policies, but few people get more than four weeks off per year. Of course, time off may be supplemented by FAM trips. New agents tend to think of these as vacations, while experienced agents sometimes refuse FAMs that include too many hotel tours or too much travel time.

7.5 Free labor

Every jurisdiction has a minimum wage. Despite this, many students get unpaid work experience by doing a two-week to three-month practicum with an agency. To avoid any wage liability, protect yourself with a written contract stating your intention to swap training for labor. Better yet, go through the placement department of a travel school to get a student. By using a travel school, the nature of your obligation to the student is abundantly clear.

8. STAFF MORALE

Running a sales team is an art in itself, one you will never finish learning about. Spend some time learning all you can about the latest way to motivate your staff and keep morale high, and try some of the following methods to get the best from your employees.

Every jurisdiction has a minimum wage. You need to know what it is.

(a) *Communicate.* Thank people in front of the rest of the staff or in writing when a job is well done. Pay attention when someone has a problem or a suggestion. Encourage staff by sending them on courses (usually the cost is slight and well worthwhile). Personal guidance can also work wonders. Never discipline a staff member within earshot of anyone else.

(b) *Consult* with your staff and ask their advice. Not only will you get great ideas from time to time but soliciting opinions also builds consensus and cooperation.

(c) *Promotions, salary increases, more responsibility* even a change in responsibility can have a powerful, beneficial effect on employees.

(d) *Rewards* for good performance are always welcome. Dinner *with* the boss may not be a wonderful experience no matter how fancy the restaurant, but dinner *on* the boss (always for two), or a thoughtful and appropriate gift, lets everyone know you care and notice how they are doing.

(e) Start an *incentive system* but be careful you encourage the right behavior (see the example of problems that might arise in section **7.1**). Put yourself in the agent's place. What is the program really encouraging? Be sure the prize is attainable and valuable. Travel and time off are prized and relatively cheap for you to award. Reward systems in which no one wins or in which the same person wins each time breed apathy or a sense of betrayal. Your staff will catch on before the contest even begins that only the top producers are going to win. In addition to rewarding the highest volume in the office, give bonuses for the most improved, the most trips to a particular destination, or the most frequent use of a particular supplier.

(f) Be aware of *symbols*. A move to a better desk or even a newer phone can communicate your pleasure at no expense to you.

For more ideas about motivating your employees see *Motivating Today's Workforce,* another title in the Self-Counsel Series.

9. TERMINATION

Consult your lawyer or local labor board regarding the laws before you fire anyone.

Some jurisdictions have probation periods for new employees in which you can let an employee go for any reason without any obligation on your part. This trial period allows you to assess whether the person fits with your organization. We strongly advise you to use this time carefully to consider your decision. If you find your new employee does not fit in, for whatever reason, do not let the situation continue. Meet the unpleasant task of firing the employee head-on. You have an obligation to yourself and your other employees to give your business the best chance for success you can.

If you need to fire or lay off employees during or after the probation period, be sure to consult your lawyer or local labor board to find out exactly what the laws are in your district.

22
MARKETING A LARGE TOUR OPERATION

Most large tour operators follow exactly the same marketing principles we outlined in chapter 12 for the individual offering a single tour. If you have a retail travel agency in addition to your tour business, here are some other suggestions to help market your tours.

1. CHOOSE A DESCRIPTIVE NAME

If you specialize in tours to Greece, choose a name conveying that fact. Every time your name is used, people will know what you do. Even if you do not specialize in a particular destination, your name can prevent a certain number of wasted phone calls. Travelers looking for a shopping extravaganza will never call a tour company called Roughing It In The Bush. Choosing your name is difficult and can take time, so start the process early. Some of the things you must consider:

(a) If you use a name that is the same as or even similar to one already in use, you risk legal confrontations. Check your phone book and your state or province's registrar of companies for existing names.

(b) If you pick a geographic area as part of your name — 49th Street Adventure Travel, for example — be sure you are not going to move.

(c) If you include a destination in your name, make sure you can service this destination well enough to continue doing it forever.

(d) A personal name in the company's identity can become a problem when you take on new partners or if you sell the business. It also ties you personally to the success or failure of your business.

There are different levels of protection you can obtain to ensure that after you have spent years cultivating a following, someone does not use your company's name to steal your business. The cost for this protection ranges from inexpensive state or provincial registrations giving you minimal protection to trademark registration that is lengthy and expensive but puts you in a strong position to fight someone who wants to use your name.

Do not apply for trademark protection in your first two or three years in business unless you have already achieved public name recognition for your fabulously profitable tour business. If that is the case, read as much as you can on trademarks and definitely see a lawyer. You may find you decide to delay getting a trademark forever. In fact, most tour operators never go to this expense.

2. MARKETING THROUGH TRAVEL AGENTS REVISITED

As we mentioned in chapter 12, you can have travel agents do your selling for you on a commission basis. Some tour operators think travel agents are worth every penny they pay them. Others hold them in contempt. If you are going to go this route, bear the following points in mind.

(a) Travel agents are a mixed blessing. Some are very good and some will be incredible time-wasters who do not want to read a brochure but will demand that you spoonfeed them every bit of information. Be prepared to serve both kinds patiently and well.

Choosing your name can take time, so start the process early.

(b) Have a well-thought-out plan for dealing with travel agents and make sure you appear professional. If you market to them in a sloppy manner, you will make no sales and waste time and money. You must inspire the agents' confidence if you expect them to give you large sums of their valued clients' money.

(c) Make sure you approach agents with promotional material at least once or twice a month. With all the competition from other tour companies, travel agents forget fast. Keep your name in front of them.

(d) If you are running specialized tours, try to target the agencies catering to the appropriate kind of client and market to them. Keep in mind, though, that picking and choosing does cost money and time. A blanket marketing campaign may be cheaper in the end, even though some of the effort is wasted.

Have a well-thought-out plan for dealing with travel agents.

(e) Market by fax if you can. Most travel agencies accept faxes as a worthwhile way to receive information. If you are generating promotional material on your computer, get one of the better automatic fax broadcast programs such as Winfax Pro. With this program you can automatically send out your information for no cost and with a minimum of work time. Always get permission from an agency before you transmit, though, as unsolicited faxes cause irritation way out of proportion to the three cents worth of fax paper that recipients feel you wasted.

(f) The industry has information distribution channels which, for a fee, will distribute your brochures, updates, and promotional material to any segment of the travel agency community. This can be expensive, but it can also be a cost-effective way to distribute information to everyone in the industry. It saves you the time it would take to develop and maintain your own data base.

(g) Normal commissions to travel agencies range between five percent and 15 percent. Price wars break out from time to time as one tour operator tries to capture more of the market share. Occasionally, all tour operators who offer a certain destination raise their commission rates at the same time. As a new tour operator, you can command some attention and probably some sales by offering a very high commission rate.

(h) Do your financial homework before you start. If paying commission creates too thin a profit margin, it does not make sense to sell through agencies.

3. TRAVEL SHOWS

We are not big fans of travel shows. Many companies have tried to pick up clients this way and have stopped. Having said that, we do recommend you try a show or two to see if this is a profitable way to market your tours. Shows are very labor intensive and very expensive, so you might want to hedge your bets and try to share the expenses with one of your suppliers. The supplier might pay the entrance fee, which can be hundreds of dollars, and it probably already has all the material you need for a booth. In exchange, you could offer to staff the booth for the whole show. If you are willing to pledge your time, you may be able to do the show virtually cash free.

Alternatively, negotiate with the show owners for a lower entrance fee or, if you are willing to wait until the last minute to find out if you will be setting up, offer to be a standby exhibitor in exchange for a lower fee. This strategy will never work for shows that always sell out, but we have used it for other events and saved ourselves thousands of dollars.

Code all brochures you hand out to indicate they were given out at the show and give your office crew a special code for sales originating there. These tracking devices will help you evaluate whether the show generated enough sales to make it worthwhile. You do not want to do this twice if it does not work.

4. WALK-IN TRAFFIC — HOW MUCH DO YOU REALLY WANT?

If you will not be offering tours to the public on a retail basis, skip this section. If you are contemplating running a retail agency with your tour operation, read on.

Contrary to what most people think, not all agencies want walk-in traffic. Although a busy place with many potential customers passing your door sounds ideal, drop-in customers present some real disadvantages. The main problem is that walk-ins generally take up more time than someone who calls you. Clients who phone will tell you what they want and then hang up to await your call back. In order to answer a client's questions, an agent must research information either in the computer or by phone. This can easily take an hour. Without a client across the desk, the agent can catch up on paperwork while on hold or

Code all brochures so you can track whether the show generated enough sales to make it worthwhile.

answer other calls while working at the computer. It would be rude to do this with a client sitting across the desk from you. As well, constant interruptions by walk-ins can be frustrating for an agent working on another client's file and can sometimes lead to costly errors.

There is also no way to smooth out the walk-in business. Potential clients will always come in clumps right around the time you have a major crisis to contend with. Inevitably, some will be peeved when they come in at lunchtime and find every chair full. With phone-in clients, you can politely explain you are extremely busy and ask if you can call them back at a specific time. Most agents feel intimidated about requesting this same courtesy from a client standing before them.

Walk-in agencies are often seen as free information centers. It is not uncommon for someone to drop in for a chat during his or her work break, only to turn around and book the trip with the agent down the street from his or her home.

These and other issues mean that walk-in traffic is not for every personality. You must be prepared to deal with an assortment of problems with a smile and infinite patience. There is no point in opening an agency catering to walk-in traffic if you are going to turn clients off with unwelcoming treatment.

Walk-ins generally take up more time than someone who calls you.

5. ATTRACTING WALK-IN TRAFFIC

If you decide that you do want walk-in traffic, you must plan how you will attract it to your office. It is easy in a busy, properly selected location. When you choose an office space, make sure your front window is as wide as possible. This is the stage on which you will fashion a tableau of artistic, fresh, people-stopping dreams. Your displays should announce proudly and clearly that you are a tour operator and travel agency at the same time as they evoke thoughts of vacation and leisure. Anything too esoteric can give the wrong message or no message at all. (One agency's window display consistently attracted clothes shoppers!) You can get some marvelous display paraphernalia from airlines and other tour operators. If you do not feel you can put together a tasteful display, hire someone to do it for you.

One tip: If the thrust of your marketing is price competition, try using a chalkboard as the centerpiece of your display to list destinations, prices, and hot specials.

6. THE BROCHURE RACK

If you have walk-in traffic, you must have a supply of brochures for clients. The brochure rack, with all its color and dreams, can be an attraction if it is placed strategically near the door or front window. Assign an employee to remove old brochures, order new ones, and keep everything arranged properly. Incidentally, a brochure rack takes up about the same amount of space as a desk and chair for another salesperson. Be sure the trade-off is profitable.

The downside of a brochure rack is that many people will use it as a library. If you plan to feature a brochure rack prominently, train your staff to use it aggressively. When people come in to look, staff should seize the opportunity to engage them in conversation. "Where are you thinking of going?" is a much better opening line than "Can I help you?" Stamp all brochures with your name to remind people who you are after they leave your office. Clients are notorious for forgetting who had that great price or service.

23
ADVERTISING

Advertising is an expensive trial and error endeavor. Yet it is a rare retail agency or tour operation that cannot benefit from advertising. The objective of advertising is to increase sales. To advertise efficiently, you must know how much sales increase for every dollar you spend on advertising. To run an effective advertising campaign, you need to —

 (a) choose a product to advertise,

 (b) choose the most effective advertising medium, such as radio or newspapers,

 (c) create an eye- or ear-catching ad to draw the prospect's attention, and

 (d) evaluate the return on your advertising dollar.

If sales do not increase, change the ad content, the medium, or the product you are advertising and try again. For a small new business with a restricted budget, hiring professional help to design an advertising campaign is probably a waste of money. The fees you pay a consultant could probably be better spent trying new ads.

1. RADIO AND TV

In our experience, the cost of radio and TV ads is not covered by the increase in sales they generate. TV has the advantage of being able to create terrific images for the viewer, but TV advertising is closed to all but a few large firms which can afford the production costs of a commercial and the cost per commercial spot. Since you may have to try several different time slots or even change TV stations or commercials before you find the right combination, your budget for a TV campaign must be substantial. A few late-night ads will not bring in enough business to pay for the ad. You must risk comparatively large sums of money before you know if you have a winner.

Generally, radio is a bust for travel ads. After we tried for a year to squeeze more prospects from our advertising budget using radio, we learned a surefire method for determining ahead of time if radio ads work for a particular station or location. Call every past travel advertiser the station has ever had and ask each one's opinion. Everyone we asked said radio was not as effective as print for them. We recommend careful research as a first step if you are considering radio advertising.

Generally, radio is a bust for travel ads.

So much for informal surveys. If you are going to advertise on radio, negotiate hard for better rates. Except for the most popular stations, most stations will give you a deal to entice you to try their service. Radio is sold in "spots" that can be 10, 15, 30, or 60 seconds long. Stations usually discourage the shorter ads since they are more work to schedule for less money. The cost of a spot depends on when the ad is run, which in turn depends on how many listeners usually tune in during that time of day. The most expensive times are during the drive to and from work. You can put together a mix of different spots but the more you vary the time, the harder it is to figure out the most efficient periods in which to concentrate your ads for a future campaign. One bonus is that production costs of the ad are usually included in the cost of a series of advertisements if the commercial is not too elaborate.

2. PRINT ADVERTISING

With print advertising, you can create your own ads with comparative ease. A simple text ad may be all you need and the magazine or newspaper will probably set the type for free. Print advertising is also low risk compared to radio and TV. With a small budget, you can get a good feel for whether to continue with the tactics you have now or change one of the variables in your advertising.

2.1 Newspapers

Newspapers are a common means of advertising travel. Their biggest advantage is flexibility. You can use graphics or text in differently sized ads to get your message across. It is also comparatively easy to change your ad as the situation changes. For instance, you may decide to advertise a certain destination only to discover your competitors have a better deal or the airlines have suddenly changed their price. In a day you can design a new ad to reflect the changing conditions.

Print advertising is low risk compared to radio and TV.

The price structure for newspaper advertising provides special contract rates which can lower your costs by a significant amount. By committing your business to a certain quantity of ad space over a certain period of time, you can reduce your per insertion cost. Normally the paper will want you to commit to a minimum number of lines of classified advertising or inches of display space per year.

Work out what this will mean on a weekly basis to see if you can come anywhere near the required amount. Some contracts are so loosely drawn that you can opt in and out of the contract rate as you like. For instance, instead of requiring a certain number of lines of advertising per year, a newspaper may simply ask that you have 15 lines of type in a given ad to receive the preferred rate. If you do not have 15 lines, you don't get the rate. Other publications will let you skip days of advertising even though the strict letter of your contract says you must advertise every day. Be sure to read and understand your obligations.

When you are choosing a newspaper in which to advertise, there are many questions you need to answer.

(a) Does the newspaper's circulation area overlap the area in which you are concentrating your marketing? Unless you want to develop new areas and have created a campaign to support this push, advertising to a far-off place might be a waste of time.

If a particular paper seems to be "pulling well," even though many of its readers are outside your marketing area, consider expanding your phone service. The installation costs and monthly charges for toll-free telephone lines have come down dramatically in recent years (from $300 to $10 for installation!), and even long-distance rates have declined dramatically. The smallest company can now afford a larger geographic presence.

On the other hand, do not overlook small community newspapers in favor of larger dailies with a wide circulation. The smaller papers are cheaper and may focus your ad more specifically on the group of people you want to reach — the people in the neighborhood of your office.

(b) Can you afford a series of ads? One ad may not be enough to test the efficacy of a particular newspaper.

(c) Does the paper fit the image you want to project? For example, if you want a biker clientele, you will want to advertise in those publications which cater to bikers.

(d) Is the paper read by the people you want to reach? The *New York Times* might seem to be a great place to advertise a tour to see the Perseid Meteors in August, but if people in your area, or astronomers, do not subscribe to the *New York Times,* you have wasted your money. This seems obvious, but you do need to ask specifically to make sure that a paper or magazine is distributed to the people you want your ad to reach.

2.2 Magazines

Magazine advertising is expensive and is not usually timely enough to be of much value to you. It may be several weeks or months between the time you design your ad and the day the magazine hits the newsstands. A lot can change in the interim. As well, monthly magazines may be on sale long after the expiry date of any travel deal you advertise. Offsetting these big disadvantages is the fact that people read magazines long after a newspaper is in the garbage. We have had calls from customers who read our ads in the dentist's office a year after the magazine was published!

3. CREATING EFFECTIVE PRINT ADVERTISING

3.1 Pick the product to advertise

Destination ads have consistently produced five or six times as many calls for us.

Step one, choose a product to advertise. Try to pick one that will tap into the largest audience possible, or the largest section of the publication's readership. Making this choice will involve a lot of guesswork in the beginning, but it's obvious that you do not want to advertise a rock-climbing expedition in a senior's paper, for example. An outdoor adventure magazine would be better.

Usually tour operators advertise a specific destination, stressing special expert knowledge or a special price. Occasionally the ad will emphasize something else, such as your operation's convenient location, stability and dependability, or overall good service. We favor destination-specific ads because they target your market so neatly. So many businesses promise good service that the public has come to see this as meaningless puffery. Over the years, destination ads have consistently produced five or six times as many calls for us as service quality ads.

3.2 Create your ad

Unless you have tons of money, skip the feel-good image ads. People already have an image of what they are going to get, based on all the advertising airlines and big tour companies do. An evocative picture in a magazine or newspaper will cost you the proceeds of dozens of sales. Instead, briefly tell the reader exactly what your tour is. State the destination. If your prices are good, publish prices. If you deliver tickets or perform some other unusual service, tell the reader. The ad must be short, snappy, and to the point.

Always include your phone number in large bold numbers at the bottom of the ad so people do not have to search for it. An address should be included only if you want drop-in traffic. Your company name and logo lend credibility to an ad and help people associate your company with your specialty. In certain places it is customary not to use them in classified ads (check the ads in the publication you are thinking of advertising in to see what other people do), and you can save a bundle over a year by forgoing your name or logo on your ads.

For your first ad, try a two- or three-inch display ad with a large headline naming your tour destination, a prominent dollar price, and a big phone number. The words "from" in small letters might precede the dollar value if you offer a range of prices. Make sure it is an excellent price compared to what other companies are advertising for that product. If your tour is particularly special, list some of the details in point form in small type.

You can use exactly the same ad in the classified section, or alter it slightly to save money. By downsizing it to a standard text-only line ad, you pay a fraction of the price of a display ad but you may get just as many clients. Try each of these tactics and compare the response.

Make your phone number large in your ads so that it's easy for people to find.

3.3 Choose the right vehicle

Advertise where everyone else advertises travel. This is where customers have been educated to look. Advertising your tour in the food section of a paper is probably not efficient unless it is a tour devoted to food.

To determine the proper advertising vehicle, go to the library and get copies of every magazine and newspaper that covers your area. Look for other advertisers, not just travel advertisers, who are in your city. Call them to see if the paper or magazine gets customers for them. Even nontravel advertisers may have some interesting feedback. When you have selected a candidate or two, contact them for rate information. Try to negotiate a better rate as a first-time advertiser, then place your ad.

3.4 Evaluate the response

When we run a new ad, we normally ask the staff to keep tallies of calls in response to the ad. This serves as an early warning system for bad ads. If there are few calls, you may want to cancel the ad early and save your cash.

The first indication an ad has "pull" is that the phone starts ringing more. This is not a measure of the success of your ad, however. It is a limited measure of how well you created your ad or how well you picked your vehicle. People obviously saw the ad and are curious enough to want to know more. Even if there are numerous calls, later analysis may show that not one person bought anything. Do not mistake action for results. Every time the phone rings with a new prospect from the ad, it costs you and your staff time to serve that person. If no sale results, you are losing not only advertising dollars but staffing dollars too.

How do you determine if an ad is worthwhile? Let's say that the week after the ad runs, everyone who calls about it buys the product you advertised. With the money you made, did you cover the cost of the ad? If the answer is no even with all the sales, your ad is definitely a bust. Also ask yourself if doubling or tripling the number of calls and sales would have paid for the ad. Every ad needs to be given a chance to perform, but if two or three times the current volume of calls will not make a difference, you probably have a dud. An ad that generates less than twice its cost should also be looked at critically. It probably did not make you money and you should watch to see if sales pick up as the ad continues. An ad that does no more than cover its own cost loses you money. We will continue an ad only if it pulls at least three times its own cost.

Do not mistake action for results.

An ad that pulls a lot of calls that do not result in sales could indicate several things. Maybe one of your competitors offered a much better price than you did on the tour you advertised. Lower your price and try again or wait until your competitor stops advertising that price. Perhaps it is too early in the season to make sales — your callers may be window-shopping. Ads for winter resort destinations prompt calls like this early in the fall. Try the ad later in the season.

To evaluate an ad, you must have a system in place that records where every sale came from. We have our staff put the source of the customer right on the invoice control sheet when they write a new invoice to record the sale (see Sample 13). Invoices are numbered and the invoice control sheet has space for the client's name, the date, the supplier used, and how the client heard about us. The manager is responsible for ensuring every invoice number has a corresponding source filled in.

Each source is coded and everyone in the office knows the codes. For instance, people who come from referrals are given the code "W/M" for "word of mouth"; clients who have dealt with us before are coded "repeat." Newspaper ads are coded with the paper name in abbreviated form and some shortened title from the ad such as "NYT — Frankfurt" or "NYT — Australia" for ads run in the *New York Times*. Make the codes easy. Stay away from cryptic references and numbering your sources. Your staff will never remember these codes and will not do a good job of tracking responses.

By keeping careful records, you can intelligently budget your advertising dollars and avoid waste. Micromanaging your advertising budget does pay off. Running an ad until you get a "feel" for whether it works is foolish. If the destination you picked requires a lot of work per inquiry and your agents are busy fielding calls, it may feel like the ad is doing its job when in fact it is just sucking up your cash.

3.5 Helpful hints for print advertising

Every magazine and newspaper, and every locale is different. You will need to experiment with the advertising vehicles in your area. We have learned the following from experience:

(a) Watch what other advertisers do time after time. This may give you a clue about what makes a successful ad or advertising campaign.

An ad that does no more than cover its own cost loses you money.

Keeping careful records means you can budget your advertising dollars and avoid waste.

SAMPLE 13
INVOICE CONTROL SHEET

Invoice #	Client Name	Date	Supplier	Source
1001	Costello	Nov 12	Air Canada	Repeat
1005	Young	April 2	Sunny Tours	Repeat

(b) There is a cumulative effect in advertising. If you advertise now, you may still be getting some response from the ad months later. However, do not let the cumulative effect fool you into thinking an ad might still work if it did not pull anything the week it ran. Once a dud ad, always a dud ad.

(c) For the same budget, run smaller ads more frequently rather than opting for bigger size and fewer times.

(d) Ads smaller than an inch and a half tend to get lost in display advertising. Conversely, ads over a quarter of a page do not have double the pulling power of ads half that size.

(e) Ads under four lines do not pull well in classified sections.

(f) Always tell all your sales staff — both inside and outside travel agents — exactly what you are advertising before the ad goes in. Your credibility goes out the window when a potential client calls about the super-special deal you advertised and no one knows what the client is talking about. There should never be exceptions to this rule.

Don't stop working your advertising budget and trying new approaches.

(g) Never run an ad without confirming that it is properly placed and correct. Request a copy of the magazine or newspaper, or arrange to have a clipping faxed to you on the day the ad first runs.

(h) Know what your competition is offering. It does no good to have side-by-side ads offering the same thing when your price is $100 higher. There will be times when you just cannot advertise because your competitors have a better deal than you do. If this happens all the time, concentrate your marketing effort on tours where you can offer special expertise or advertise in different newspapers and magazines.

(i) Do not include your address in the ad. With good telephone and fax communication it is not important, and leaving it out will save you money by saving ad space.

(j) Seasonal considerations and timing may play a part in advertising for your area. For instance, we never advertise on long weekends. Few people read papers then, and we have noticed a marked decrease in calls. Days on either side of a long weekend are dead too, especially in the summer. The week between Christmas and New Year's Day can be slow, especially if Christmas is in the middle of the week. To save money, you may want to cancel all your advertising during the holiday season. Experiment a bit.

(k) Finding your first consistently winning ad may take some time. Do not get discouraged. It does take a lot of work. Once you have your first really successful ad, it is easier to go through the trial and error. No matter how successful your ads become, do not stop working your advertising budget hard and trying new approaches.

4. CO-OP ADVERTISING

Many suppliers will share advertising costs with you if you are running an ad that advertises their product exclusively. They may put up as much as 50 percent of the cost of the ad. If you want to arrange such a co-op ad, you must have a well-thought-out proposal which includes information on the kind of ad and the number of times it will run. Generally, suppliers do not require a written proposal, but it is advisable to get confirmation in writing that they will pick up the agreed-on percentage of the bill.

If you are selling your tours through travel agencies, they might expect you, in turn, to help them out by paying for a share of a co-op ad. You should be able to get a clear picture of how the ad pulls by looking at the agency's sales figures.

5. PIGGYBACK ON SOMEONE ELSE'S MARKETING

Look for opportunities to share the costs of reaching your audience with someone else. A prime example is a firm that pays part of a bank's statement mailing-cost each month and in exchange inserts a blurb of its own in the envelope. The key to a successful campaign is to get an apparent endorsement from the bank at a low per-piece cost.

If an organization or business approaches you with this idea, you must first determine whether or not you will be reaching customers who would normally buy from you. There is no sense advertising a trekking tour in Nepal to a group of people with mobility restrictions. Few sales will result.

Look for opportunities to share the costs of reaching your audience.

Along the same lines, if another company or organization is running a contest, you might donate one of your tours as a prize. In exchange, you and the tour will receive exposure in ads promoting the contest.

6. DIRECT MAIL

Many small tour operations depend on direct mail, even though this form of advertising can be expensive and time-consuming. A direct mail campaign, including postage, handling and stuffing, production of the mailing piece, and the waste of undelivered pieces, may run you as much as $1 per piece delivered. However, if it is done correctly, a direct mail campaign pinpoints groups of people who are most interested in the products you sell. It can also be cost-effective compared with other advertising. We recommend you cultivate a mailing list of prospects. Start with names of past customers and people who respond to other marketing you do, then build on it regularly from there.

Our experience shows that blanketing an area with handbills does not work. Stuffing every mailbox in an area with a one-page advertisement can easily cost $250, when you consider the cost of distribution, printing, and artwork. This means you must make approximately $2,500 in gross sales to receive the $250 in commission that will cover the cost of the advertisement. On top of that is the cost of staff time to service the calls that do come in.

7. ADVERTISING HOTLINES

For many years we ran a telephone travel hotline, a recorded message that listed terrific discounts on last-minute cheap seats from various tour operators. The newspaper advertising we used to support the hotline was short and inexpensive. Sometimes ads consisted of nothing more than the headline "Travel Hotline" and a phone number. This saved a bundle of advertising money and, over time, the hotline acquired a following of its own. Even when we did not advertise the hotline, we still made sales, as word of mouth spread the number for us.

This can be an ideal method for selling retail products as well as your tours and can cut down on your advertising expenditures significantly.

Hotlines do have some disadvantages, however. For one thing, they require a special commitment — you must be there every week to change the recording or find someone else to do it for you, and staff members will spend a minimum of two hours each week to research and record the hotline deals. People begin to depend on it and will let you know if it is not changed regularly. They will also complain if there is nothing worthwhile on the recording, though occasionally there are

Make good use of key words and search engines in your advertising on the Internet.

no deals to record. If you run tours less than once a week and do not have a retail operation in addition to your tour business, you will need to be creative so the public does not get bored with stale messages on your hotline.

8. ADVERTISING ON THE WORLD WIDE WEB

As most of the world knows, World Wide Web pages are all the rage and are continuing to gain popularity daily. If you decide to open a Web site, make the investment to learn how to use this tool to full advantage, keep current on changes and improvements, and be aware of the following points for your advertising:

(a) You must make a commitment to change the page as often as prices or destinations change. There was a court case where an airline was fined a large sum of money for failing to honor an out-of-date price.

(b) Web pages, like any other form of advertising, are useless unless you know how to get people to see your page. This requires some computer marketing skills. Make good use of key words and search engines.

(c) Many clients are still uncomfortable with the security of using their credit cards over the net. You may still need to have staff to do the booking procedures over the phone.

For more information, see chapter 13, "Using the Internet."

9. NEWSLETTERS AND OTHER PERIODIC MAILINGS

For those who really want to communicate with their clients, this may be an ideal method, but it requires a serious commitment and a love of writing. A haphazard attempt to entice prospects will waste money and a tremendous amount of time. Because of the amount of time and energy a newsletter requires, we recommend you use other methods of advertising until you have your business up and running and the initial pressure is off. Our experience is that a newsletter is almost as expensive as TV and radio on a per sale basis, but it does produce loyal clients. Unlike TV, you can start small and expand the newsletter later if it is successful. If you are already using direct mail as your primary marketing channel, a newsletter may be just the right advertising vehicle.

10. PROMOTIONS — PREMIUM GIVEAWAYS AND CONTESTS

Premium giveaways are expensive and are not used extensively in the travel industry by small tour operators. Contests must comply with your state or provincial gambling legislation, which could add hassles and headaches. Fulfillment houses can put a part or whole contest together for you, but this adds more expense.

If you are intent on using the contest avenue, contact the airlines. With the right promotion package, you might be able to talk one of them into supplying part of the prize in exchange for piggybacking on your media campaign. Be warned: airlines are approached often. To make headway you must have a well-thought-out proposal that will show a superb advertising benefit for the airline. Airlines love radio and TV campaigns, especially if you foot the bill.

11. PROMOTIONS — CHARITABLE DONATIONS

By donating a small percentage of each sale to the charity of their choice, you may be able to sway members of an association to book with you. The amount you choose to donate is up to you and the association. As part of the deal, the association must advertise you to their members in any association communications. Every time anything is sent out to association members, a reminder can be put in of your commitment to help the charity they have chosen. Many people will support a company that makes this kind of offer.

12. DIRECTORIES

An advertisement in a directory may be around for a year, which means your ad cannot list prices. Nor can you change the ad if your business or marketing thrust changes. You are limited to messages that amount to puffery in the public's mind or to lists of the destinations you serve. The Yellow Pages reach a tremendous number of people, but the advertising rates are expensive. We have not found this to be an effective vehicle for tour operations or retail outlets.

13. DISCOUNT COUPONS

Some tour operators, but few retail travel agencies, use discount coupons even though the cost of production and distribution is high

No amount of advertising will overcome faulty pricing, a bad choice of products, or rotten service.

when compared to other means of letting the public know about discounts. The big advantage over most other types of advertising is that coupons have a long shelf life. People tack them up on the fridge and use them six months later. Unfortunately, any discount you offer cuts into the commission you make, limiting the size of the discount you can give. For example, if you offer a $50 discount, you could be giving away half your commission on a $1,000 sale (a 10 percent commission on $1,000 is $100, and only $50 after the coupon).

In conclusion, remember that no amount of advertising will overcome faulty pricing, a bad choice of products to sell, or rotten service. Advertising is an important part of your marketing effort, but not all of it.

24
AN ENDING AND A BEGINNING

Travelling is not just seeing the new; it is also leaving behind. Not just opening doors; also closing them behind you never to return. But the place you have left forever is always there for you to see whenever you shut your eyes.

— Jan Myrdal, *The Silk Road*

Although you have reached the end of this book, it is really just the beginning of your journey. We hope you have discovered some new ideas and inspirations. We wish you safety in your travels, joy in your new experiences, and success in your business — whatever you choose to make it.

APPENDIX 1
USEFUL ORGANIZATIONS AND ASSOCIATIONS

1. UNITED STATES

American Automobile Association (AAA)
1000 AAA Drive
Heathrow, FL 32746
Tel: (407) 444-7000
Fax: (407) 444-7380
www.aaa.com

Regional AAA offices can be found in most medium or large towns. They are a good source of information and detailed maps, although you need to be a member to access these services for free.

American Bus Association
#1050 - 1100 New York Avenue N.W.
Washington, DC 20005-3934
Tel: (202) 842-1645
Toll free: 1-800-283-2877
Fax: (202) 842-0850
www.buses.org

American Hotel and Motel Association
#600 - 1201 New York Avenue N.W.
Washington, DC 20005-3931
Tel: (202) 289-3100
Fax: (202) 289-3199
www.ahma.com

Chamber of Commerce of the United States
Although each town usually has its own chamber of commerce,
the general number is worth noting.
1615 H Street N.W.
Washington, DC 20062
Tel: (202) 659-6000
Fax: (202) 463-5836
www.uschamber.com

1.1 Convention and visitors bureaus

As with chambers of commerce, check each destination (especially if it
is a major center or is located close to a major center) to see what it can
offer you. Here are two general numbers to get you started.

(a) **International Association of Convention and
Visitors Bureaus**
#702 - 2000 L Street N.W.
Washington, DC 20036-4990
Tel: (202) 296-7888
Fax: (202) 296-7889
www.iacvb.org

(b) **Western Association of Convention and
Visitors Bureaus**
#240 - 1730 I Street
Sacramento, CA 95814
Tel: (916) 443-9012
Fax: (916) 443-8065
www.wacvb.com

Cruise Lines International Association (CLIA)

#1407 - 500 5th Avenue
New York, NY 10110
Tel: (212) 921-0066
Fax: (212) 921-0549
www.cruising.org

National Tour Association/Foundation

546 E. Main Street
Box 3071
Lexington, KY 40596-3071
Tel: (606) 226-4444
Fax: (606) 226-4321
www.ntaonline.com

This organization focuses on the development, promotion, and increased use of leisure travel that is packaged by tour operators. It offers numerous professional educational programs and industry statistics, and maintains a research library on the tour guiding profession.

Pacific Asia Travel Association (PATA)

International Office
1000 Telesis Tower
1 Montgomery Street
San Francisco, CA 94104
Tel: (415) 986-4646
Fax: (415) 986-3458
www.pata.org

PATA focuses mainly on inbound traffic to the Pacific Rim market.

Travel Industry Association of America

1100 New York Avenue N.W. Suite 450
Washington, DC 20005-3934
Tel: (202) 408-8422
Fax: (202) 408-1255
www.tia.org

This association promotes tourism to and within the United States and publishes a quarterly survey of how economic conditions affect travel plans among Americans. The United States Travel Data Center is a branch of the association, which compiles data about the tourism industry. Reports can be purchased by nonmembers, and a catalogue is available.

United States Tour Operators Association (USTOA)
342 Madison Ave, Suite 1522
New York, NY 10173
Tel: (212) 599-6599
Fax: (212) 599-6744
www.ustoa.com

World Travel and Tourism Tax Policy Center (WTTTPC)
c/o Travel, Tourism, and Recreational Resource Center
172 Natural Resources Building
Michigan State University
East Lansing, MI 48824-1222
Tel: (517) 432-2636
Fax: (517) 432-2296
www.traveltax.msu.edu

WTTTPC acts as a barometer of how taxes impact the travel industry and offers up-to-the-minute information about tax rates and structures worldwide.

2. CANADA

Association of Canadian Mountain Guides
Box 8341
Canmore, AB T1W 2V1
Tel: (403) 678-2885
Fax: (403) 609-0070
www.acmg.ca

Association of Tourism Professionals
See: Pacific Rim Institute of Tourism

Canadian Association of Tour Operators (CATO)
1 First Canadian Place, 100 King St. W., Suite 700
Toronto, ON M5X 1C7
Tel: (416) 304-0521
Fax: (416) 681-9500

CATO represents the interests of Canadian tour operators, works to improve industry standards, evaluates opportunities to improve revenue, and provides assistance in legal matters to its members.

Canadian Automobile Association — National (CAA)
#200 - 1154 Hunt Club Road
Ottawa, ON K1V 0Y3
Tel: (613) 247-0117
Fax: (613) 247-0118
www.caa.ca

Each province also has its own local branch (e.g., BCAA in British Columbia) that provides maps and other travel services to members.

Canadian Bus Association
451 Daly Ave
Ottawa, ON K1N 6H6
Tel: (613) 238-1800
Fax: (613) 241-7428

Canadian Tourist Guide Association of British Columbia
1423 Howe Street
Vancouver, BC V6Z 1R9
Tel: (604) 669-0851
Fax: (604) 669-0853

Members meet monthly for informational and educational advancement. Promotes tour guide certification and acts as a voice for tour guiding professionals.

2.1 Chambers of commerce

Although each town usually has its own chamber of commerce, this is the general number.

Canadian Chamber of Commerce
350 Sparks St., Suite 501
Ottawa, ON K1R 7S8
Tel: (613) 238-4000
Fax: (613) 238-7643
www.chamber.ca

Pacific Asia Travel Association (PATA)
Western Canada Office
#110 - 1020 Mainland Street
Vancouver, BC V6B 2T4
Tel: (604) 682-8083
Fax: (604) 682-2025

PATA focuses mainly on inbound traffic to the Pacific Rim market.

Pacific Rim Institute of Tourism (PRIT)
1185 W. Georgia, Suite 800
Vancouver, BC V6E 4E6
Tel: (604) 682-8000
Fax: (604) 688-2554
www.prit.bc.ca

PRIT offers training and support to all tourism professionals, maintains an extensive resource centre covering all aspects of travel and tourism, and played a major role in the development of Canadian industry standards.

Western Canada Motorcoach Association
P.O. Box 4520, Station "C"
Calgary, AB T2T 5N3
Tel: (403) 244-4489
Fax: (403) 224-2340

Western Tour Directors Association of Canada
#111 - 22950 - 116th Avenue
Maple Ridge, BC V2X 2T7
Tel/Fax: (604) 463-0890

The association is active in promoting industry standards and professionalism among tour guides.

3. INTERNATIONAL

Asia Association of Convention and Visitors Bureau

As with chambers of commerce, check each destination (especially if it is a major center or is located close to a major center) to see what it can offer you. Here are three general numbers to get you started.

P.O. Box 2297 GPO
35th Floor, Jardine House
Connaught Place Central, Hong Kong
Tel: (852) 801-7111
Fax: (852) 801-4877

International Association of Tour Managers
397 Walworth Road
London, UK SE 172AW
Tel: (171) 703-9154
Fax: (171) 703-0358

International Chamber of Commerce
38 Cours Albert 1 er
Paris, France F-75008
Tel: 1-4953-2828
Fax: 1-4953-2859
www.iccwbo.org

International Federation of Tour Operators
170 High Street
Lewes, East Sussex
UK, BN7 1YE
Tel: 1273-47-722
Fax: 1273-48-3746

International Hotels Association (IHA)
80 Rue de la Roquette
Paris, France 75544
Tel: 1-47-0084-57
Fax: 1-47-0064-55

Japan National Tourist Organization (JNTO)
2-10-1 Yuraku-cho
Chiyoda-ku
Tokyo 100, Japan
Tel: 3-3216-1901
Fax: 3-3214-7680
www.jnto.go.jp

World Federation of Tourist Guide Lecturers' Association
Stubenring 8-10
A-1010 Vienna, Austria
Tel: 1-5145-0257
Fax: 1-5145-0258

World Tourism Organization
Capitan Haya, 42
E28020 Madrid, Spain
Tel: 1-571-0628
Fax: 1-571-3733
www.world-tourism.org

3.1 World Travel and Tourism Council (WTTC)

WTTC is a global coalition that works with governments to promote job creation in an open and competitive market. It provides research and economic analysis of the travel and tourism industry.

(a) WTTC Registered Office
20 Grosvenor Place
London, UK SW1X 7TT
Tel: 44-171-838-9400
Fax: 44-171-838-9050
www.wttc.org

(b) Claussee de la Hulpe 181, Box 10
Brussels, Belgium
Tel: 32-3-660-2067
Fax: 32-3-660-9170

APPENDIX 2
A PRELIMINARY LIST OF TOUR OPERATORS

It would be impossible to list all tour operators and tour companies, so the following is meant as a primer only. Your own search will lead you to many more and for this reason we strongly recommend you keep records as you discover new companies. If you are computer oriented, any commercial data base program will allow you to create a useful list. Otherwise, file cards arranged alphabetically are still an effective way to keep yourself up to date.

1. UNITED STATES

Brendan Tours
15137 Califa Street
Van Nuys, CA 91411
Toll free: 1-800-421-8446
Fax: 818-902-9876
www.brendantours.com

Collette Tours
162 Middle Street
Pawtucket, RI 02860
Tel: (401) 728-3805
Fax: (401) 728-1380
Toll free: 1-800-468-5955
www.collettetours.com

Elderhostel USA
75 Federal Street
Boston, MA 02110
Tel: (877) 426-8056
Fax: (877) 426-2166
www.elderhostel.org

Globus/Cosmos
5301 South Federal Circle
Littleton, CO 80123
Toll free: 1-800-221-0090
Res: 1-800-323-3796 (admin)
Fax: (303) 798-5441 (admin)
www.globusandcosmos.com

Grand Circle Travel
347 Congress Street
Boston, MA 02210
Toll free: 1-800-221-2610
Fax: (617) 346-6770
www.gct.com

Holland America Line Westours
300 Elliott Avenue W.
Seattle WA 98119
Tel: (206) 281-3535
Toll free: 1-800-637-5029
Fax: (206) 281-0351
www.hollandamerica.com

Maupintour
1421 Research Park Dr., Suite 300
Lawrence, KS 66049
Mail only: P.O. Box 807
Lawrence, KS 66044
Tel: (785) 331-1000
Fax: (785) 331-1057
Toll free: 1-800-255-4266
www.maupintour.com

Overseas Adventure Travel
625 Mount Auburn Street
Cambridge, MA 02138
Tel: (617) 876-0533
Toll free: 1-800-221-0814
Fax: (617) 492-1723
www.oattravel.com

Princess Cruises
#1800 - 10100 Santa Monica Boulevard
Los Angeles, CA 90067
Toll free: 1-800-527-6200
Fax: (661) 284-4745
www.princess.com

Tauck Tours
276 Post Road W.
Westport, CN 06880
Mail only:
P.O. Box 5027
Westport, CN 06881
Tel: (203) 226-6911
Toll free: 1-800-468-2825 (res)
www.tauck.com

Trafalgar Tours
11 E. 26 Street
New York, NY 10010
Tel: (212) 689-8977
Toll free: 1-800-854-0103
Fax: (212) 725-7776
www.trafalgartours.com

2. CANADA

Alba Tours International
130 Merton St.
Toronto, ON M4S 1A4
Tel: (416) 485-1700
Toll free: 1-800-465-4472
Fax: (416) 485-0728 (PR dept)
www.sunquest.ca

Brewster Transportation and Tours
P.O. Box 1140
Banff, AB T0L 0C0
Tel: (403) 762-6700
Fax: (403) 762-6750
www.brewster.ca

Collette Tours
701 Evans Ave., Suite 707
Etobicoke, ON M9C 1A3
Tel: (416) 626-1661
Fax: (416) 626-2788

Elderhostel Canada
4 Cataraqui St., Suite 300
Kingston, ON K7K 1Z7
Tel: (613) 530-2222
Fax: (613) 530-2096
www.elderhostel.org

Jade Tours
3190 Steeles Ave. E., Suite 110
Markham, ON L3R 1G9
Tel: (905) 948-9483
Toll free: 1-800-387-0387
Fax: (905) 948-3893

Globus/Cosmos
1061 Eglington Avenue W.
Toronto, ON M6C 2C9
Tel: (416) 787-1281 (res),(416) 787-1284 (admin)
Fax: (416) 787-7491
www.globusandcosmos.com

Regent Holidays
6205 Airport Road, Building A, Suite 200
Mississagua, ON L4V 1E1
Tel: (905) 673-0777
Toll free: 1-800-263-8776 (admin), 1-800-387-4860 (res)
Fax: (905) 673-1717
www.regentholidays.com

Trafalgar Tours (Canada)
355 Eglington Avenue E.
Toronto, ON M4P 1M5
Tel: (416) 322-8466
Toll free: 1-800-387-2680
Fax: (416) 322-8148

APPENDIX 3
USEFUL MAGAZINES AND PUBLICATIONS

This is just a sampling of the many and varied magazine resources available. There are literally hundreds of consumer and trade publications available which can increase your knowledge and expand your creativity for designing tours. Remember, no matter how obscure you think your destination is, someone probably publishes a magazine or newsletter about it. An afternoon spent browsing the various magazine directories in any major library will net you a long list of potential resources.

1. UNITED STATES

ASU Travel Guide
1525 Francisco Boulevard E.
San Rafael, CA 94901
www.asuguide.com

Best Fares Discount Travel Magazine
Box 14261
Arlington, TX 76094-1261
Toll free: 1-800-635-3033
www.bestfares.com

Condé Nast Traveler
360 Madison Avenue
New York, NY 10017
www.conceirge.com/

Consumer Reports Travel Letter
Subscriptions Director
Box 53629
Boulder, CO 80322-3629
Toll free: 1-800-234-1970

Eco Traveler
7730 S.W. Mohawk
Tualatin, OR 97062
www.ecomall.com

Group Travel Leader
340 South Broadway
Lexington, KY 40508
www.grouptravelleader.com

Journal of Travel and Tourism Marketing
10 Alice Street
Binghamton, NY 13904-1580

Mature Group Traveler
100 Prospect Street
Stanford, CT 06901

The Thrifty Traveler
Box 8168
Clearwater, FL 34618
Toll free: 1-800-532-5731
www.thriftytraveler.com

Tour & Travel Marketplace
600 Community Drive
Manhasset, NY 11030

Tour & Travel News/TTG North America
Box 1190
Skokie, IL 60076
Toll free: 1-800-447-0138

Travel Industry Monitor
111 W. 57th Street
New York, NY 10019

Travel & Leisure
1120 Avenue of the Americas
New York, NY 10036

Travel Marketing
607 South 4 Street
Dekalb, IL 60115

Travel Trade
15 W. 44 Street, 6th Floor
New York, NY 10036
www.traveltrade.com

Travel Weekly
500 Plaza Drive
Secaucus, NJ 07096

2. CANADA

Canadian Travel Press
310 Dupont Street
Toronto, ON M5R 1V9
www.travelpress.com

Educational Travel
Athabasca University
P.O. Box 10,000
Athabasca, AB T0G 2R0

Road Explorer (formerly *Ontario Motor Coach Review*)
#600 - 920 Yonge Street
Toronto, ON M4W 3C7

Travel Impulse
9336 - 117th Street
Delta, BC V4C 6B8
www.suntrackercafe.com

Travelweek Bulletin
Travel Trade Publication
282 Richmond Street E., Suite 100
Toronto, ON M5A 1P4
Toll free: 1-800-727-1429

3. INTERNATIONAL

Asia Travel News
101 Muhammadi House
Chundrigar Road
Karachi, Pakistan

Asia Travel Trade
190 Middle Road #11-01
Fortune Center
Singapore 0718
Singapore

Business Traveller
22 Redan Place
London, UK W2 4SZ

Group Travel Organizer
250 Kennington Lane
London, UK SE 11 5RD
www.touristguides.org.uk/links.html

OTHER TITLES IN THE
SELF-COUNSEL BUSINESS SERIES

PREPARING A SUCCESSFUL BUSINESS PLAN
Rodger D. Touchie
$15.95

At some time, every business needs a formal business plan. Usually, until the need for money arises, business plans remain informal collections of memos, magazine articles, personal diaries, and mental notations. You can use this book and the worksheets in it to focus your organizational priorities and better understand the keys to preparing a successful business plan.

Includes:

- Understanding basic elements of business planning

- Building strong business foundations

- Identifying your target audience

- Creating a mission statement

- Communicating your expectations effectively

- Developing a marketing strategy

- Preparing a financial plan

- Preparing for future growth and expansion

GETTING PUBLICITY
Tana Fletcher and Julia Rockler
$18.95

If you'd like to know all the inside secrets for attracting publicity to your business, your association, or yourself, you need this book. Step-by-step instructions illustrate just what it takes for any enterprise to generate media attention.

Aimed specifically at individuals and organizations whose ambitions are bigger than their bankrolls, *Getting Publicity* emphasizes low-cost, do-it-yourself promotional strategies, and is filled with inexpensive and practical tips for capitalizing on the power of publicity.

Includes:

- Becoming your own publicist

- Putting together a publicity plan

- Creating publicity opportunities

- Understanding the media: print, broadcast, and Internet

- Announcing a new product

- Mastering the media interview

- Writing and public speaking

WRITING TRAVEL BOOKS AND ARTICLES

Richard Cropp, Barbara Braidwood,
and Susan M. Boyce
$15.95

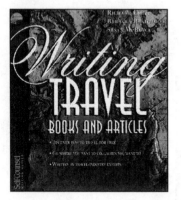

Do you love to travel to exotic and exciting destinations? Is writing your passion? Imagine being paid to do both as a travel writer! Offering guaranteed job satisfaction, travel writing has many fringe benefits such as getting behind-the-scenes information and travelling to your favourite destinations.

Written by experienced travel writers, this guide will show you how to get those all-important free trips and get your travel writing published. Ideal for the novice writer, and full of helpful tips for the experienced travel writer, this information-packed book includes:

- Finding sponsors
- Getting your first article published
- Publishing on the Internet
- Common mistakes of new travel writers.

ORDER FORM

All prices are subject to change without notice. Books are available in book, department, and stationery stores. If you cannot buy the book through a store, please use this order form. (Please print.)

Name_____

Address _____

_____

Charge to: ❏ Visa ❏ MasterCard

Account Number _____

Validation Date _____

Expiry Date _____

Signature _____

Shipping and handling will apply.

In Canada, 7% GST will be added.

In Washington, 7.8% sales tax will be added.

Yes, please send me the following:

_____ *Preparing a Successful Business Plan*

_____ *Getting Publicity*

_____ *Writing Travel Books and Articles*

Please add $3.00 for postage and handling.

❏ Check here for a free catalogue.

IN THE USA
Self-Counsel Press, Inc.
1704 N. State Street
Bellingham, WA 98225

IN CANADA

Please send your order to the nearest location:

Self-Counsel Press	Self-Counsel Press
1481 Charlotte Road	4 Bram Court
North Vancouver, BC	Brampton, ON
V7J 1H1	L6W 3R6

Visit our Web site: *www.self-counsel.com*